P9-EAJ-308

DATE DUE

DEMCO 38-296

GEORGE WHITEFIELD CHADWICK

George Whitefield Chadwick. Photo courtesy of the family and heirs of George Whitefield Chadwick.

GEORGE WHITEFIELD CHADWICK

CHADWICK

A Bio-Bibliography

BILL F. FAUCETT

Bio-Bibliographies in Music, Number 66
Donald L. Hixon, *Series Adviser*

GREENWOOD PRESS
Westport, Connecticut • London

Riverside Community College
Library
4800 Magnolia Avenue
Riverside, CA 92506

ML 134 .C413 F38 1998

Faucett, Bill F.

George Whitefield Chadwick

Library of Congress Cataloging-in-Publication Data

Faucett, Bill F.
    George Whitefield Chadwick : a bio-bibliography / by Bill F.
Faucett.
        p.   cm.—(Bio-bibliographies in music, ISSN 0742–6968 ; no.
66)
    Includes discography (p.   ) and indexes.
    ISBN 0–313–30067–4 (alk. paper)
    1. Chadwick, G. W. (George Whitefield), 1854–1931—Bibliography.
I. Title. II. Series.
ML134.C413F38   1998
780′.92—dc21
    [B]   97–42482
                MN

British Library Cataloguing in Publication Data is available.

Copyright © 1998 by Bill F. Faucett

All rights reserved. No portion of this book may be
reproduced, by any process or technique, without the
express written consent of the publisher.

Library of Congress Catalog Card Number: 97–42482
ISBN: 0–313–30067–4
ISSN: 0742–6968

First published in 1998

Greenwood Press, 88 Post Road West, Westport, CT 06881
An imprint of Greenwood Publishing Group, Inc.

Printed in the United States of America

· The paper used in this book complies with the
Permanent Paper Standard issued by the National
Information Standards Organization (Z39.48–1984).

10 9 8 7 6 5 4 3 2 1

The author and the publisher gratefully acknowledge permission to use
material from the unpublished journal of George W. Chadwick.

To
Julie, Billy, and Adam

Contents

viii   Contents

Preface

This volume follows the general format of other volumes in Greenwood Press's Bio-Bibliographies in Music series. Following a chapter about Chadwick's life and music, a bibliography of his music, titled "Works and Performances," records details of his compositions, their premieres, other performances, and critical reception. Also included in this book is a discography, followed by a discography bibliography which features critical reviews of the discography. A general bibliography catalogs books and articles that relate to Chadwick's life, career and music, while a bibliography of Chadwick's own writings follows. Finally, I have included two music indices, one each for songs and choral music.

In the Works and Performances section compositions are categorized by genre and then placed in alphabetical order. Each work is denoted with an identifying label beginning with the letter "W" (for "Work"). This chapter includes information on the composition's dates, dedication information, publishing details, holograph location, instrumentation, current availability, and other pertinent information. The instrumentation information given for large compositions follows the customary order: piccolo, flutes, oboes, English horn (eh.), clarinets, bass clarinet, bassoons, contrabassoon; horns, trumpets, trombones, tuba; timpani and other percussion; other instruments; and strings.

Premieres and other performances, when known, are listed following each composition's details. Performances are listed chronologically and are designated by the "Work" number followed by sequential lower-case letters. Details of the performance record include dates, performers, conductors, locations, and other important information, as available. Following the performance listing, a bibliography of writings that pertain to the composition and its performance, mostly critical reviews, is designated with "WB" for "Works Bibliography."

Entries are annotated, arranged chronologically, and cross-referenced with the performance entries.

This book also provides an inventory of Chadwick's music for band ("WR") whether arranged by Chadwick or another person, as well a listing of Chadwick's own arrangements of music by other composers ("WA").

A Discography ("D") chapter provides the details of Chadwick's recorded music, while the Discography Bibliography ("DB") gives the locations of recording reviews and includes annotated references to reviews of recordings in the Discography. Both chapters are organized, like the Works and Performances chapter, first by genre and then by the title of the work under consideration. Following that, listings in the Discography are chronological, while citations in the Discography Bibliography are arranged alphabetically by the reviewer's last name and cross-referenced with entries in the Discography.

The General Bibliography contains books and articles that consider aspects of Chadwick's life, career, and music without being direct commentaries on specific performances of his music. The listing is chronological and each entry is preceded with the identifier "B" (for "Bibliography").

The Bibliography of Writings by Chadwick is listed chronologically, and each entry is preceded by "C" (for "Chadwick"). I have also included in this section of the book Chadwick's interviews in the printed press if they are of substantial length.

The sheer quantity of Chadwick's songs and works for chorus makes any effort to organize them a cumbersome task. Many of these compositions were published in individual leaves and then later re-released singly or included in one or more collections. Further, some were first issued in a collection and then later sold as individual compositions. The present Music for Chorus and Songs sections of the Works and Performances chapter lists most items in their collection versions, while those that were published only individually are so listed. The reader may assume that most of the individual works from each collection were released alone at one time or another. The Choral Music Index and Song Title Index cross-reference all compositions in the listing and will help the researcher locate a specific work by title.

Throughout the book there are references to Chadwick's *Journals* and *Memoirs*. He kept daily records of his activities for many years, and I have referred to these as the *Journals*. They include his thoughts about his and other composers' music, information about financial transactions, and even facts about the weather and baseball. In the 1920s, advancing age compelled Chadwick to begin the compilation of his *Memoirs* for the benefit of his family and posterity. Over the past several years I have been afforded a great deal of access to these materials and have included herein information that is appropriate to this volume.

Over the course of his productive career, Chadwick worked with many publishers. While the Works and Performances catalog indicates only an abbreviated name of each publishing firm, the full name of each company and its location is presented herewith:

C. C. Birchard, Boston; Boston Music Company, Boston; J. Church, Cincinnati; Oliver Ditson, Boston; H. W. Gray, New York; T. B. Harms, New York; J. B. Millet, New York; Novello, London; L. Prang, Boston; G. Schirmer, New York; Arthur P. Schmidt, Boston and Leipzig; Charles Scribner, New York; Silver Burdett, Boston; B. F. Wood, Boston.

Further, while manuscript locations, when known, are included here, many of the orchestral works are currently available either for purchase or rental from Luck's Music Library (Madison Heights, Michigan) or from the Edwin A. Fleisher Collection of the Free Library of Philadelphia. I have indicated the catalog number of available compositions in the Works and Performances chapter.

For the locations of manuscripts and other archival materials, the following library abbreviations will apply:

CtY	Yale University (New Haven, Connecticut)
DLC	Library of Congress (Washington, D. C.)
MB	Boston Public Library (Boston, Massachusetts)
MBCM	New England Conservatory (Boston, Massachusetts)
MS	Springfield City Library (Springfield, Massachusetts)
NN	New York Public Library (New York, New York)
NRU-Mus	Sibley Music Library, Eastman School of Music (Rochester, New York)

Acknowledgments

I would like to thank the family and heirs of George Whitefield Chadwick for their constant encouragement of my interest in his music. Special thanks to Theodore Jr. and Elsie Chadwick for their warm hospitality to me and my family during several extended visits to their home. Their generosity with information, family lore, photographs, and other materials, is truly remarkable; I especially thank them for permission to quote from Chadwick's *Journals* and *Memoirs*. Without their enthusiastic cooperation much less would be known about the great Yankee composer and his music.

I am grateful to Steven Ledbetter who similarly encouraged my efforts and whose still invaluable *George W. Chadwick: A Sourcebook* has served as a launch pad for my own work over the last decade. His enthusiasm, careful research, and willingness to share information has not only heightened my own interest, but has led directly to the recent Chadwick renaissance. Ledbetter's advice has always been sound and enlightening, and his untiring efforts on behalf of Chadwick are remarkable and inspiring. I truly appreciate his input.

Don Hixon, my adviser from Greenwood Press, provided valuable information and guidance during the latter stages of this book's development for which I am very appreciative. Special thanks to Charles Freeman, a doctoral student at The Florida State University, for his willingness to send me important documents and information, always efficiently compiled and always in a timely manner. Victor Yellin continues to be a fountain of knowledge about all things Chadwick, and I appreciate his insights and encouragement. Jean Morrow, Director of Libraries, New England Conservatory, went well out of her way to assist me. She cheerfully provided copies of programs, details regarding manuscripts and other Conservatory holdings, and responded to countless miscellaneous requests. This project would not have been possible without her.

Professor Douglass Seaton of The Florida State University read and commented on the life and works chapter of this volume. As always, the value of his input is inestimable.

Many others assisted with this work by providing everything from scores and large chunks of information to tiny tidbits of data. All have been essential to my efforts and I sincerely appreciate their help. Thanks to: The staff of the Palm Beach County Library, Royal Palm Beach branch, especially David P. Darnell and Cheryl Morris Gray; Libby Nemota of the Inter-Library Loan section of the same library was extremely helpful; Robert Benedikt and Erich Mamson; Phyllis Danner, Sousa Archives for Band Research, The University of Illinois at Urbana-Champaign; Zoraya Mendez, Print Licensing Manager for G. Schirmer and Associated Music Publishers, New York; Diane O. Ota, Curator of Music, Boston Public Library; Julie Englander, The Newberry Library, Chicago; Neeme Jarvi, conductor, The Detroit Symphony Orchestra; MGySgt. Mike Ressler, Chief Librarian, The United States Marine Band ("The President's Own"), Washington, D.C.; Michael Pisani, Watanabe Special Collections, Sibley Music Library, Eastman School of Music; Sidney Grolnic, Music Librarian, and Kile Smith, Curator of the Fleisher Collection at the Free Library of Philadelphia; Wayne D. Shirley, Music Specialist, and William C. Parsons, Music Specialist, of The Library of Congress; Joan Bedard, Worcester Historical Museum; Natalie Palme, The Harvard Musical Association; Virginia Eskin, pianist; Barbara Wolff and Melanie Wisner of the Houghton Library at Harvard University; Mary W. Pitt, Beardsley and Memorial Library, Winsted, Connecticut; Robert Schmieder, Campus Writer, New England Conservatory; Dr. Myron Welch, Director of Bands, The University of Iowa; Dr. Thomas Stoner, Connecticut College; Dr. Theodore C. Davidovich, Westfield State College; Richard Cormier, conductor, The Tampa Bay Chamber Orchestra; Leif Bjalund, Music Director, Waterbury Symphony Orchestra; Norman Lovely, Worcester Public Library; Alan Karass, Music Librarian, The College of Holy Cross; Francesca M. Blasing, director of communications, Music Teachers National Conference; Kendall L. Crilly, Music Librarian, Yale University; Kate Culkin, Archival Assistant, New York University; Cynthia Murphy, Associate Librarian, The Springfield Museums; Mary Elizabeth Rame, Archivist, Eastman School of Music; Joan D. Krizack, Archivist, Northeastern University; Robert O. Johnson, CCM Library, University of Cincinnati; Robin Baker, archivist, Handel & Haydn Society, Boston; Mary C. Plaine, Librarian, Baltimore Symphony Orchestra; Teri A. McKibben, publications manager, and Scott A. Rocke of the Cincinnati Symphony Orchestra; Mark Loftin, Bard College; Rosanne Swire, General Manager, New England Philharmonic; Patricia O'Kelly, National Symphony Orchestra; Richard Wandel, New York Philharmonic; Kimberly Barncastle, Los Angeles Philharmonic; Jane Terry,

Indianapolis Symphony Orchestra; Carol S. Jacoabs, The Cleveland Orchestra; Timothy Flynn and Frank Villella, Chicago Symphony Orchestra; Steven J. Astle, San Francisco Symphony; Julie Eugenio, The Philadelphia Orchestra; Ingrid Nelson, The Minnesota Orchestra; Linda L. Acosta, The Saint Louis Symphony Orchestra; Nick Jones, Atlanta Symphony Orchestra; and Gino Francesconi, Carnegie Hall.

Finally, special thanks to my wife, Julie, for her patience, indulgence, and good-humor throughout this project. She makes any difficulty, scholarly or otherwise, much easier to bear.

GEORGE WHITEFIELD CHADWICK

Life, Works and Style

"George Whitefield Chadwick came from good
old orthodox New England stock, and was
unmistakably a Yankee."

Dr. Hamilton C. MacDougall, 1931.

Life

George Whitefield Chadwick was born on 13 November 1854 in the industrial
town of Lowell, Massachusetts. His mother, Hannah Godfrey Fitts Chadwick,
died within days of his birth, leaving Chadwick's father, Alonzo Calvin
Chadwick, alone to care for the newborn and George's older brother, Fitts Henry.
Alonzo Chadwick married Susan Collins less than three months later, on 3
February 1855. For unknown reasons, during the next two years George resided
with his grandparents. He was reunited with his father and stepmother in 1857,
whereupon they moved 15 miles upriver to the town of Lawrence,
Massachusetts.

Apparently Chadwick's first musical experiences occurred when he was quite
young, for his parents were competent and enthusiastic amateur musicians.
Louis Charles Elson, his friend, colleague, and sometime critic, wrote that both
of his parents were musical. Alonzo had taught in an academy and singing
school near Concord, New Hampshire, while Chadwick's mother sang in the
church choir. Further, Elson noted that Chadwick's extended family was "more
or less active in the old style of psalmody."

Alonzo Chadwick was a member of the Lawrence Musical Association and was one of many area singers to lend his talents to Patrick S. Gilmore's enormous musical spectacle, the 1869 Boston Peace Jubilee. In addition, Chadwick's older brother, Fitts Henry, played the organ and gave George his first lessons on that instrument. Fitts Henry also participated in the Boston Oratorio Class [Society] and various other community musical organizations.

If Chadwick displayed an interest in music at an early age, his academic achievements were less impressive. He dropped out of high school in 1871 only to flounder briefly in Alonzo Chadwick's insurance business. Chadwick presumably developed some administrative acumen while working for his father, a man who had risen from the ranks of the laboring class to found his own establishment. But the more important aspect of this business experience may have been Chadwick's frequent trips into Boston and other cities, during which he made efforts to attend concerts and partake of cultural events not available in Lawrence.

Chadwick entered New England Conservatory as a "special student" in 1872. Special students enjoyed the benefits of studying with the faculty without the rigors of formal entrance requirements and without following a curriculum that resulted in a degree. In reality, special students enabled the then-struggling conservatory to increase its cash-flow by giving voice and piano lessons to those with modest musical ambitions. But Chadwick approached his studies more seriously and took advantage of a full spectrum of offerings. He studied organ with George E. Whiting (1840-1923), piano with Carlyle Petersilea (1844-1903), and theory with Stephen A. Emery (1841-1891), each of whom was a respected figure in Boston's musical circles.

In addition to his conservatory studies, Chadwick supplemented his education by taking occasional organ lessons with the esteemed Dudley Buck (1839-1909), who may have served as a role model for him. In the 1870s Buck was just beginning his career as a composer, but he was well known as a performer and teacher and had spent several years in Germany. Buck had also spent a year in Paris, an unusual destination for a young American musician in those days. But Buck, who in 1875 would become Assistant Conductor with the Theodore Thomas Orchestra, was one of the very few American artists versatile enough to carve a living out of music in the days before musical activities were supported by the academy.

After a scant four years of formal music training and without the benefit of a degree, in 1876 Chadwick found himself in a position to accept a job at the Michigan Conservatory, the music department of Olivet College in Olivet, Michigan, southwest of Lansing. Chadwick was listed as Conservatory Director on concert programs and flyers and obviously had an opportunity to establish an important career in Michigan. There he taught a number of basic music subjects, performed regularly, and was no doubt a valued administrator.

It is from his time at the Michigan Conservatory that the first evidence of Chadwick's interest in composing appears. Although a fire destroyed many of the conservatory's records from the period, a program dated 6 November 1876, lists a performance of his **Canon in E-flat**. This is the earliest extant listing that we have for Chadwick as composer, but he had harbored the desire to compose from his earliest days at New England Conservatory and almost certainly did so--the **Canon in E-flat** is listed on the program as opus 16, no. 1.

Chadwick remained at the conservatory for only a single year, perhaps recognizing that he could not develop as a composer without further, more intensive study. Ever savvy to musical politics and with a clear understanding of what Americans expected from composers, Chadwick must have realized that his career in music in the United States would be limited without European credentials.

Chadwick arrived in Berlin in 1877, hoping to study with the renowned organist Karl August Haupt (1810-1891), who had exerted a strong influence on John Knowles Paine (1839-1906). But Paine's musical experiences in Europe had been mainly related to organ performance, and Chadwick quickly realized that Haupt was not competent to teach him composition, which by this time had become Chadwick's main interest. Although there was no shortage of composition teachers in Berlin at the time, Chadwick removed to Leipzig and the Royal Conservatory of Music, where he began lessons with Salomon Jadassohn (1831-1902) and Carl Reinecke (1824-1910), which continued until 1879.

Both Jadassohn and Reinecke were eminent figures when Chadwick met them. Jadassohn had studied piano with Liszt and was highly regarded as a theorist and composer, although much of his renown was acquired following Chadwick's matriculation. Reinecke had joined the conservatory in 1860 and also enjoyed an enviable reputation as conductor of the Leipzig Gewandhaus Orchestra.

Of the two, Chadwick was drawn to the younger Jadassohn. They shared a similar fun-loving spirit, and Jadassohn, though by no means an avant-garde composer, was not as overtly conservative as Reinecke. Chadwick was probably attracted to Jadassohn's mastery of traditional compositional technique, tempered by a willingness to deviate from the rules for the purposes of dramatic expression.

Chadwick's most important compositions from his student days include two string quartets and the concert overture **Rip Van Winkle**. While clearly student works, they served to solidify his position as a young American up-and-comer with his German teachers and classmates, as well as with the German press. The critical accounts of Chadwick's chamber works and the overture are unusually favorable.

Following his two-year stay in Leipzig, Chadwick found himself traveling around Europe with a group of artists who referred to themselves as the "Duveneck Boys." They were mostly painters led by a spiritual mentor, the American artist Frank Duveneck (1848-1919). No doubt Duveneck's free-spirited nature struck the young Chadwick as wonderfully Romantic, but one can only speculate on the extent to which this experience impacted Chadwick's music. Chadwick himself did not discuss this period of his life at length.

Chadwick's adventures with the Duveneck Boys were centered around France and have been credited with infusing into Chadwick's music a certain Gallic style, and indeed to an extent this is true, although French traits were slow to appear in his compositions. In any number of his works after about 1895, especially in the great "American" works like **Symphonic Sketches** and **Suite Symphonique**, French influences can be plainly heard. But surely some of his Frenchness can be attributed to the increasing popularity of the impressionistic style in the United States and the notoriety of French music's greatest proponent, Claude Debussy.

Taken with the French lifestyle and apparently impressed by that nation's musical and artistic outlook, Chadwick briefly considered study in Paris with Cesar Franck. He returned to Germany in the fall of 1879, however, and resumed his compositional studies, this time with Joseph Rheinberger (1839-1901) at the Hochschule fur Musik in Munich. Why Chadwick chose Munich over Paris is a matter for speculation. As the end of the nineteenth century neared, Germany was still a most important center of musical activity, and Chadwick, an extraordinarily self-disciplined individual, may have been attracted to Rheinberger's stern pedagogical methodology. At the same time, Munich, then as now, offered a less hectic, more carefree lifestyle than northern Germany, while still providing a sound musical education.

Rheinberger was a conservative after the manner of Jadassohn and Reinecke, but he directed his students with more vigor. Whereas music courses in Leipzig required no small amount of self-direction, Rheinberger was known as a taskmaster and a skilled craftsman who infused his own works with creative polyphony and astonishing formal clarity. Moreover, Chadwick undoubtedly benefited from Rheinberger's extensive knowledge of the classics from both the instrumental and choral traditions, and from his unusual work ethic, for Rheinberger, like Chadwick, was prolific.

Chadwick returned to Boston in March 1880 and immediately busied himself with the task of establishing a career. After opening a teaching studio, his first order of business was to secure performances of the works that had made him successful in Germany. **Rip Van Winkle** was given two performances even before his return to Boston, and Chadwick undoubtedly played no small part in making sure that the public and critics alike were aware of the triumphant reception it received in Leipzig. He certainly added to his reputation when, in May 1880, he conducted the work publicly himself. The energetic young composer did not rest on his already-completed work, however; rather he set about completing his now-forgotten **First Symphony**. At that time a symphony by an American composer was a novelty. While the work is derivative and sometimes uninspired, following its sole performance reviewers were nevertheless quick to note that the symphony was a valuable early contribution by a gifted young musician.

In addition to his compositional activities, Chadwick was also busy as a performer. He took the position of Musical Director at Boston's Clarendon Street Baptist Church in early 1881, and the following year became the organist at Park Street Church. Through the years he would serve a number of different churches as organist. Chadwick also assumed teaching duties at New England Conservatory in 1882, where it had been reported that he would " . . . be at the head of a department of practical composition" (See: B6). His appointment led to a fifty-year association with that institution.

Perhaps following the model of Dudley Buck, throughout his career Chadwick harbored a desire to conduct professionally. He often conducted his own music and additionally held a number of conducting posts throughout his life. One early and important assignment occurred when John Knowles Paine asked Chadwick to conduct Paine's own **Oedipus Tyrannus** in 1881. In addition, Chadwick led various community musical associations in the 1880s, including the Arlington Club (Boston) and the Schubert Club (Salem).

One of Chadwick's most important early conducting experiences was with the Boston Orchestral Club, which he led from 1887 to 1892. Although the group was intended to offer competition to the Boston Symphony Orchestra, its short season and uneven quality of musicianship, coupled with its inability to match the Boston Symphony in economic terms, made it only marginally competitive. Nevertheless, Chadwick was able to hone his conducting skills and perform a varied repertoire in front of audiences which were beginning to appreciate his considerable contributions to the cultural life of the city.

In 1890 Chadwick began his nine-year tenure as Music Director of the Springfield Festival. This large annual festival was regarded at the time as one of the best such events in the nation. Eventually Chadwick was confronted with difficulties that he thought would be impossible to overcome, the quality of the singing and the difficulty of attracting accomplished singers being the festival's greatest limitation. For their part, many of the participant's began to sense Chadwick's resentment toward them, and a public scandal started to brew. The *Springfield Graphic* (Massachusetts) noted some of the difficulties:

> The musical association chorus is sadly in need of male voices, but it is safe to say that there are men who enjoy singing with the chorus who do not enjoy Mr. Chadwick's sarcasm, which at times verges on impoliteness. Mr. Chadwick is immensely funny, and his wit is keen; but there is a kind and courteous treatment that even bass and tenor singers appreciate. Perhaps this is only a symptom of Bostonese manners.

In 1899 Chadwick left the Springfield Festival and accepted an appointment as Music Director of the Worcester Festival, also a highly regarded event. Musical circumstances in Worcester were not drastically different from those in Spring-field, and in many ways Chadwick's task was just as difficult. Nevertheless, by the time he relinquished his post in 1901, he had overseen a number of performances of his own music and improved the quality of the festival.

Chadwick's most important career step occurred in 1897 when he was appointed Director of New England Conservatory by a unanimous decision of its board of directors. When Chadwick took over, the conservatory was in difficult straits. It had just experienced a scandal which culminated in the resignation of Chadwick's predecessor, the highly-regarded pianist Carl Faelten (1846-1925). Further, the conservatory was desperately low on funds, and contributions were not forthcoming in the wake of the upheaval.

Chadwick was by this time a mature forty-two years old and was known to all as talented, personable, frank, and energetic. While he lacked a college education, he nevertheless had been schooled in Boston as well as in Europe's finest conservatories and could even boast a directorship at the Michigan Conservatory. Chadwick was a nationally-recognized musical figure, and, in retrospect, the conservatory board's choice seems inevitable. Chadwick had all of the necessary musical tools to lead the conservatory, and his humor and self-confidence, the board must have thought, would enable him to hobnob with Boston's elite and perhaps bring in much-needed funding.

In their recent history of New England Conservatory, *Measure by Measure*, Bruce MacPherson and James Klein note that Chadwick ". . . had transformed an impoverished piano and voice academy into a modern conservatory. That work made him the the most important figure in the school's history." Chadwick instituted a number of changes that made the conservatory more closely resemble the German conservatories of his experience. Students were required to take more music history and theory classes, and a variety of performing ensembles were established. Further, Chadwick began to involve members of the Boston Symphony Orchestra in the training of students on the various orchestral instruments, and before long the conservatory's ensembles were of a respectable calibre.

Chadwick himself was an inspiring teacher, and a number of America's best young musical minds sought him out for instruction. Student reports convey an image of Chadwick as a demanding, fair-minded, and witty mentor. Among his students were Horatio Parker, William Grant Still, Mabel Daniels, Edward Burlingame Hill, Daniel Gregory Mason, and many others. Still's experience with Chadwick is seemingly typical; the young African-American composer was given a great deal of creative latitude with his musical ideas, and Chadwick simply discussed weaknesses and made suggestions, leaving Still's own style intact. Another of Chadwick's important pedagogical contributions was his textbook, **Harmony: A Course of Study**, which remained in wide use a number of years after his death.

In addition to greatly enhancing the quality of New England Conservatory's music programs, Chadwick endeavored to make the conservatory experience a more social one by instituting clubs and activities to keep his students busy during those rare occasions when they were not practicing or attending concerts. Under Chadwick's guidance, New England Conservatory founded the Alpha chapter of what is now the nation's pre-eminent music fraternity, Phi Mu Alpha Sinfonia.

The fifteen-year period from 1885 to 1900 saw the creation of several of Chadwick's most popular pieces. The **Symphony No. 2 in B-flat Major** was composed over several years beginning in 1883 and was premiered in 1886. Its sparkling, pentatonic second-movement melody has made it famous, and today it seems an obvious precursor to Dvorak's "American" style. The serious nature of **Melpomene** made that work one of Chadwick's most-often performed compositions in his day. With Wagnerian hints and dramatic aims, the work is a masterpiece of nineteenth-century orchestral music and can withstand comparison to anything Europe has to offer from that time. Chadwick reached the height of his creativity in the field of chamber music with the **Third, Fourth**, and **Fifth String Quartets** and the **Piano Quintet**. Each was admired and performed widely, but, inexplicably, after the turn of the century Chadwick composed only short, occasional chamber works. Some of Chadwick's most compelling choral works date from this time, **Phoenix Expirans, The Lily Nymph**, and his **Columbian Ode** perhaps being the best and best known.

After 1897 Chadwick's administrative concerns left him little time for composing during the academic year. Although after 1900 much of his music was begun or completed in the summer months at his residence in West Chop on the extreme northern tip of Martha's Vineyard, his inventive powers did not subside. He composed much of his best music after the turn of the century, and only during the Great War was there a significant decline in his output.

Although the 1880s and 1890s had been very productive, many of Chadwick's finest works were written between 1900 and 1915. Several of his best orchestral compositions fall into this period, such as **Sinfonietta in D major**, **Suite Symphonique**, **Aphrodite**, and **Tam O'Shanter**. A number of less well-known works, like **Cleopatra** and the **Theme, Variations, and Fugue** for organ and orchestra, were also written during these years. As numerous and as impressive as Chadwick's works for orchestra are, though, he seems to have pinned his hopes for even greater success on his stage works, particularly **Judith** and **The Padrone**.

The tale from the Apocrypha of Judith and Holofernes provided Chadwick with an excellent dramatic vehicle, as did **The Padrone**, a riveting story of Italians in the north end of Boston. While **Judith** received a number of performances during Chadwick's day and was generally admired by the public, it fell out of fashion by the onset of the Great War, although it continued to be mentioned in most discussions of Chadwick's legacy. **The Padrone**, on the other hand, received its first complete performance only in 1996, and, while its realistic subject matter would no doubt would have exerted a marked influence on the history of American opera, its plot may have contributed to its rejection for performance in the days when Italian musicians and administrators held much sway over what was performed in American opera houses. At any rate, the failure of **The Padrone** to attain a performance and Chadwick's subsequent disappointment, coupled with growing tension in Europe and his advancing age, caused a marked slowing in the pace of his activities.

World War I took its toll on Chadwick. Both of his sons, Theodore and Noel, were active soldiers early on in the conflict, but Theodore actually saw battle at Verdunne and elsewhere in Europe, and Chadwick was constantly worried about him. The emotional stress visited upon him made it difficult to compose, and in a *Journal* entry from 1916 Chadwick wrote, "I do not feel that I accomplished anything this year. For the first time since I can remember, I find myself with nothing to write" (1 January 1916). Chadwick frequently mentioned the conflict and admitted his personal difficulties in a 1918 entry: "And every day comes news of our New England boys, some of them our friends, being killed or wounded. Ma [Ida May Chadwick] is wonderful and I think I should go to pieces except for her steadfast courage. We live on hope. . . . " (25 November 1918).

Chadwick's output slowed considerably in the years from 1916 to 1918. His only major orchestral work was the tone poem **Angel of Death**, a darkly moving work. **Love's Sacrifice** was Chadwick's final stage work, a "pastoral opera" that Allen Langley reports to have been largely completed by one of Chadwick's composition classes at New England Conservatory. Perhaps the best composition of the period is the patriotic and beautiful **Land of Our Hearts**, to John Hall Ingham's dramatic text.

By the early 1920s Chadwick had tired of composing. With things running smoothly at the conservatory, which by then was a model institution for the nation, Chadwick had little to do but busy himself with attending concerts, taking in the odd performance of his own music here and there, and indulging his love for entertaining friends and participating in Boston's very active club life. He did write three interesting works for baritone and orchestra, a combination he had found attractive earlier in his career. **Lochinvar** of 1896 was considered a fine achievement, and Chadwick's affinity for the combination was heightened by his friendship with two of the era's leading baritones, Max Heinrich (1853-1916) and David Bispham (1857-1921). While they did not garner a permanent place in the repertoire, works like **Pirate Song**, **Drake's Drum**, and **Joshua** exhibit Chadwick's always-careful attention to architectural detail and interesting moments throughout. Other works from Chadwick's later years include the **Anniversary Overture**, a piece that was generally considered by critics as academic and old-fashioned; the charming miniature set **Tre Pezzi**, a work which deserves modern reconsideration; and the gorgeous **Elegy**, a richly-textured symphonic memorial to Chadwick's former student and longtime friend Horatio Parker.

Chadwick's character has often been commented upon, but aspects of his personal life have rarely been considered. His *Journals* confirm Chadwick's congeniality and good humor. He loved sports, and often took in baseball and football games, and even the occasional round of golf. In his later years, having become an established figure, he enjoyed Boston's club life, fine dining, and entertaining friends. He and his wife, Ida May, traveled and vacationed regularly with Mr. and Mrs. Horatio Parker; other musical figures, such as Arthur Foote and "Eddie" Hill (Edward Burlingame Hill) were regular companions. Chadwick derived a great deal of joy from his friendship with John Philip Sousa, whom he found likable and possessed of a sympathetic sense of humor. Chadwick's advancing age disturbed him tremendously and gave way to an annual opportunity to comment with sarcastic humor: "65th Birthday. Cheer Up! The worst is yet to come." (*Journal*, 13 November 1919). Chadwick, who was known to take a drink now and then, commented on one of the most pressing social issues of the day in a 1923 entry: "The prohibition question is more unsettled than ever. After four years of this fanatical despotism, there is more drunkenness, more 'dope,' more crime, and more rum to be had than ever" (*Journal*, 31 December 1923).

Following Chadwick's death in 1931 several memorial essays were authored by his friends, students and admirers. One of the best was offered by Hamilton C. MacDougall, one of Chadwick's counterpoint pupils at New England Conservatory. Writing in the organists' periodical *The Diapason*, MacDougall penned a brief but enlightening and highly personal account of Chadwick. MacDougall wrote:

> The brief time [ca. 1900] I had lessons from him showed me what a clear thinker he was, how destitute of all pomposity, bluster and self-conceit . . . . He was very good company and at home with artistic and literary folk of all degrees; a retentive memory and a wide acquaintance with many clever musicians and well-known people in all walks of life provided him with a fund of anecdotes always apropos of the conversation and always entertaining.

MacDougall continued with a detailed account of Chadwick's death:

> Chadwick's death was sudden. On Saturday, April 4, he was in his usual, though by no means robust, health, and the Chadwicks were entertaining friends at dinner. [At] About ten [o'clock] he excused himself to go to bed. Mrs. Chadwick, hearing a noise, went to the room where he had fallen and tried to help him up, but he died in her arms.

Chadwick's funeral was held at Boston's Trinity Church on 7 April 1931. Honorary pallbearers included his long-time friend and conservatory colleague Wallace Goodrich, the composers Frederick Shepherd Converse, Charles Martin Loeffler, and Edward Burlingame Hill, and the admired American conductor-composer Henry Hadley.

Chadwick was very well known in his own day, and, of course, was particularly beloved in his adopted city of Boston. He had received two honorary degrees, one from Yale University (1897), and one from Tufts University (1905). His hometown of Lawrence, Massachusetts, had shown its pride in the composer by founding a Chadwick Club. In 1907 it boasted 42 members and sponsored at least one orchestra performance at which Chadwick conducted his own concert overture, **Euterpe**. Later he was elected to the American Academy of Arts and Letters and the National Institute of Arts and Letters, which awarded him its Gold Medal in 1928 (now in the possession of his heirs). To this day New England Conservatory remembers Chadwick each year by awarding an outstanding senior the "The George Whitefield Chadwick Medal."

Chadwick's musical legacy is strengthening as a renewed interest in his life and music has led to important recordings of some of his finest compositions. Books, articles, and dissertations are starting slowly to appear, and most confirm his genius. George Chadwick was an unusual man with numerous talents and interests. He could be gruff, sarcastic, and dishearteningly honest with friends and students, but he was nearly always able to endear himself to others, whether with a wry smile, a joke, interesting conversation, or a captivating composition. MacDougall noted another of Chadwick's traits, one observed by his many admirers, and thought it a fitting summary of the composer's entire life:

> I have left to the last what seems to me Chadwick's most remarkable quality of mind and music, his youth. He was 76 years old as time goes, but a most active and original mind, a most vivid personality, [and] an intense vitality gave youth to his music.

Works and Style

Chadwick and his music remain enigmatic, even though he was one of the most prolific composers that the United States ever produced. During a career that spanned over fifty years, Chadwick was widely considered the "Dean of American Composers," and he remained among the most esteemed musicians in America until after World War I. He composed in nearly every genre, including opera, chamber music, choral works, and songs, and he had a special affinity for orchestral music. The major genres to which Chadwick did not contribute are the concerto and the solo sonata.

Chadwick's music can be categorized into four main style periods. (1) The Mainstream Period, 1879-1894; (2) The Americanism/Modernism Period, 1895-1909; (3) The Dramatic Period, 1910-1918, and; (4) The Reflective Years, 1919-1931.

Dubbing Chadwick's first period (1879-1894) of creative activity "mainstream" is somewhat misleading, for a number of his compositions from this period display a more eclectic technique and vision than the word suggests. Generally, from the beginning of his serious work as a composer until the completion of his **Third Symphony**, his works exhibit hallmarks of an early- to mid-nineteenth century musical technique and resemble in many respects those works with which he probably became familiar as a student in Leipzig. Specifically, Chadwick favored sonata form, diatonic harmony, and regular rhythms and phrases in his music.

Chadwick's symphonies constitute an important body of nineteenth-century orchestral works, and their merits are only now being discovered. The **Symphony [No. 1] in C Major, Symphony No. 2 in B-flat Major,** and **Symphony in F (No. 3)** adhere to the accepted principles of conservative composition, and follow the four-movement outline that by Chadwick's time had become routine. The works also follow the sonata plan rather carefully, and Chadwick's models were drawn from the works of Beethoven, Mendelssohn, Schumann, and Brahms, and, to a lesser extent, even Wagner.

There are some important original aspects of the symphonies, however. While the first is clearly the work of a novice orchestral composer, both the **Second Symphony** and the **Third Symphony** employ pentatonicism, clever and knowledgeable use of the orchestral forces, bountiful melody, and a certain robust character that makes them stand out among other American symphonies of the period. The Scotch-Irish gaiety and remarkable orchestration of the **Second Symphony** have contributed mightily to the attention that Chadwick has received in recent years.

Among his most important early overtures are **Rip Van Winkle, Melpomene**, and **Thalia**. **Rip Van Winkle** was Chadwick's first orchestral work and set the stage for his fame both in Europe and in America. Set around Washington Irving's famous tale, the overture was acclaimed for its sturdy craftsmanship and clever handling of materials. While it moves a bit slowly at certain points and some of the themes are less than inspiring, there is evidence of ingenuity. The same might be said of **Melpomene**, one of Chadwick's most important works during his own lifetime.   **Melpomene** garnered many performances and was lauded for its "seriousness." The fact that it sounded in many passages like Wagner contributed to its success, but it is a rich, lush work that can stand on its own beside other music of the period. The marginal success of Chadwick's comedy overture **Thalia** is a bit surprising. Chadwick was seen by some as the American heir apparent to Mendelssohn in the area of lighter composition, and the work is full of memorable melody. Nevertheless, its simple use of materials has made it among the least heralded of all of Chadwick's major works in the genre.

Like **Rip Van Winkle**, Chadwick's **First** and **Second String Quartets** date from his student days in Leipzig, but they show surprising inventiveness and a secure knowledge of developmental procedures. The third movement of the **First Quartet** utilizes a popular American dance ("Shoot the Pipe"), while the fourth movement of the **Second Quartet** is an attractive and ingenious display of rhythmic propulsion. This from a young man not yet twenty-five years of age who had begun composing in earnest less than five years earlier.

The **Third String Quartet** displays a marked improvement over the first two in its handling of the instruments. While Chadwick's basic style has changed little, the work is more distinguished in its themes than the **First Quartet**, less derivative than the **Second**, and contains more interesting writing than was found in either of his earlier efforts. Further, the sound overall is more genuinely American than anything Chadwick had composed up to that time.

Chadwick's final major chamber work, the **Quintet for Piano and Strings**, is a lyrical, often wistful creation that utilizes the instruments in a relatively standard manner. Chadwick's melodic gifts are in evidence, and the work lacks any hint of "Americanism," a fact which may have resulted in its popularity at the turn of the century. But here the instrumentation is less comfortable, even at times a bit plodding, and the rhythmic drive that has been a hallmark of his music seems suppressed. Nevertheless, it is one of the most important American chamber works from the nineteenth century and deserves more attention than it is presently getting.

Chadwick composed three stage works during this period, including two lost comic operas, **The Peer and the Pauper** and **A Quiet Lodging**. A third stage work, **Tabasco**, which Chadwick dubbed a "burlesque opera," survives. **Tabasco** features a humorous plot, comically-named characters, and light, popular-style music that, at the outset, seems very unexpected from the composer of the orchestral and chamber works. But Chadwick was drawn to its rather exotic, Middle Eastern-inspired plot, and his own wry wit and gift for setting down catchy tunes could not have been given a better outlet.

Among Chadwick's music for soloists, chorus and orchestra one piece stands out. **The Lily Nymph** kept alive the nineteenth century preoccupation with mystical themes, and Chadwick's tale of knights and nymphs is not without several beautiful moments. But even though the music, couched in a curious mixture of techniques borrowed from impressionism and Mendelssohn, succeeds, the story is loose and unbelievable.

In the second style period (1895-1909) of Chadwick's career two related musical strains began to assert themselves more aggressively: Americanism and modernism. Americanism had been hinted at in at least two of Chadwick's earlier works, the **Second Symphony** and the **Third String Quartet**. But in this period mere hints give way to a full-blown reconsideration of nationalism and its possibilities in music. Chadwick's modernistic thinking displays itself in his freer treatment of sonata form, and even its abandonment in some compositions.

Although in recent years it has received no attention, at its premiere the concert overture **Adonais** was considered one of Chadwick's most modern works up to that time. The highly regarded critic William Foster Apthorp stated,

> It is the most modern in spirit of anything I know from his pen. . . .
> He has outgrown the classic idea, his time for being modern has come,
> and he follows the new instinct with complete willingness and
> frankness. . . . The very character of the thematic material in **Adonais**
> is modern, in sharp contrast to the classic reserve shown in the
> **Melpomene** [overture]; the expression is more outspoken, more
> purely emotional and dramatic.

Its "modernisms" included a multi-sectional structure, muted effects in the
strings, and the use of a harp and other "color" instruments and effects to provide
an ethereal quality, rhythmic ambiguity, and sporadic chromaticism. Combined,
these attributes make this his most compelling dramatic work since
Melpomene.

Chadwick continued to explore the symphonic genre with his **Symphonic
Sketches, Sinfonietta**, and **Suite Symphonique**. All are in the
conventional four-movement pattern, but Chadwick departed from tradition by
utilizing light, sometimes even humorous themes, elements of programma-
ticism, impressionism, modalism, and non-functional harmony. The orchestration is clever and unexpected; bass clarinet cadenzas, saxophone solos, full-
blown solos for brass instruments, and large percussion batteries can be found in
much of this music. Moreover, the often-pentatonic melodies that Chadwick
weaves throughout his orchestral palette are completely captivating.

Chadwick's **Fourth** and **Fifth String Quartets** are both elegantly
constructed, often vigorous compositions that were quite renowned in their own
day. The **Fourth**, composed on the heels of Dvorak's String Quartet in F (Op.
96, "American"), displays a more overtly American sensibility than the **Fifth**.
Full length folk-style themes abound, and the pentatonic third-movement fiddle
tune, surrounded by simple harmonies, is infectious.

Judith stands out as the first of Chadwick's major works for the stage, but it
has been almost completely neglected since his death. A curious blend of opera
and oratorio, the work borrows for its plot the tale from the Aprocrypha of
Judith and Holofernes. It is a melodic, sometimes chromatic work that
successfully depicts both the exotic and the erotic, and has been considered a
musical relative of Saint-Saens's **Samson et Delilah**.

Ecce jam noctis, for chorus and orchestra, is one of Chadwick's few attempts
at setting Latin. Composed for Yale's 1897 commencement ceremony, at which
Chadwick was awarded an honorary degree, the work suffers from a sometimes
awkward setting of the language, with which Chadwick had had little experience.
Nevertheless, it features a striking, contemplative orchestral introduction and a
number of delightful rhythmic twists, particularly the section in which the

triple-meter strings are pitted against the static, homophonically-set chorus. The work nicely demonstrates Chadwick's considerable ingenuity with limited musical materials.

Lochinvar is an arresting essay for baritone and orchestra. The obvious Celtic flavor of the piece led observers to neglect its interesting manipulation of musical materials, including duple versus triple metrical shifts, translucent orchestration, and smooth, flowing vocal line. Chadwick's combination of the baritone voice with the violin soloist just before the "Introduction and Strathspey" section is one of his most inspired creations.

In his third style period (The Dramatic Period, 1910-1918), Chadwick abandoned overtures and symphony-like compositions to produce dramatic, pictorial, and highly programmatic works. These unusually episodic compositions are based on extraordinarily vivid extramusical ideas. It is clear that by this point in his career Chadwick was more interested in effect than in architecture; he was now giving in completely to a trend in his music that had begun in the 1890s with the loosening of his formal structures.

His two major orchestral works of this period are the tone poems **Aphrodite** and **Tam O'Shanter**, both for large orchestra. While they are very different in terms of the messages they attempt to communicate, these two important compositions share many of the same traits. Both are highly programmatic and rely on Chadwick's genius for orchestration and melodic invention. Both are also highly sectional, episodic, and provide excellent depictions of their intended subjects. **Aphrodite** is one of the finest evocations of the sea ever penned, and **Tam O'Shanter**, based on the famous tale by Robert Burns, is a thrilling and effective depiction that may stand on an equal footing with anything produced by Richard Strauss.

Chadwick's **Angel of Death** for large orchestra features few of the effects he used in his earlier works from this period. His ruminations on death are surprisingly robust until the final section, and although special effects are used (muted strings, glissandi, etc.) throughout the work, Chadwick maintains the listener's interest with eleven key changes and interesting motivic development.

Chadwick's most important stage work from this period is **The Padrone**, his realistic tale of life among the immigrant Italians in the north end of Boston. Chadwick considered this among his finest works and apparently was convinced that it was not selected for performance by New York's Metropolitan Opera because its subject matter was too close to the real-life experiences of the Met's Italian management. What separates **The Padrone** from other stage works by Chadwick is its verismo style, that is, its realistic action integrated with a lyrical score that lends the entire work a powerful effect. Only within the last several years is this masterpiece of American operatic literature finally getting its due hearing.

Chadwick wrote a number of patriotic works during the Great War, including **These to the Front**, **The Fighting Men**, and perhaps his best known such composition, **Land of Our Hearts**. Composed for chorus and orchestra, the latter work features an easily sung and gently flowing syllabic setting of a poem by John Hall Ingham. Chadwick's mixed-meter music is clever from the beginning and the orchestration is transparent yet powerful throughout. No doubt the words "Yield us strength to suffer and to dare" had special meaning to the composer, whose son soldiered during the war. And while it seems dated by today's standards, the triumphant and martial ending on ". . . one blood, one Nation everlastingly" is very effective.

What little music Chadwick composed following the Great War, during his fourth period (1919-1931), shows a return to the conservative style of his earlier years. He was no longer writing as the creative artist that he had once been but was by this time a highly-regarded elder musician who was spending his efforts on fulfilling commissions and writing occasional works. The **Anniversary Overture**, intended to celebrate Chadwick's twenty-fifth anniversary as director of New England Conservatory, was considered "scholarly" at its premiere, but critics also noted its warmth and congeniality. Indeed it is rather conventional, but it exhibits a mastery of a nineteenth-century style that was losing its appeal to musicians of a younger generation.

Chadwick's diminutive orchestral set, **Tre Pezzi**, features charming themes sometimes cloaked in rather pedestrian and predictable counterpoint. Several occasional works, like **Fathers of the Free**, **Commemoration Ode**, and the **Fanfare** for brass instruments, display Chadwick's trademark craftsmanship, but they do not exhibit the ingenious sparkle of his earlier music.

More difficult to place within style periods are Chadwick's compositions for piano and organ and his numerous songs. His keyboard works, many of which were published, show a wide spectrum of interests and reveal Chadwick to have had a greater facility in this arena than many have given him credit for. Usually Chadwick's own keyboard skills are remarked upon disdainfully, and it is true that he had not mastered the piano or organ; Chadwick did not care to practice and seems to have made no secret of the fact. Nevertheless, it must be remembered that, for a while at least, he earned his living as an organist, and played the instrument professionally for years. Further, he performed his own **Piano Quintet** several times, and that is no small task for even an accomplished pianist.

The piano works fall mainly into three categories: transcriptions of his own orchestral works, characteristic pieces, and pedagogical pieces. Of the first category there are but two extant examples, transcriptions of **Aphrodite** and **Melpomene**. They are finely built and show an understanding of the genre. Multi-movement characteristic compositions like **Five Pieces for Pianoforte** and **Six Characteristic Studies** feature evocative titles like "Les Grenouilles" ("The Frogs") and "Congratulations," and elegant pianistic writing. The fetching **Chanson orientale**, from 1895, is an early example of an American composer utilizing techniques of eastern exoticism. Chadwick's pedagogical pieces range from compositions intended for the very young, like **Diddle, Diddle Dumpling** and **Ten Little Tunes for Ten Little Friends** to the more advanced **The Aspen**.

Chadwick's organ compositions are slightly more conservative than the piano works and reflect the needs of a working church organist and pedagogue. The music includes polyphonic pieces like **Canzonetta** and **10 Canonic Studies (Op. 12)**, as well as a number of works suitable for church performance, including preludes, marches (or processionals), and pastoral movements.

Chadwick was an enthusiastic composer of songs, and his vast corpus, approaching 150 in number, awaits a thorough scholarly treatment. As a group, the songs defy simple chronological categorization; composed over nearly fifty years, they encompass a huge variety of styles, and include sacred songs, art songs, occasional songs (i.e., songs for holidays and other special events), simple limericks and ditties, and comic songs. Chadwick took full advantage of the freedom offered by the song genre; he appreciated the flights of fancy enabled by a good text (several of which he wrote himself), as well as the freedom from the severe formal writing that marked so much of his instrumental work. The following paragraphs can only hope to offer a brief glimpse into Chadwick's work in this genre.

Like many composers in his day, Chadwick was drawn to the exotic. A number of his songs reflect a fascination with foreign cultures, including **Bedouin Love Song**, a mysterious Middle-Eastern evocation. The song features a thinly-conceived, extremely active accompaniment, which underpins a syllabic text setting (a hallmark of Chadwick's vocal style) and haunting melodic gestures. Similarly, **Mexican Serenade**, wryly marked "a la Tango," features, in addition to a clever text involving armadillos and revolutions, a fluid use of habanera and ragtime rhythms.

"The Trilliums," from Chadwick's collaboration with Arlo Bates titled **A Flower Cycle**, is a fine example of the composer's art-song style. Again utilizing a simple, mostly syllabic word setting, Chadwick paints an elegant melody on a background of 6/8 meter with several jarring shifts into duple simple rhythm. The song ends with an ingenious moment of word-play when

an extended trill is heard on the word "Trillium." Another important collaboration with Bates resulted in the collection **Lyrics from "Told in the Gate"**
and one of Chadwick's most heralded songs, "Sweetheart, Thy Lips are Touched
with Flame." The title alone was rather evocative for Victorian New England
sensibilities, and the song itself is a rather lusty affair. A love song, the work is
a dramatic, even mildly erotic piece, with a sense of pathos wonderfully captured
by the chromatic, densely-written, indeed, almost orchestral, accompaniment.

Other songs effectively display Chadwick's wide range of expression. Folk
songs like "The Northern Days," and the works which comprise his **Songs of
Brittany** show a marked talent for declamation and for sentimentality without
effusiveness. Chadwick's **Three Nautical Songs** feature captivating
accompaniments and a good grasp of light-hearted English sea chantey style,
while a keen sense of humor is evident in "Joshua" (to be pronounced, as the
author carefully notes, "Josh-u-ay") and in the clever **Four Irish Songs**.

Works and Performances

I. Original Compositions

ORCHESTRAL MUSIC

W1. **ADONAIS**, Elegiac Overture (Sketches begun at West Chop, summer 1897; completed January 27, 1899, at New England Conservatory)

Dedication: "In memoriam Frank Fay Marshal" [d. July 26, 1897]
Unpublished
Ink holograph: DLC (score); MBCM (copy of score; parts)
Availability: Fleisher cat. no. 6394
For: 3 (3rd doubles picc.). 2. 2. 2./
         4. 2. 3. 1./
         timp. 1 perc. harp. strings.

The title of this work was suggested by Percy Bysshe Shelley's poem, *Adonis: An Elegy on the Death of John Keats* (1821).

Premiere

W1a.   2/3 February 1900; Boston Symphony Orchestra, Wilhelm Gericke, cond.; Music Hall, Boston.

Other Selected Performances

W1b.   24 November 1916; New England Conservatory Orchestra, "Eben Jordan Memorial Concert," G. W. Chadwick, cond.;

Jordan Hall, Boston.

W1c.   9 March 1917; New England Conservatory Orchestra, Wallace Goodrich, cond; Jordan Hall, Boston.

W1d.   19 May 1931; New England Conservatory Orchestra, "George Whitefield Chadwick Memorial Concert," Wallace Goodrich, cond.; Jordan Hall, Boston.

W1e.   4 May 1934; New England Conservatory Orchestra, "Edwin Perkins Brown Memorial Concert," Wallace Goodrich, cond.; Jordan Hall, Boston.

W1f.   11 December 1940; New England Conservatory Orchestra, Wallace Goodrich, cond.; Jordan Hall, Boston.

W1g.   24 April 1951; New England Conservatory Orchestra, Malcolm Holmes, cond.; Jordan Hall, Boston.

Bibliography

WB1.   W. F. A. [William Foster Apthorp]. "Music and Drama -- Boston Symphony Orchestra." *Boston Evening Transcript* February 5, 1900: 8. Review of the premiere. "It is the most modern in spirit of anything I know from his pen . . . . his time for being modern has come . . . . there is a certain Wagnerish flavor to some passages . . . ." (See: W1a)

WB2.   L. C. E. [Louis C. Elson]. "Musical Matters -- The Symphony Concert -- Chadwick's 'Adonais'." *Boston Daily Advertiser* February 5, 1900: 8. Review of the premiere. "Skill in treatment is not lacking, but the contrapuntal work is not obtruded to the detriment of the psychological idea." This work ". . . may be spoken of in the same breath with Brahms' 'Tragic Overture'." (See: W1a)

W2.   ANDANTE (1882)

Dedication: None
Unpublished
Holograph: Score not located; parts at MBCM
Availability: Fleisher cat. no. 2280s (under the title "Intermezzo")
For: string orchestra

Adapted from String Quartet No. 2 (1878), movement no. 2, "Andante espressivo ma non troppo lento." (See: W31)

Premiere

W2a.   13 April 1882; Boston Philharmonic Orchestra, G. W. Chadwick, cond.; Music Hall, Boston.

Other Selected Performance

W2b.   17 February 1924; People's Symphony Orchestra, All-Chadwick program, G. W. Chadwick, cond.; St. James Theatre, Boston.

Bibliography

WB3.   "Theatres and Concerts." *Boston Evening Transcript* April 14, 1882: 1. Review of the premiere. "Mr. Chadwick's Andante, arranged, with some modifications, from the Andante of his string quartet, is as charming as ever, and was very nicely played." (See: W2a)

WB4.   "Entertainments -- Philharmonic Society's Concert." *Boston Post* April 14, 1882: 1. Review of the premiere. "An Andante movement for string orchestra . . . was performed under the direction of the composer in an acceptable manner, and proved a very pleasing composition." (See: W2a)

WB5.   "Editorial -- Philharmonic Concert." *Musical Record* 186 (April 22, 1882): 476. Comment on the premiere. "Mr. Chadwick conducted his Andante for Strings very artistically." (See: W2a)

WB6.   Elson, Louis C. "Review of Recent Concerts." *The Musical Herald* 3/5 (May 1882): 122. Review of the premiere. It is ". . . a beautiful work of modern melodic vein . . . ." (See: W2a)

WB7.   "People's Symphony." *Boston Daily Advertiser* February 17, 1924: D/4. Announcement regarding the People's Symphony Orchestra concert, February 17, 1924. (See: W2b)

WB8.   H. T. P. [Henry T. Parker] "Week-End Round Over Bostonian Concert-Giving." *Boston Evening Transcript* February 18,

1924: 8. Review of the People's Symphony Orchestra concert, February 17, 1924. "... the assembled pieces bore witness to the range of his musical mind and imagination." (See: W2b)

W3.   **ANGEL OF DEATH**, Symphonic Poem (Begun 1917; completed January 3, 1918)

Dedication: Walter Damrosch
Unpublished
Ink holograph: DLC (score); MBCM (copy of score; parts)
Availability: Fleisher cat. no. 6447
For: 2. 2. eh. 2. bass clar. 2./
          4. 2. 3. 1./
          timp. 3 perc. 2 harps (unison). strings.

This composition was inspired by the sculpture *Angel of Death and the Sculptor* (bronze, 1891) by the American artist Daniel Chester French (1850-1931). The work is located at Forest Hills Cemetery, Jamaica Plains, Massachusetts.

Premiere

W3a.   9 February 1919; New York Symphony Society, "Theodore Roosevelt Memorial Concert," Walter Damrosch, cond.; Aeolian Hall, New York.

Other Selected Performances

W3b.   13 November 1919; Boston Symphony Orchestra, Pierre Monteux, cond.; Cambridge, Massachusetts.

W3c.   2/3 January 1920; Chicago Symphony Orchestra, "Theodore Thomas Memorial Concert," Frederick Stock, cond.; Chicago, Illinois.

W3d.   3/4 February 1922; Saint Louis Symphony Orchestra, Rudolph Ganz, cond.; Saint Louis, Missouri.

W3e.   6 March 1930; Eastman-Rochester Orchestra, Howard Hanson, cond.; "American Composers Series"; Kilbourn Hall, Rochester, New York.

Bibliography

WB9. "Plans of the Musicians." *New York Times* February 2, 1919: IV/4. Announcement of the premiere by the New York Symphony Society. (See: W3a)

WB10. "Music and Musicians." *Boston Evening Transcript* February 7, 1919: 12. Notice of the premiere performance. "It seems a pity that music written by a Bostonian composer and suggested by a Bostonian monument should seek and receive first performance in New York and not from the Boston orchestra." (See: W3a)

WB11. "Concerts of the Week." *New York Times* February 9, 1919: IV/5. Announcement of the premiere performance. (See: W3a)

WB12. "Concerts of a Day -- Roosevelt Memorial Observed by Symphony and Opera Folk." *New York Times* February 10, 1919: 11. Review of the premiere. ". . . a brief but epic piece of music inspired by D. C. French's sculpture." (See: W3a)

WB13. Krehbiel, Henry E. "Music -- Symphony Society Gives Concert as Memorial to Roosevelt." *New York Tribune* February 10, 1919: 11. Review of the premiere. "He does not despise the new order of dissonant harmony, yet he differs from the ambitious, more youthful and less learned members of his guild in knowing how to handle his material. He sets his goal and pursues it directly, fluently. He does not fumble. The 'Angel of Death' is interesting because it is good music." (See: W3a)

WB14. "News of Music." *Boston Evening Transcript* February 10, 1919: 17. Discussion of the New York premiere featuring comments excerpted from various New York newspapers. (See: W3a)

WB15. Hale, Philip. "Berlioz First on Program." *Boston Herald* November 15, 1919: 13. Review of the November 13, 1919 Boston performance. "Mr. Chadwick himself says: 'It may be that the last part suggests eventually the artist's ascent to the Parnassus of which he dreamed. But it might also be a meorial [*sic*] for evry [*sic*] artist who has given his life during the war . . . .' " And, "The work is firmly knit, soundly constructed, sonorous, and as such it was warmly received by the audience." (See: W3b)

WB16. "Mme. Frijsh Sings with the Symphony." *Boston Globe* November 15, 1919: 5. Review of the November 13, 1919 Boston performance. "Mr. Chadwick deserved the applause that compelled him to rise in his place and bow . . . . The piece is one of the best recent American compositions." (See: W3b)

WB17. H. T. P. [Henry Taylor Parker]. "Week-End Concerts." *Boston Evening Transcript* November 17, 1919: 13. Review of the November 13, 1919 Boston performance. Next to Ernest Bloch's music, which was also featured on the program, *Angel of Death* " . . . could only seem colorless, unindividual, routine." (See: W3b)

WB18. Warner, A. J. "Chadwick Music in Kilburn [*sic*] Hall." *Rochester Times-Union* March 7, 1930. Review of the March 6, 1930 concert in Rochester, New York. (See: W3e)

W4. ANNIVERSARY OVERTURE (N.E.C. 1897-1922) (1917?)

Dedication: No formal dedication; this work commemorates Chadwick's 25th (silver) anniversary as Director at New England Conservatory
Unpublished
Ink holograph score and parts: MBCM
For: 2 (2nd doubles picc). 2. eh. 2. bass clar. 2. contrabssn. [manuscript part; ad lib.]./
4. 3. 3. 1./
timp. 2 perc. celesta. 2 harps (2nd ad lib.). strings.

The string parts of this composition reveal that its original title was *Illyria*. It may have been completed as early as 1917.

Premiere

W4a. 7 June 1922; Norfolk Festival Orchestra, G. W. Chadwick, cond.; Music Shed, Norfolk, Connecticut.

Other Selected Performances

W4b. 27/28 October 1922; Chicago Symphony Orchestra, Frederick

Stock, cond.; Chicago, Illinois.

W4c.   15/16 December 1922; Boston Symphony Orchestra, Pierre
        Monteux, cond.; Symphony Hall, Boston.

W4d.   13/14 January 1923; New York Philharmonic, Henry Hadley,
        cond.; Carnegie Hall, New York City.

W4e.   28 February 1923; New England Conservatory Orchestra, G.
        W. Chadwick, cond.; Symphony Hall, Boston.

W4f.   10/11 January 1924; Saint Louis Symphony Orchestra,
        Rudolph Ganz, cond.; Saint Louis, Missouri.

Bibliography

WB19.   H. M. H. "Magnificent Playing and Singing Mark Climax of
        Norfolk Music Festival." *Winsted* (Connecticut) *Evening
        Citizen* June 8, 1922: 1. Review of the premiere performance.
        "The overture . . . was artistically and efficiently directed by its
        composer. A splendid climax was achieved in this symphonic
        study. Mr. Chadwick . . . received a composer's wreath and a
        generous ovation from the audience." (See: W4a)

WB20.   Thompson, Oscar. "American and British Works Given First
        Performances at Norfolk, Conn." *Musical America* 36/3 (June
        17, 1922): 1, 5-6. Review of the premiere. "Though the
        work is said to have had its inception and even to have been
        virtually completed a number of years ago, the composition as
        revealed under the composer's direction, has characteristics not
        infrequently found in the piece d'occasion." (See: W4a)

WB21.   H. T. P. [Henry Taylor Parker]. "Concert Chronicle -- From
        Mr. Chadwick." *Boston Evening Transcript* December 14,
        1922: II/5. Preview of the Boston Symphony Orchestra
        performances, December 15/16, 1922. "The music adheres in
        the main to the accepted pattern of such concert overtures and
        abounds in scholarly devices . . . ." (See: W4c)

WB22.   "Boston Work in Symphony Bill." *Boston Daily Advertiser*
        December 16, 1922: 16. Review of the Boston Symphony
        Orchestra performance, December 15, 1922. The writer finds
        in the work ". . . sound, scholarly and agreeable writing,
        dramatic, but never shocking . . . . intensely lyrical and

dramatic . . . ." (See: W4c)

WB23.   H. T. P. [Henry Taylor Parker]. "Current-Chronicle -- A Full Week-End Variously Harvested." *Boston Evening Transcript* December 18, 1922: 7. Review of the Boston Symphony Orchestra performance, December 15/16, 1922. *Anniversary Overture* is a work " . . . in which Mr. Chadwick making music, is eager and warm again." (See: W4c)

WB24.   "Programs of the Coming Week." *New York Times* January 7, 1923: VII/5. Announcement of the New York performances, January 13 and 14, 1923. (See: W4d)

WB25.   "Music -- Local Programs of the Week." *New York Times* January 14, 1923: VII/4. Announcement of New York performance, January 14, 1923. (See: W4d)

WB26.   "Composer Chadwick Guest." *New York Times* January 15, 1923: 18. Review of the New York performance, January 14, 1923. " . . . a packed house called for the Boston composer to bow repeatedly after a performance of his Anniversary Overture." (See: W4d)

W5.   **APHRODITE**, Symphonic Fantasie (Sketched July 5 to August 3, 1910; orchestration begun June 27, 1911; completed August 26, 1911, at West Chop)

Dedicated: Mr. and Mrs. Carl Stoeckel
Published: Schmidt, 1912 (publ. plate no. 9816)
Pencil holograph: DLC (score); MBCM (parts)
Availability: Fleisher cat. no. 5253; Luck's cat. no. 05187
Duration: 28 minutes
For: 3. 2. eh. 2. bass clar. 2. contrabsn./
          4. 4. 3. 1./
          timp. 2 perc. harp. celesta. strings. offstage trumpets
             and field drums

This composition was inspired by the marble bust of the Greek Goddess of Love and Beauty, Aphrodite (Venus), donated to the Boston Museum of Fine Arts by Francis Bartlett. The lengthy unsigned descriptive poem that precedes the score is by Chadwick.

(See also: W38)

Premiere

W5a.   4 June 1912; Norfolk Festival Orchestra, G. W. Chadwick, cond.; Music Shed, Norfolk, Connecticut.

Other Selected Performances

W5b.   13/14 December 1912; American Composers' concert; Chicago Orchestra, Frederick Stock, cond.; Chicago, Illinois.

W5c.   4/5 April 1913; Boston Symphony Orchestra, Karl Muck, cond.; Symphony Hall, Boston.

Bibliography

WB27.   "Army of Over 8,000 Music-Lovers Filed Through Whitehouse Gates in Four Nights." *Winsted* (Connecticut) *Evening Citizen* June 9, 1911: 1. Preview notice. "Next year a new orchestral composition . . . will be produced. It is on a classical subject, in which style of music Mr. Chadwick has become pre-eminent. The poem from which he conceived the idea of the new composition is also his own work." (See: W5a)

WB28.   "Would Make Norfolk One of the World's Musical Centers." *Winsted* (Connecticut) *Evening Citizen* June 5, 1912: 1. Review of the premiere. "Mr. Chadwick's composition . . . was highly praised by the composers and American musical critics present. The composition is already in print and will be played several times next season by leading orchestras of the United States." (See: W5a)

WB29.   G. W. J. [George W. Judson] "County Choral Union's Rendition of 'A Tale of Old Japan' was Tremendous Success from Every Standpoint." *Winsted* (Connecticut) *Evening Citizen* June 5, 1912: 1. Review of the premiere. " . . . it displays a quality of popular appeal which is quite certain to win for it the success it richly deserves. There is variety, mingled strength and tenderness, blithesomeness and martial rigor, and in parts a playful quality . . . ." (See: W5a)

WB30.   Aldrich, Richard. "Norfolk Festival a Choral Triumph." *New York Times* June 9, 1912: II/10. Review of the premiere. "The musical ideas have beauty and distinction. There is a true

power in their development. There are many passages of a
tonal richness and color that signally illustrates Mr.
Chadwick's skill in orchestration." (See: W5a)

WB31.   H. T. P. [Henry Taylor Parker]. "Mr. Chadwick's New Tone
Poem and its Uneven Quality." *Boston Evening Transcript*
April 5, 1913: III/14. Review of the Boston Symphony
Orchestra performance, April 4, 1913. " . . . in spite of a
measure of imagination with harmonies and timbres,
progressions and dissonances, the outcome is no more than
well-made and appropriate music." (See: W5c)

WB32.   Hale, Philip. "New Fantasie at Symphony." *Boston Herald*
April 5, 1913: 8. Review of the Boston Symphony Orchestra
performance, April 4, 1913. Commenting on Chadwick and
the music's picturesque nature: "The most fastidious
composer may yet welcome the opportunity of writing
program music for motion pictures." (See: W5c)

WB33.   Elson, Louis C. "Aphrodite a Brilliant Work." *Boston Daily
Advertiser* April 5, 1913: 5. Review of the Boston Symphony
Orchestra performance, April 4, 1913. "Aphrodite is a
symphonic poem in modern vein and is one of the most
ambitious of the composer's scores . . . . The form itself is a
new departure, for it is a series of short, connected tone
pictures, applying the idea of a suite . . . . Five times was Mr.
Chadwick obliged to rise from his seat in the audience and bow
his acknowledgements." (See: W5c)

W6.   **CLEOPATRA**, Symphonic Poem (Sketched June 20 to August 23,
1904; orchestrated October 15 to December 31, 1904)

Dedication: none
Unpublished
Ink holograph: DLC (score); MBCM (copy of score and parts)
Availability: Fleisher cat. no. 6445
For: 3 (3rd doubles picc). 2. eh. 2. bass clar. 2./
          4. 3. 3. 1./
          timp. 5 perc. harp. celesta (ad lib.). strings.

According to his *Memoirs*, Chadwick was inspired to compose this
work after reading Plutarch's *Life of Antony*.

Premiere

W6a.   29 September 1905; Worcester Festival Orchestra, Franz
Kneisel, cond.; Mechanics Hall, Worcester, Massachusetts.

Other Selected Performances

W6b.   14/15 December 1906; Boston Symphony Orchestra, Karl
Muck, cond.; Symphony Hall, Boston.

W6c.   3 January 1907; Boston Symphony Orchestra, Karl Muck,
cond.; Providence, Rhode Island.

W6d.   12 January 1907; Boston Symphony Orchestra, Karl Muck,
cond.; Carnegie Hall, New York City.

W6e.   15 January 1907; Boston Symphony Orchestra, Karl Muck,
cond.; Springfield, Massachusetts.

W6f.   22/23 February 1907; Cincinnati Symphony Orchestra, G. W.
Chadwick, cond.; Music Hall, Cincinnati, Ohio.

W6g.   16 May 1907; Royal Philharmonic Society, Frederic Cowen,
cond.; Queen's Hall, London.

W6h.   27/28 March 1908; Chicago Orchestra, Frederick Stock, cond.;
Chicago, Illinois.

Bibliography

WB34.   Hale, Philip. "Symphony and Mme. Eames' Recital."
Sunday Herald (Boston) December 16, 1906: 7. Review of the
Boston Sympony Orchestra performance, December 14/15,
1906. "In certain ways the symphonic poem is more modern
in its sentiment than are the other works of the composer's
later period: it is bolder in its harmonic treatment, it is freer,
it is richer in color." (See: W6b)

WB35.   "Boston Symphony Orchestra." *New York Times* January 6,
1907: IV/5. Announcement of the Boston Symphony
Orchestra's performance in New York City, January 12, 1907.
(See: W6d)

WB36.   "The Boston Orchestra." *New York Times* January 13, 1907:

I/9. Review of the Boston Symphony Orchestra's performance in New York City, January 12, 1907. " . . . it may be doubted whether it will stand as one of the most authoritative products of his own genius, which is one of the strongest that America possesses in music." (See: W6d)

WB37. "Chadwick at Symphony." *Cincinnati Enquirer* February 22, 1907: 7. Notes that Chadwick will be in the audience for the Cincinnati Symphony performances, February 22 and 23, 1907. (See: W6f)

WB38. "Concerts." *Times* (London) May 17, 1907: 6. Review of the London performance of May 16, 1907. "It is a clearly designed rhythmical work, built up on a few simple melodies which, though they are not very striking, are at any rate not very commonplace, and the orchestration is straightforward and attractive except in one or two places where strong colour is somewhat misapplied." (See: W6g)

WB39. Hubbard, W. L. [William Lines]. "News of the Theatres -- Thomas Orchestra." *Chicago Tribune* March 28, 1908: 8. Review of the March 27, 1908 concert in Chicago. ". . . although the two themes symbolic of the two lovers are wanting somewhat in distinctiveness, the manner in which the themes are handled and the instrumental color employed make the score brilliant and attractive." (See: W6h)

W7. ELEGY (1920)

Dedication: "In memoriam Horatio Parker [d. December 18, 1919] "
Unpublished; solo organ version published in *American Organ Monthly* 1/3 (May 1920): 29-33.
Ink and pencil holograph: DLC (score); MBCM (parts)
Availability: Fleisher cat. no. 6581
Duration: 8 minutes
For: 3. 2. eh. 2. 2./
        4. 2. 3. 0./
        timp. bass drum. harp. organ [ad lib.]

(See also: W58)

Selected Performances

W7a.   20 December 1925; "In memoriam Louis A. Coolidge"; New

England Conservatory Orchestra, Wallace Goodrich, cond.; Jordan Hall, Boston.

W7b. Circa 1990 [precise date not on program]; The Community of Jesus Orchestra, Dr. Richard J. Pugsley, cond.; Cape Cod, Massachusetts.

W8. **EUTERPE,** Overture (Sketches begun at West Chop, July 26, 1903; completed November 4, 1903)

Dedication: Samuel S. Sanford
Published: Schirmer, 1906 (publ. plate no. 18209)
Pencil holograph: DLC (score); MBCM (parts); NRU-Mus holds a
    manuscript copyist's score that includes editorial markings by
    Chadwick
Availability: Fleisher cat. no. 1996; Luck's cat. no. 06538
Duration: 14 minutes
For: 2. 2. 2. 2./4. 2. 3. 1./timp. strings.

This composition, titled after the Greek muse of lyric poetry, was originally intended as a finale movement to Chadwick's *Sinfonietta*, which was being composed at this time.

Premiere

W8a. 22/23 April 1904; Boston Symphony Orchestra, G. W. Chadwick, cond.; Symphony Hall, Boston.

Other Selected Performances

W8b. 27/28 January 1905; Chicago Orchestra, Frederick Stock, cond.; Chicago, Illinois.

W8c. 8 March 1907; New England Conservatory Orchestra, G. W. Chadwick, cond.; Jordan Hall, Boston.

W8d. 20 March 1907; New England Conservatory Orchestra, "Auspices of the Chadwick Club," G. W. Chadwick, cond.; Lawrence, Massachusetts.

W8e. 2 January 1914; Philharmonic Society of New York, Josef Stransky, cond.; Carnegie Hall, New York City.

W8f. 1 August 1915; "American Composers' Day," Panama-Pacific

International Exposition; The Exposition Orchestra, G. W. Chadwick, cond.; Festival Hall, San Francisco, California.

W8g.   17 February 1924; People's Symphony Orchestra, All-Chadwick program, G. W. Chadwick, cond.; St. James Theatre, Boston.

W8h.   28 March 1924; New England Conservatory Orchestra, G. W. Chadwick, cond.; Jordan Hall, Boston.

W8i.   9 May 1924; New England Conservatory Orchestra, Wallace Goodrich, cond.; Jordan Hall, Boston.

W8j.   20 April 1976; Indianapolis Symphony Orchestra, Oleg Kovalenko, cond.; at Butler University's "Romantic Festival," Indianapolis, Indiana.

W8k.   15 May 1994; New England Philharmonic Orchestra, Jeffrey Rink, cond.; Framingham State College, Framingham, Massachusetts.

W8l.   21 May 1994; New England Philharmonic Orchestra, Jeffrey Rink, cond.; Sanders Theatre, Cambridge, Massachusetts.

Bibliography

WB40.   "New Overture by Chadwick." *Sunday Herald* (Boston) April 24, 1904: 16. Review of the premiere. "The work will not enlarge his reputation, for it is not conspicuously imaginative or brilliant: it has rather the character of a well-made 'occasional' overture . . . ." (See: W8a)

WB41.   R. R. G. "Music and Drama." *Boston Evening Transcript* April 25, 1904: 9. Review of the premiere. While the reviewer thought the music well planned, " . . . the overture did not seem interesting although it was agreeable . . . ." (See: W8a)

WB42.   "The Philharmonic Plays." *New York Times* January 3, 1914: 8. Review of the New York Philharmonic performance, January 2, 1914. Only brief mention of *Euterpe*, but with works on the program by Goldmark, Brahms, R. Strauss, and Chadwick, the concert was "distinctly modern." (See: W8e)

WB43. Mason, Redfern. "As to Music and Musicians." *San Francisco Examiner* August 1, 1915: 26. Announcement of the August 1, 1915 performance in San Francisco. Notes that Chadwick will be conducting his own works [*Melpomene* was also on the program]. (See: W8f)

WB44. Mason, Redfern. "Composers of America Display Art." *San Francisco Examiner* August 2, 1915: 6. Review of the August 1, 1915 performance. Chadwick's music exhibits ". . . the classic attitude of mind without so much as a hint of Americanism." (See: W8f)

WB45. H. T. P. [Henry Taylor Parker] "Week-End Round Over Bostonian Concert-Giving." *Boston Evening Transcript* February 18, 1924: 8. Review of the People's Symphony presentation, February 17, 1924. " . . . the assembled pieces bore witness to the range of his musical mind and imagination." (See: W8g)

W9. EVERYWOMAN WALTZ (Completed March 8, 1909)

Dedication: none
Published: Harms, 1911 (as the entr'acte in the piano-vocal score of *Everywoman.*)
Holograph score: not located; MBCM holds the holograph piano-vocal version and parts
For: 3. 2. 2. 2./4. 2. 3. 0./timp. 5 perc. harp. strings.

This work was originally titled *S. S. Waltz*, suggesting that Chadwick may have intended to employ it in his *Suite Symphonique*, which was being composed during this period.

(See also: W68)

Premiere

W9a. 9 February 1911; Hugo Frey, Music Director; Parsons Theatre, Hartford, Connecticut (as part of the premiere of the stage work). (See also: W68a)

Other Selected Performance

W9b. 10 May 1912; New England Conservatory Orchestra, G. W. Chadwick, cond.; Jordan Hall, Boston.

W10. JOSHUA (MARCH) (alternative title: **JERICHO MARCH**) (ca. 1919)

Dedication: None
Published: Boston: New England Conservatory Press, 1995 [Archival
        Manuscript Edition]; chorus version, Ditson, 1919
Pencil holograph score and parts: MBCM
Premiere: Unknown
For: picc. 2. 2 [ad lib.]. 2. 2./
          4. 2. 3. 0./
          timp. snare. bass drum. cymbals. strings.

This work, an orchestral version of the song *Joshua*, was originally
titled *Jericho March*; the title was later changed to *Joshua*. This version
may be performed with or without vocalist. (Words by Richard Darwin
Ware.)

(See also: W82, W100, W138, and W234)

Selected Performance

W10a.   Circa 1990 [precise date not on program]; The Community of
        Jesus Orchestra, Dr. Richard J. Pugsley, cond.; Cape Cod,
        Massachusetts [Instrumental version; program located at
        MBCM.]

W11. MELPOMENE, Dramatic Overture; (Sketches completed July 15,
        1887, in Nantucket, Massachusetts; orchestration begun July 15,
        1887; completed September 30, 1887)

Dedication: Wilhelm Gericke
Published: Schmidt, 1891 (publ. plate no. 2794)
Ink holograph: DLC (score); DLC also holds holograph sketches
Availability: Fleisher cat. no. 158; Luck's cat. no. 05263
Duration: 12 minutes
For: picc. 2. 1. eh. 2. 2./
          4. 4 [trumpet 3 and 4 parts are in manuscript, apparently added
              following publication]. 3. 1./
          timp. 2 perc. strings.

This work is titled after the Greek muse of tragedy. The title is
transliterated from the original Greek which appears on the holograph.

(See also: W45 and WR3)

Premiere

W11a. 23/24 December 1887; Boston Symphony Orchestra, Wilhelm Gericke, cond.; Music Hall, Boston.

Other Selected Performances

W11b. 15 April 1888; Arion Society concert, Frank van der Stucken, cond.; Steinway Hall, New York City.

W11c. 1 August 1888; Symphony Capelle; Copenhagen [complete details not discerned; this performance is recorded on the last page of the holograph score in the composer's hand].

W11d. 1/2 March 1889; Boston Symphony Orchestra, Wilhelm Gericke, cond.; Music Hall, Boston.

W11e. 2 April 1889; Boston Symphony Orchestra, Wilhelm Gericke, cond.; Philadelphia, Pennsylvania.

W11f. 12 July 1889; Exposition Universelle concert, Frank van der Stucken, cond.; Grande Salle des Fetes, Trocadero Palace, Paris.

W11g. 8/9 April 1892; Chicago Orchestra, Theodore Thomas, cond.; The Auditorium, Chicago, Illinois.

W11h. 6 July 1893; World's Columbian Exposition "Concert of American Music" (Concert Series No. 29), The Exposition Orchestra, Theodore Thomas, cond.; Music Hall, Chicago, Illinois.

W11i. 18 January 1895; Cincinnati Symphony Orchestra, Frank van der Stucken, cond.; Pike Opera House, Cincinnati, Ohio.

W11j. 13 June 1895; Royal Philharmonic Orchestra, Sir Alexander MacKenzie, cond.; London.

W11k. 10/11 January 1896; New York Philharmonic, Anton Seidl, cond.; Carnegie Hall, New York City.

W11l. 14 March 1896; Boston Symphony Orchestra, Wilhelm Gericke, cond.; Music Hall, Boston.

W11m. 21/22 October 1898; Boston Symphony Orchestra, Wilhelm Gericke, cond.; Music Hall, Boston.

W11n. 16/17 December 1898; Chicago Orchestra, Theodore Thomas, cond.; Chicago, Illinois.

W11o. 20 October 1903; Jordan Hall inaugural concert; Boston Symphony Orchestra, G. W. Chadwick, cond.; Jordan Hall, Boston.

W11p. 19 February 1905; Handel and Haydn Society concert [featuring "a full orchestra from the Boston Symphony Orchestra"], Emil Mollenhauer, cond.; Symphony Hall, Boston.

W11q. November 1905 [precise date unknown]; Concordia Choral Society concert in honor of Chadwick; G. W. Chadwick, cond.; [precise location undetermined], Leipzig.

W11r. 14/17 February 1911; New York Philharmonic, Gustav Mahler, cond.; Carnegie Hall, New York City.

W11s. 7 April 1911; New England Conservatory Orchestra, G. W. Chadwick, cond.; Jordan Hall, Boston.

W11t. 14/15 November 1913; Chicago Orchestra, G. W. Chadwick, cond.; Chicago, Illinois.

W11u. 11/12 December 1914; Saint Louis Symphony Orchestra, Max Zach, cond.; Saint Louis, Missouri.

W11v. 5/6 March 1915; Chicago Orchestra, Frederick Stock, cond.; Chicago, Illinois.

W11w. 30 June 1915; Ninth Biennial Convention of the Federation of Music Clubs, "Festival of American Music," G. W. Chadwick, cond.; Trinity Auditorium, Los Angeles, California.

W11x. 1 August 1915; Panama-Pacific International Exposition, "American Composers' Day," The Exposition Orchestra, G. W. Chadwick, cond.; Festival Hall, San Francisco, California.

W11y. 14 December 1917; Minneapolis Symphony Orchestra,

"America" program, Emil Oberhoffer, cond.; The Auditorium, Minneapolis, Minnesota.

W11z.   14 November 1918; New York Philharmonic, Josef Stransky, cond.; Carnegie Hall, New York City.

W11aa. 17 November 1918; New York Philharmonic, Josef Stransky, cond.; Brooklyn Academy of Music, Brooklyn, New York.

W11bb. 23 April 1920; New England Conservatory Orchestra, Wallace Goodrich, cond.; Jordan Hall, Boston.

W11cc. 1/2 April 1921; Boston Symphony Orchestra, Pierre Monteux, cond.; Symphony Hall, Boston.

W11dd. 13 February 1921; New York Philharmonic, Henry Hadley, cond.; Carnegie Hall, New York City.

W11ee. 18 December 1925; New England Conservatory Orchestra, Wallace Goodrich, cond.; Jordan Hall, Boston.

W11ff. 6 May 1930; New England Conservatory Orchestra, Wallace Goodrich, cond.; Jordan Hall, Boston.

W11gg. 10/11 April 1931; Chicago Symphony Orchestra, Frederick Stock, cond.; Chicago, Illinois.

W11hh. 19 October 1938; New England Conservatory Orchestra, Wallace Goodrich, cond.; Jordan Hall, Boston.

W11ii. 14 December 1940; Chicago Symphony Orchestra, Hans Lange, cond.; Orchestra Hall, Chicago, Illinois.

W11jj. 7 April 1946; Handel and Haydn Society concert featuring members of the Boston Symphony Orchestra, Thompson Stone, cond.; Symphony Hall, Boston.

W11kk. 12/14 December 1946; Cleveland Orchestra, Rudolph Ringwall, cond.; Severance Hall, Cleveland, Ohio.

W11ll. 23-26 October 1958; New York Philharmonic, Leonard Bernstein, cond.; Carnegie Hall, New York City.

Bibliography

WB46. Ticknor, Howard Malcolm. "Last Night's Symphony -- The New 'Melpomene' Overture Takes Honors." *Boston Sunday Globe* December 25, 1887: 4. Review of the premiere. "Mr. Chadwick has infused the genius of tragedy into this. Not of bitter, bloody, murderous, material tragedy, but the tragedy of deep gloom . . . ." (See: W11a)

WB47. "Theatres and Concerts -- Boston Symphony Orchestra." *Boston Evening Transcript* December 27, 1887. Review of the premiere. " . . . the vigor, the poetic suggestiveness of the music strike [the listener] at once. Here there is an exuberance of energy that takes hold of you forcibly, and carries you away . . . ." (See: W11a)

WB48. "Amusements." *New York Times* April 15, 1888: 16. Announcement of Arion Society concert, April 15, 1888. "The programme is one of great promise." (See: W11b)

WB49. "Music in America." *The Musical Times* (London) 554/30 (April 1, 1889): 230-231. Commenting on the March 2, 1889 performance: " . . . the Boston critics speak very highly of this composition." (See: W11d)

WB50. "Theatres and Concerts -- Boston Symphony Orchestra." *Boston Evening Transcript* March 4 1889: 6. Review of the Boston Symphony Orchestra performance, March 2, 1889. "It is surely a beautiful and noble composition from beginning to end. The work is serious, earnest and intense in expression, without either dryness or bombast, and brilliant without triviality." (See: W11d)

WB51. Proteus [Louis Charles Elson]. "Music in Boston." *The Musical Visitor* (April 1889): 94-95. Review of the March 1/2, 1889 performances in Boston. *Melpomene* ". . . won the heartiest of applause, and deserved it, for it is altogether the best score of the composer. It is full of graphic, highly dramatic touches, and will take rank among the standard concert overtures." (See: W11d)

WB52. "Amusements -- Notes of the Week." *New York Times* July 21, 1889: 2. Notice of the Paris Exhibition concert, July 12, 1889. "Mr. Frank van der Stucken gave his first orchestral

concert of American music at the Trocadero in Paris, July 12."
The program also included works by Arthur Foote, Edward
MacDowell, John K. Paine, and others. (See: W11f)

WB53. "American Music in Paris." *The Musical Visitor* (August
1889): 206. This article on the July 12, 1889 performance in
Paris contains information about the event itself, but only
general comments about the music performed. Although
published after the concert, the article reads like a preview.
(See: W11f)

WB54. A. G. "From Paris." *Musical Herald* (September 1889): 212.
Notes that the July 12, 1889 performance of American music
at the Exposition Universelle was ". . . a successful program
in every respect." (See: W11f)

WB55. "Concert of American Composers." *Chicago Tribune* July 7,
1893: 8. Review of the World's Columbian Exposition
performance, July 6, 1893. ". . . a long, elaborate, and well
worked composition, containing many charming movements
[*sic*]." (See: W11h)

WB56. "Philharmonic Society." *The Musical Times* (London) 36
(July 1, 1895): 454-455. Review of the June 13, 1895
performance in London. "He studied in Germany for some
time and he evidently [*sic*] knows his Wagner. Mr.
Chadwick has written much in various departments of art, and
the present Overture shows that he is an earnest, conscientious
musician, with much command of tragic expression, the
climax being even powerful." (See: W11j)

WB57. "Notes of Music." *New York Times* January 5, 1896: II/12.
Announcement of January 10 and 11, 1896 concerts by the
New York Philharmonic. (See: W11k)

WB58. "Philharmonic Society Rehearsal." *New York Times* January
11, 1896: 5. Comments on rehearsals in preparation for the
January 10 and 11, 1896 concerts by the New York
Philharmonic. Among the selections were "Mr. Chadwick's
rather rambling overture . . . ." (See: W11k)

WB59. "Music and Drama -- Music Hall: Boston Symphony
Orchestra." *Boston Evening Transcript* March 16, 1896: 5.
Review of the March 14, 1896 performance in Boston. In this

work " . . . Chadwick has preserved just enough of the classic musical spirit, of the classic modes of musical expression, to give the strenuous romanticism which is, after all, the most salient trait in the composition just the due tinge of tragic dignity." (See: W11l)

WB60. "News of the Theatres -- Chicago Orchestra." *Chicago Tribune* December 17, 1898: 5. Review of the December 16, 1898 performance in Chicago. "The work betrays much intelligent training in the best modern schools of orchestration. Few tone effects are left untried; the music is dramatic in treatment, and there is neither an obvious following of any particular master nor a striving after originality for originality's sake. But when that is said the possibilities of praise are exhausted." (See: W11n)

WB61. "No Other Like It -- Jordan Hall, Conservatory of Music, Dedicated." *Boston Daily Globe* October 21, 1903: 1. Report on the Jordan Hall inaugural concert, October 20, 1903. Conductor Chadwick ". . . received a handsome ovation." (See: W11o)

WB62. "Leipsic [*sic*] Discovers a Boston Composer." *Boston Globe* December 29, 1905. Includes comments about the November 1905 performance in Leipzig. "As he [Chadwick] had only an orchestra from one of the regimental bands of the garrison, the performance must have proceeded under some difficulties. . . ." (See: W11q)

WB63. "The Philharmonic Society." *New York Times* February 12, 1911: VII/7. Preview of the February 14 and 17, 1911 concerts by the New York Philharmonic. "Chadwick's overture of Melpomene enjoys the distinction of being the first American work performed by the London Philharmonic." (See: W11r)

WB64. "The Philharmonic Society." *New York Times* February 15, 1911: 7. Review of the February 14, 1911 concert by the New York Philharmonic. " . . . it is worth rehearing oftener-- a finely conceived and vigorous work with some adimrable [*sic*] instrumental effects." (See: W11r)

WB65. H. E. K. [Henry E. Krehbiel]. "Music." *New York Daily Tribune* February 18, 1911: 7. Review of the February 17,

1911 performance by the New York Philharmonic. ". . . though it is orthodox in form it says beautiful things so well that its orthodoxy as well as its age need not be held as criminal accusations against it." Krehbiel also notes that Mahler had difficulty deciding whether or not the composition should be on the program. (See: W11r)

WB66. Gunn, Glenn Dillard. "Concerning the New Compositions, the Public and the Orchestra." *Chicago Tribune* November 9, 1913: sec. 8, p. 5. Announcement that Chadwick's music will be included on the Chicago Symphony Orchestra's programs of November 14/15, 1913, ". . . devoted entirely to compositions by members of the institute . . . ." [National Institute of Arts and Letters, to which Chadwick had recently been elected]. (See: W11t)

WB67. Gunn, Glenn Dillard. "Orchestra Patrons Hear Music of the Immortals." *Chicago Tribune* November 15, 1913: 9. Review of the Chicago Symphony Orchestra performance, November 14, 1913. "Chadwick has the talent to refine popular music while preserving its fluency and elevating its sentiment." And, "Chadwick, Parker, and Foote betray an interesting family resemblance in their music . . . ." The concert included music by Horatio Parker, Arthur Foote, Edgar Stillman Kelley, Edward MacDowell, and Frederick Stock. (See: W11t)

WB68. Mason, Redfern. "As to Music and Musicians." *San Francisco Examiner* August 1, 1915: 26. Announcement of the August 1, 1915 performance in San Francisco. Notes that Chadwick will be conducting his own works [*Euterpe* was also on the program]. (See: W11x)

WB69. Mason, Redfern. "Composers of America Display Art." *San Francisco Examiner* August 2, 1915: 6. Review of the August 1, 1915 performance. "Melpomene is a beautiful overture. Its fault, if fault it be, is that of being too perfectly knit." (See: W11x)

WB70. H. E. K. [Henry E. Krehbiel]. "Music." *New York Daily Tribune* November 15, 1918: 9. Review of the New York Philharmonic performance, November 14, 1918. Krehbiel notes that *Melpomene*, ". . . American music long in the repertory, opened it [the concert] right worthily . . . ." (See: W11z)

WB71. "Chicago Symphony Honors George W. Chadwick's Memory." *Musical Courier* 102/16 (April 18, 1931): 32. Review of the Chicago Symphony performances, April 10 and 11, 1931. "This aristocratic, dignified music was reverently presented . . . ." (See: W11gg)

WB72. "Bernstein Directs Preview Concert." *New York Times* October 24, 1958: 40. Brief discussion of the October 23, 1958 concert of the New York Philharmonic. (See: W11ll)

W12. THE MILLER'S DAUGHTER, Song and Overture (Completed June, 1886)

Text: Alfred Tennyson (1809-1892)
Dedication: Joshua Page
Unpublished
Ink holograph score and parts: MBCM
For: Baritone
         2. 2. 2. 2./4. 2. 0. 0./timp. strings.

From Tennyson's poem "The Miller's Daughter" in *The Lady of Shalott and Other Poems* (1832).

(See also: W244 and W252)

Premiere

W12a.   18 May 1887; Loring Club, "American Concert"; [conductor not determined]; San Francisco, California.

Other Selected Performances

W12b.   10 December 1890; Manuscript Society concert, Perry Averill, baritone, Frank van der Stucken, cond.; Chickering Hall, New York City.

W12c.   14 January 1892; Boston Philharmonic Orchestra, Thomas E. Clifford, baritone, Bernhard Listemann, cond.; Tremont Theatre, Boston.

Bibliography

WB73. "Loring Club Concert -- An Excellent Programme." *San Francisco Chronicle* May 15, 1887: 7. Announcement of the premiere performance, May 18, 1887. The article does not discuss the music at length, but notes that two part-songs [unidentified] by Chadwick would also be featured. Included on the program were works by Dudley Buck, Arthur Foote, and George Whiting. [No review of this performance was located.] (See: W12a)

WB74. "Musical Notes." *New York Times* December 7, 1890: II/13. Announcement of the first concert of the Manuscript Society, ". . . a new organization whose object is the performance of unpublished works by composers living in America." The writer states that this event ". . . promises to be one of the most interesting entertainments of the season . . . ." (See: W12b)

WB75. "Amusements -- The Manuscript Society." *New York Times* December 11, 1890: 4. Review of the Manuscript Society concert. "Mr. Chadwick's treatment of the familiar poem is most ingenious and musical. He has set the Miller's Daughter as a song and he made use of the song theme as the cantabile of his overture, of which the allegro, a vigorous movement, is plainly designed to express the happiness of the lovers. The overture is made to conclude after the good old-fashioned manner of love stories, with a clever introduction of the opening measures of Mendelssohn's 'Wedding March.' It is a very dainty conceit and very neatly handled." (See: W12b)

WB76. "Theatres and Concerts." *Boston Evening Transcript* January 15, 1892: 4. Review of the Boston Philharmonic concert, January 14, 1892. "Mr. Chadwick has done such good work before that one may pass over his Miller's Daughter in silence. It is a work that in no wise adds to his reputation, neither need it detract from it." (See: W12c)

WB77. Hale, Philip. "Music -- The Philharmonic Orchestra." *Boston Journal* January 15, 1892: 4. Review of Boston Philharmonic concert, January 14, 1892. ". . . the programme-book stated that it was first produced in San Francisco . . . . His themes are not happily invented, his development of them is dry and scholastic, and his instrumentation is conventional and uninteresting. In a word, the work is dull." (See: W12c)

W13. A PASTORAL PRELUDE (1890)

Dedication: H. [Horatio] W. Parker
Unpublished
Ink holograph: DLC (score); MBCM (parts)
Availability: Fleisher cat. no. 6633
For: picc. 2. 2. eh. 2. 2./4. 2. 0. 0./timp. strings.

Preambular words are by William Wordsworth, *Ode: Intimations of Immortality from Recollections of Early Childhood* ("Feel the Gladness of the May!" [line 175]) (1804).

Premiere

W13a.   29/30 January 1892; Boston Symphony Orchestra, Arthur Nikisch, cond.; Music Hall, Boston.

Other Selected Performances

W13b.   25/26 January 1895; Chicago Orchestra, Theodore Thomas, cond.; Chicago, Illinois.

Bibliography

WB78.   "The Symphony Concert." *Boston Journal* February 1, 1892: 5. Review of the premiere. "The instrumentation shows a very practiced hand and it is often ingenious." (See: W13a)

WB79.   "Theatres and Concerts." *Boston Evening Transcript* February 1, 1892: 5. Review of the premiere. ". . . here we have a bright, lively, chattering movement, full enough of a certain rusticity . . . but in no wise suggestive of that peaceful repose . . . ." (See: W13a)

W14. RIP VAN WINKLE, Overture (Completed March 18, 1879; revised version completed April 19, 1929)

Dedication: Joseph Jefferson (1829-1905)
Ink holograph: original version is held at DLC (score) and MBCM
         (parts); the revised version (also in ink) is held at NRU-Mus
Publisher: revised version printed by Eastman School of Music of the
University of Rochester; distributed by Birchard, 1930 (score) and

1931 (parts); (publ. plate no. 86)
Availability: Fleisher cat. no. 2590
Duration: 11 minutes
Original version for: 2. 2. 2. 2./4. 2. 3. 0./timp. strings.
Revised version for: picc. 2. 2. 2. 2./4. 2. 3. 1./timp. 3 perc. strings.

Inspired by the tale by Washington Irving (1783-1859). The dedicatee, a well-known actor, portrayed Rip to great acclaim in the 1860s and 1870s.

(See also: W51 and WR6)

Premiere

W14a.   20 June 1879; Ninth Hauptprufung of the Royal Conservatory of Leipzig; G. W. Chadwick, cond.; Saale des Gewandhauses, Leipzig.

Other Selected Performances

W14b.   17 September 1879; Concert-Kapelle des Konigliche Belvedere, Bernhard Gottlober, cond.; Bruhl'schen Terrasse, Dresden, Germany.

W14c.   11 December 1879; Harvard Musical Association concert, Carl Zerrahn, cond.; Music Hall, Boston.

W14d.   29 January 1880; Harvard Musical Association concert, Carl Zerrahn, cond.; Music Hall, Boston.

W14e.   6 May 1880; Triennial Festival of the Handel and Haydn Society, G. W. Chadwick, cond.; Boston.

W14f.   31 January 1883; Boston Philharmonic Society, Bernhard Listemann, leader; Music Hall, Boston.

W14g.   27 September 1889; Worcester Festival Orchestra, G. W. Chadwick, cond.; Mechanics Hall, Worcester, Massachusetts.

W14h.   17 February 1924; People's Symphony Orchestra, All-Chadwick program, G. W. Chadwick, cond.; St. James Theatre, Boston.

W14i.   14 June 1929; New England Conservatory Orchestra, G. W.

Chadwick, cond.; Jordan Hall, Boston.

W14j.   6 March 1930; Eastman-Rochester Orchestra, Howard Hanson, cond.; "American Composers Series"; Kilbourn Hall, Eastman School of Music, Rochester, New York.

W14k.   6 May 1930, New England Conservatory Orchestra, Wallace Goodrich, cond.; Jordan Hall, Boston.

W14l.   21 May 1931; Eastman-Rochester Orchestra, "American Music Festival," Howard Hanson, cond.; Rochester Philharmonic Orchestra; Kilbourn Hall, Rochester, New York.

W14m.   31 January-2 February 1956; Cincinnati Symphony Orchestra, Thor Johnson, cond.; Music Hall, Cincinnati, Ohio.

W14n.   4 May 1995; Detroit Symphony Orchestra, Neeme Jarvi, cond.; Orchestra Hall, Detroit, Michigan.

Bibliography

WB80.   Bernsdorf, G. "Hauptprufungen am Konigl. Consertavorium der Musik zu Leipzig." *Signale fur die Musikalische Welt* 37/41 (June 1879): 642-4. Review of the premiere. "Von den Ouverturen haben wir als die weitaus beste die des herrn George W. Chadwick aus Boston--zu dem amerikanischen Marchen 'Rip van Winkle'--zu bezeichnen; sie bietet frischen Inhalt, gutgegliederte Architectonic und geschickte Orchestrirung." ["Of this year's compositions from the conservatory, the overture to 'Rip van Winkle' by George W. Chadwick of Boston, is by far the best. The contents are fresh, it is architecturally well knit and adroitly orchestrated." Translated by Chadwick in his *Memoirs*, 1877-1890.] (See: W14a)

WB81.   V. B. "Correspondenzen." *Neue Zeitschrift fur Musik* 75/2 (4 July 1879): 288. Reprint, Scarsdale, N.Y.: A Schnase, 1964. Review of the premiere. "Das studium der [Mendelssohn's] Sommernachtstraummusik scheint ihm anhaltende befruchtende Freude berreitet zu haben." ["The study of Midsummer Night's Dream seems to have given him constant and fruitful pleasure."] (See: W14a)

WB82.   *Musikaliches Wochenblatt* 10 (4 July 1879): 334. Review of the premiere. "Auch ohne letzteres zu kennen, haben wir vor dem Werk des Hrn. Chadwick Respect bekommen. Dasselbe hat bei gutem musikalischen Fluss entschieden Farbe und Physiognomie, ist mehr als das Resultat gewissenhaften Studiums. Der junge Autor hat eigene poetische Intentionen . . . ." ["Although few of us were familiar with Washington Irving's tale of 'Rip van Winkle,' this work called for respect because it betrayed more than conscientious study and showed that the young American had his own poetic intentions and that his music has color and physiognomy . . . ." Translated by Chadwick in his *Memoirs, 1877-1890.*] (See: W14a)

WB83. "Musical Intelligence." *Dwight's Journal of Music* 39/1006 (November 8, 1879): 184. Notes that the composition "won the palm" at the Leipzig Conservatory in June 1879 and is being considered for performance by the Harvard Musical Association's Concert Committee. (See: W14c)

WB84. "Music and the Drama." *Boston Daily Advertiser* December 12, 1879: 1. Review of the December 11, 1879 performance. "The overture impressed us as ingeniously constructed, with clearly treated melodic forms, and scored in a learned but not pedantic manner . . . . the modern German school of orchestra [composition] has had greater influence on the young author than that of Beethoven or even of Schumann." (See: W14c)

WB85. "Music and the Stage." *Daily Evening Traveller* (Boston) December 12, 1879: 3. Review of the December 11, 1879 performance. "Mr. Chadwick's overture is by no means a great work, but it is scholarly and contains great promise of a brilliant future . . . . The scoring is rich, and shows how strongly the composer is under the influence of the modern school . . . ." (See: W14c)

WB86. "Musical." *Boston Evening Transcript* December 12, 1879: 1. Review of the December 11, 1879 concert. "Its rich sonority, reflecting the modern spirit among composers, and an expert knowledge of instrumentation and the artistic taste and skill with which a few graceful commonplaces were worked over to fill out a work of important dimensions, prove musicianly gifts and scholarly acquirements of an order rare among our countrymen." (See: W14c)

WB87.   "Music in Boston." *Dwight's Journal of Music* 39/1009
(December 20, 1879): 205. Review of the December 11, 1879
concert. Chadwick's composition " . . . more than justified
the interest with which it was anticipated. It is a fresh, genial,
and thoroughly well-wrought, consistent, charming work."
(See: W14c)

WB88.   "Recent Concerts." *The Musical Herald* 1/1 (January 1880):
21. Review of the December 11, 1879 concert. "It is a
scholarly production, gracefully written, and produced a very
favorable impression." (See: W14c)

WB89.   "Musical -- The Harvard Symphony Concert." *Boston
Evening Transcript* January 30, 1880: 4. Review of the
January 29, 1880 concert. The composition " . . . sustains the
good impression created by its first performance." (See:
W14d)

WB90.   "Harvard Musical Association." *Dwight's Journal of Music*
40/1013 (February 14, 1880): 30-31. Review of the January
29, 1880 concert. The overture was a "welcome repetition"
and "improved upon acquaintance." (See: W14d)

WB91.   "Musical -- Triennial Festival." *Boston Evening Transcript*
May 7, 1880: 1. Review of the May 6, 1880 performance.
Chadwick's work was ". . . led by the composer himself with
verve and splendid effect." (See: W14e)

WB92.   "Haydn and Handel Festival -- Third Day of the Music
Triennial in Boston." *New York Times* May 7, 1880: 2.
Review of the May 6, 1880 performance. "This overture has
been given twice before at the Harvard Symphony concerts and
has been greatly admired." (See: W14e)

WB93.   "Third Concert, Thursday Afternoon." *Dwight's Journal of
Music* 50/1020 (May 22, 1880): 86. Review of the May 6,
1880 performance. On Chadwick's conducting: "He held the
orchestra well in hand, and was warmly received as soon as the
public became aware who the conductor was." (See: W14e)

WB94.   "Concerts of the Month." *The Musical Herald* 1/6 (June
1880): 139. Review of the May 6, 1880 performance. " . . .
the orchestra played . . . under the direction of the talented
composer, Mr. Chadwick, who proved himself a good

conductor, keeping the players well together, and giving the shading and expression in thorough manner." (See: W14e)

WB95. "The Worcester (Mass.) Music Festival." *The Musical Visitor* (September 1889): 234. Announcement that Chadwick will conduct his work at the Worcester Festival, September 27, 1889. (See: W14g)

WB96. Warner, A. J. "Chadwick Music in Kilburn [*sic*] Hall." *Rochester Times-Union* March 7, 1930. Review of the March 6, 1930 performance in Rochester, New York. (See: W14j)

WB97. Downes, Olin. "Chadwick Work Played at Festival." *New York Times* May 22, 1931: 28. Notes the performance of *Rip Van Winkle* at the Eastman School of Music's "American Music Festival." (See: W14l)

WB98. Downes, Olin. "American Music at the Rochester Festival." *New York Times* May 31, 1931: X/8. Review of the May 21, 1931 performance. "The placing of this composition at the beginning of a program of works by young Americans was not merely an act of formal homage to a celebrated musician who in his later years was correctly designated as the dean of the American school. The overture was given its place with an admirable sense of fitness on the part of a younger generation of [*sic*] aims quite divergent from those of Mr. Chadwick, but nevertheless appreciative of the clear form and architecture of the piece, and its direct melodic manner." (See: W14l)

WB99. Guinn, John. "DSO, Lortie Find Vitality of Liszt Concerto." *Detroit Free Press* May 5, 1995: 7D. Review of the May 4, 1995 performance. "Jarvi opened the program with Chadwick's *Rip Van Winkle*, music to nap by." (See: W14n)

W15. SCHON MUNCHEN ("Beautiful Munich"), Symphonische Walzer a la Strauss (Completed October 28, 1880)

Dedication: Minnie E. Smith
Unpublished
Holograph score and parts: MBCM
For: 3. 2. 2. 2./4. 2. 3. 0./timp. strings.

This waltz was later used in Chadwick's comic operetta, *The Peer and the Pauper* (1884). (See: W72)

Premiere

W15a. 7 January 1881; Boston Philharmonic Orchestra, Bernhard Listemann, cond.; Music Hall, Boston.

Other Selected Performances

W15b. 17 June 1885; All-American pops concert in honor of Bunker Hill Day; [conductor undetermined]; Music Hall, Boston.

W15c. 1 August 1915, Panama-Pacific International Exposition, "American Composers' Day," Festival Hall, San Francisco, California, The Exposition Orchestra, G. W. Chadwick, cond. [Although the program for this performance reads only that a "Symphonic Waltz" by Chadwick was performed, this composition seems the most likely choice.]

Bibliography

WB100. "Musical." *Boston Evening Transcript* January 8, 1881: 3. Review of the premiere. "Mr. Chadwick's Beautiful Munich, a 'symphonic waltz' . . . was performed from the composer's manuscript. It is melodious and pretty, but how symphonique was not obvious . . . ." (See: W15a)

WB101. "Philharmonic Orchestra." *Dwight's Journal of Music* 41/1037 (January 15, 1881): 14-15. Review of the premiere. ". . . graceful, genial, charming set of waltzes, after the Strauss Vienna style, showing a clever, ready hand in such light composition--useful practice for a more serious work . . . ." (See: W15a)

WB102. "Dramatic and Musical Notes." *Boston Daily Advertiser* June 17, 1885: 4. Preview of the June 17, 1885 concert. " . . . popular concert will be made up exclusively of selections by Boston composers . . . ." Included works by Arthur Foote, Horatio Parker, and John K. Paine. (See: W15b)

WB103. "Dramatic and Musical Notes." *Boston Daily Advertiser* June 18, 1885: 4. Review of the June 17, 1885 performance. "Mr. Chadwick's Beautiful Munich waltz hints that all his study time abroad was not given over to counterpoint and theory, but the practical relationship of melody and rhythm to the poetry of motion claimed something of his care. The introduction is charmingly suave . . . ." (See: W15b)

W16. SERENADE IN F (1890)

Dedication: St. Louis Musical Club
Holograph and parts: MBCM
Unpublished
Availability: Fleisher cat. no. 2240s; Luck's cat. no. 06080
For: string orchestra

Movements: Allegro grazioso (F)
                  Andantino (B-flat)
                  Tempo di menuetto (d)
                  Finale: Presto non troppo (F)

Selected Performances

W16a. 21 April 1930; New England Conservatory Orchestra,"Concert of Compositions of George W. Chadwick," Francis Findlay, cond.; Jordan Hall, Boston.

W16b. 8 November 1988; American Music Ensemble Vienna, Hobart Earle, cond.; Minoritensaal, Graz, Austria.

W16c. 19 January 1997; Tampa Bay Chamber Orchestra, "The American Connection," Richard Cormier, cond.; Grand Salon, University of Tampa, Tampa, Florida.

Bibliography

WB104. Loft, Kurt. "Orchestra Engaging at New Home." *Tampa Tribune* January 20, 1997. Review of the January 19, 1997 performance. "Chadwick's buoyancy seldom surfaced, and the protracted finale fell flat." (See: W16c)

W17. SINFONIETTA IN D MAJOR (Sketched ca. summer, 1903; orchestration begun February 11, 1904; completed May 3, 1904)

Dedication: [Although not formally dedicated, the program for the February 24, 1905, concert at New England Conservatory stipulates that the work was written especially for the conservatory orchestra.]
Holograph: NRU-Mus (score); MBCM (parts)

Published: Schirmer, 1906 (publ. plate no. 18210)
Availability: Fleisher cat. no. 1997; Luck's cat. no. 05264
Duration: 21 minutes
For: 3 (3rd doubles picc). 2. 2. 2./
          4. 2. 3 (ad lib.). 0./
          timp. 4 perc. harp. strings.

Movements: Risolutamente (D)
                Canzonetta: Allegretto (a)
                Scherzino: Vivacissimo e leggiero (F)
                Finale: Assai animato (D)

(See also: WR8)

Premiere

W17a.   21 November 1904; [Members of the Boston Symphony
        Orchestra], All-Chadwick concert, G. W. Chadwick, cond.;
        Jordan Hall, Boston.

Other Selected Performances

W17b.   24 February 1905; New England Conservatory Orchestra, G.
        W. Chadwick, cond.; Jordan Hall, Boston.

W17c.   26 December 1907; Saint Louis Symphony Orchestra, Max
        Zach, cond.; Saint Louis, Missouri.

W17d.   2 January 1910; New York Symphony, Walter Damrosch,
        cond.; The New Theatre, New York City.

W17e.   11/12 February 1910; Boston Symphony Orchestra, Max
        Fiedler, cond.; Symphony Hall, Boston.

W17f.   15 May 1913; New England Conservatory Orchestra, G. W.
        Chadwick, cond.; Jordan Hall, Boston.

W17g.   12 November 1922; People's Symphony Orchestra, Emil
        Mollenhauer, cond.; St. James Theatre, Boston.

W17h.   28 February 1923; New England Conservatory Orchestra, G.
        W. Chadwick, cond.; Symphony Hall, Boston.

W17i. 25/26 April 1930; Boston Symphony Orchestra, Serge
Koussevitzky, cond.; Symphony Hall, Boston.

W17j. 18 March 1932; New England Conservatory Orchestra,
Wallace Goodrich, cond. (movement no. 1 only); Jordan Hall,
Boston.

W17k. 20 June 1932; New England Conservatory Orchestra, Wallace
Goodrich, cond. (movement no. 1 only); Jordan Hall, Boston.

W17l. 19 March 1938; New England Conservatory Orchestra,
Wallace Goodrich, cond. (movement no. 1 only); Jordan Hall,
Boston.

W17m. 10 February 1955; Baltimore Symphony Orchestra, Samuel
Carmell, cond.; Douglas High School, Baltimore, Maryland.

W17n. 18/19 January 1995; National Symphony Orchestra, "Meet the
Orchestra" program, Michael Morgan, cond.; John F. Kennedy
Center for the Performing Arts, Washington, D. C.

Bibliography

WB105. R. R. G. "Music and Drama -- Jordan Hall: Mr. Chadwick's
Concert." *Boston Evening Transcript* November 22, 1904:
15. Review of the premiere. "In the sinfonietta [*sic*] . . . Mr.
Chadwick has perhaps reached his high water mark. He has, at
all events, been content to forget that, a pupil of Rheinberger,
he can write admirable counterpoint, and thus has depended
more on his own individuality." (See: W17a)

WB106. "Chadwick Plays New Symphony." *Boston Herald* November
22, 1904: 7. Review of the premiere. ". . . certain characteristics associated with the American are salient in this
sinfonietta--a directness of speech, an undisguised liking for
simple sentiment, a peculiar humor, a gayety that approaches
recklessness and snaps fingers, a common sense dealing with
aesthetic problems. This music is human, virile." (See:
W17a)

WB107. "Concerts of the Week." *New York Times* January 2, 1910:
V/15. Announcement of the New York Symphony concert,
January 2, 1910. "It was first performed at a concert of the

New England Conservatory shortly after its composition in
1904. It has had several hearing in Europe." (See: W17d)

WB108. H. E. K. [Henry E. Krehbiel]. "Music -- The Symphony
Society." *New York Daily Tribune* January 3, 1910: 7.
Review of the New York Symphony concert, January 2, 1910.
"Mr. Chadwick's music is academical, and academic influences
are anathema in minds attuned to modern ideas. Mr. Damrosch
was a brave man to produce it, although his audience . . .
enjoyed it . . . ." (See: W17d)

WB109. "The New York Symphony -- A Sinfonietta by Chadwick
Played Here for the First Time." *New York Times* January 3,
1910: 9. Review of the New York Symphony concert,
January 2, 1910. "Mr. Chadwick has written tunefully,
unafraid. His orchestration is appropriate to the ideas he had to
express, translucent, euphonius, igenious [*sic*]. His treatment
of the timbres of the wood wind [*sic*] instruments is especially
pleasing. The little work is delightful to hear in these days
when serious musicians dare so seldom to be anything less
than portentous . . . ." (See: W17d)

WB110. "Sinfonietta by Chadwick Falls Flat at Concert." *Boston
Journal* February 12, 1910: 9. Review of the Boston
Symphony Orchestra performance, February 11, 1910. "It is
not so remarkable either for charm of theme or for strength of
general interest. Usually Mr. Chadwick's works have an
attractiveness well sustained from beginning to end. Yesterday
the interest of the audience rose and fell . . . . The applause
was perfunctory. There was no calling for the composer."
(See: W17e)

WB111. Downes, Olin. "Symphony Concert." *Boston Post* February
12, 1910: 15. Review of the Boston Symphony Orchestra
performance, February 11, 1910. "The pieces are in the nature
of a divertimento. There is consistent employment of some
material that has an Oriental twang, but these sighs and
roulades need not be taken too seriously . . . . the prevailing
character of the music, with its lively, snappy motives, is a
little Scotch and more plain, home-brewed American." (See:
W17e)

WB112. H. T. P. [Henry Taylor Parker] "Music and Musicians --
Bruckner and Chadwick Again." *Boston Evening Transcript*

February 14, 1910: 11. Review of the Boston Symphony Orchestra performance, February 11, 1910. "Mr. Chadwick's piece was warmly received; and had not sickness kept him from the hall, he might justly have risen to make his acknowledgement . . . ." (See: W17e)

WB113. Henderson, W. J. "In the World of Music." *The Sunday Herald* (Boston) February 16, 1910: 8. Comments on the Boston Symphony Orchestra performance, February 11, 1910. ". . . a bit of lovely musical landscape, filled with the sunshine of a happy disposition and vocal with the songs of spontaneous fancy." (See: W17e)

WB114. W. S. S. [Warren Storey Smith]. "Concert-Chronicle -- Renewing Mr. Chadwick." *Boston Evening Transcript* November 13, 1922: 8. Review of the People's Symphony Orchestra performance, November 12, 1922. "Few American composers would have the blend of scholarship, humor and fancy requisite to the writing of it . . . . It has buoyancy, picturesqueness, and a judicious admixture of sentiment." (See: W17g)

WB115. H. T. P. [Henry Taylor Parker]. "Age Honored, Youth Heard, Heights Won." *Boston Evening Transcript* April 26, 1930: 14. Review of the Boston Symphony Orchestra performance, April 25, 1930. ". . . Ravel himself might envy the fancy and felicity of the distant horns against the sustaining viola at the end of the slow movement." Of the other composers represented on the program: "Not one was, or is, so masculine as this Chadwick in his forties and fifties before symphonic poems sapped him." (See: W17i)

WB116. A. H. M. [Alfred H. Meyer] "Student Players Try Modern Music." *Boston Evening Transcript* March 19, 1932: II/5. Review of the New England Conservatory Orchestra performance of March 18, 1932. The writer comments on Chadwick's ". . . . straightforward forthrightness, his bright-rhythmed, [and] natively flavored good humor . . . ." (See: W17j)

W18. SUITE SYMPHONIQUE (Sketched 1904-1906; completed 1909)

Dedication: Frederick A. Stock and the Theodore Thomas Orchestra of Chicago

Holograph: not located; manuscript parts at MBCM
Published: Schmidt, 1911 (publ. plate no. 9276)
Availability: Fleisher cat. no. 5260; Luck's cat. no. 09994
Duration: 36 minutes
For: 3 (3rd doubles picc). 2. 2. 2. alto sax./
          4. 3. 2. 1./
          timp. 6 perc. harp. strings.

Movements: Allegro molto animato (E-flat)
                Romanza: Andantino espressivo (B-flat)
                Intermezzo e Humoreske: Poco allegretto (g)
                Finale: Allegro molto ed energico (E-flat)

In his *Memoirs* (March 27, 1907), Chadwick stated that *Suite Symphonique* began with the "Romanza" which borrowed material from his Fifth String Quartet. The "Intermezzo e Humoreske" was crafted from ideas he had never put to use. The first movement, which had been submitted to the competition of the National Federation of Music Clubs in 1910 under the title *La Vie Joyeuse*, had been conceived as an independent concert overture. The whole was completed with an original finale. In his *Journal* (February 22, 1909), Chadwick wrote that "This work has covered a great deal of time . . . ." He went on to note that, while the "Romanza" did originate from the Fifth String Quartet, some interludes and variations were composed at West Chop in 1907. Further, the second theme of the third movement dates from ". . . 1904 or earlier--There is no record of it in the sketch books." Finally, he states that the finale themes date from April 15, 1906.

This composition was awarded 1st Prize in the annual composition contest sponsored by the National Federation of Music Clubs for "Best Orchestral Work by an American Composer," 1911. Judges for the competition were Frederick Stock, Henry Hadley, and Victor Herbert.

Premiere

W18a. 29 March 1911; Philadelphia Symphony Orchestra, G. W. Chadwick, cond.; Academy of Music, Philadelphia, Pennsylvania.

Other Selected Performances

W18b. 13-15 April 1911; Boston Symphony Orchestra, G. W. Chadwick, cond.; Symphony Hall, Boston.

W18c. 12 January 1912; Minneapolis Symphony Orchestra, Emil Oberhoffer, cond.; The Auditorium, Minneapolis, Minnesota.

W18d. 2 and 4 February 1912; New York Symphony, G. W. Chadwick, cond.; Century Theatre, New York City.

W18e. 2/3 February 1912; Chicago Symphony Orchestra, Frederick Stock, cond.; Chicago, Illinois.

W18f. 31 January/1 February 1913; Saint Louis Symphony Orchestra, Max Zach, cond.; Saint Louis, Missouri.

W18g. 7 February 1913; San Francisco Symphony Orchestra, Henry Hadley, cond.; Cort Theatre, San Francisco, California.

W18h. 17 February 1924; People's Symphony Orchestra, All-Chadwick program, G. W. Chadwick, cond. (second movement only); St. James Theatre, Boston.

Bibliography

WB117. "Special Concert in Honor of Convention." *Philadelphia Inquirer* March 30, 1911: 2. Review of the premiere. "It is a fluently written, skillfully constructed and interesting work. . . . It is all highly attractive, and the suite may be expected to find a frequent and welcome place on the program of the concert room." (See: W18a)

WB118. "Philadelphia Orchestra." *Evening Bulletin* (Philadelphia) March 30, 1911: 4. Review of the premiere. The *Suite* " . . . is nobly conceived and written with deep and true musicianship on a foundation of pure melody. It has few complexities, for, while by no means superficial, it preserves, in all its most impressive effects, the charm of simplicity and directness . . . . through all and pervading all still shines the radiant beauty of the melody that gives his worthy prize-winning composition its greatest charm." (See: W18a)

WB119. "Federation Hears Orchestra Concert." *Public Ledger* (Philadelphia) March 30, 1911: 2. Review of the premiere. "The work is throughout of a cheerful, insouciant temper, blithely refusing to take itself very seriously anywhere, outside of the grave and deliberate Romanze which constitutes the melodious second movement." (See: W18a)

WB120. "Music and Musicians -- Mr. Chadwick's New Suite Played and Well Received in Philadelphia." *Boston Evening Transcript* April 5, 1911: 24. This report on the premiere includes excerpts from various Philadelphia press reviews. (See: W18a)

WB121. H. T. P. [Henry Taylor Parker]. "The Symphony Concert -- Two New Pieces of American Music." *Boston Evening Transcript* April 14, 1911: 12. Review of the Boston Symphony Orchestra performance, April 13, 1911. "Mr. Chadwick's invention of melody flags, and the slow movement, a Romance, barely escapes a rather thin and commonplace sweetness in matter and in manner. It is simplicity and sentiment carried to the perilous verge, even though the instrumental turf be velvety." (See: W18b)

WB122. Downes, Olin. "Two Novelties by Symphony." *Boston Post* April 14, 1911: 12. Review of the Boston Symphony Orchestra performance, April 13, 1911. "The first and third movements of this suite are labored. In the last movement there are occasionally delightful passages, but it is not the opinion of this writer that the composition increases Mr. Chadwick's reputation as a composer." (See: W18b)

WB123. "American Music Crop." *Musical America* 13/24 (April 22, 1911): 18. Notes that Chadwick conducted his own work at the Boston Symphony Orchestra performances of April 13-15, 1911. (See: W18b)

WB124. Downes, Olin. "Fiedler Plays New American Overture." *Musical America* 13/24 (April 22, 1911): 1, 32. Review of the Boston Symphony Orchestra performances of April 13-15, 1911. Although much of the review is given over to consideration of Henry F. Gilbert's *Comedy Overture on Negro Themes*, Downes notes that "Mr. Chadwick conducted his work and was repeatedly recalled afterwards." (See: W18b)

WB125. Gunn, Glenn Dillard. "Music and Drama -- Orchestra Introduces a Remarkable Pianist." *Chicago Tribune* February 3, 1912: 7. Review of the Chicago Symphony Orchestra performance, February 2, 1912. ". . . a deliberate effort to lift the idiom of American popular music to higher artistic levels without sacrificing salient characteristics." Gunn writes that, happily, "A message of profound significance is to be discovered nowhere . . . ." (See: W18d)

WB126. "New York Symphony -- Mr. Chadwick Conducts his New Symphonic Suite." *New York Times* February 3, 1912: 11. Review of the New York Symphony performance, February 2, 1912. "It is in the form of a symphony; the fact that its content is somewhat lighter and at some moments more jocose than composers are in the habit of putting into a symphony no doubt led the composer to let it go as a suite." (See: W18d)

WB127. H. E. K. [Henry E. Krehbiel]. "Musical Comment." *New York Daily Tribune* February 5, 1912: 7. Review of the New York Symphony performance, February 2, 1912. "What is this Americanism which seems more palpable in Mr. Chadwick's music than in that of any of his colleagues . . . ? It quite eludes description. It is felt, not comprehended . . . . Mr. Chadwick's music is certainly American." (See: W18d)

WB128. H. T. P. [Henry T. Parker]. "Chadwick Suite is Typically American." *Musical America* 15/14 (February 10, 1912): 21. Review of the New York Symphony performance, February 2, 1912. "The prevailing atmosphere of Mr. Chadwick's composition is characteristically American. It deserves many a repetition . . . ." (See: W18d)

WB129. H. T. P. [Henry Taylor Parker]. "Week-End Round Over Bostonian Concert-Giving." *Boston Evening Transcript* February 18, 1924: 8. Review of the People's Symphony presentation, February 17, 1924. Only the "Romanza" movement was given. "It is gentle, tender, musing, half-smiling, quite honest, making no parade of its warmth." (See: W18h)

W19. SYMPHONIC SKETCHES (1895-1904 [mvt. I, 1895; mvt. II, 1895; mvt. III, 1902-1904; mvt. IV, 1896])

Dedication: Frederic [*sic*] S. Converse
Holograph: DLC (score); MBCM (parts)
Published: Schirmer, 1907 (publ. plate no. 18211)
Availability: Fleisher cat. no. 5260 (complete) and 123 ("Jubilee" only); Luck's cat. no. 09131 (complete), 07914 ("Hobgoblin" only), 07915 ("Jubilee" and "Noel" only), and 07916 ("A Vagrom Ballad" only)

Duration: 29 minutes
For: picc. 2. 2. eh. 2. bass cl. 2./
          4. 2. 3. 0./
          timp. 5 perc. xylo. harp. strings

Movements: Jubilee: Allegro molto vivace (A)
                  Noel: Andante con tenerezza (D-flat)
                  Hobgoblin: Allegro vivace (F)
                  A Vagrom Ballad: Moderato. Alla Burla (a); Molto
                        vivace-Prestissimo (A)

In an entry in his *Memoirs* (April 26, 1896), Chadwick confessed that he wrote the verses which precede each movement.

(See also: WR9, WR10, WR11, WR12 and WR13)

Premiere

W19a.   21 November 1904; Members of the Boston Symphony Orchestra, All-Chadwick concert, G. W. Chadwick, cond.; Jordan Hall, Boston (movements 1-3 only).

Other Selected Performances

W19b.   7/8 February 1908 (First complete performance); Boston Symphony Orchestra, Karl Muck, cond.; Symphony Hall, Boston.

W19c.   21/22 January 1910; Chicago Symphony Orchestra, G. W. Chadwick, cond.; Chicago, Illinois.

W19d.   19 May 1915; Boston Symphony Orchestra, Karl Muck, cond.; San Francisco, California.

W19e.   1 August 1915; Panama-Pacific International Exposition, "American Composers' Day," The Exposition Orchestra, G. W. Chadwick, cond.; Festival Hall, San Francisco, California. [The program for this performance reads "Symphonic Sketch" without indicating which one.]

W19f.   29 December 1916; Baltimore Symphony Orchestra, Gustav Strube, cond.; Lyric Theatre, Baltimore, Maryland ("Noel" only).

W19g. 22 March 1918; Boston Symphony Orchestra, Karl Muck, cond.; Symphony Hall, Boston.

W19h. 1 March 1922; New England Conservatory Orchestra, G. W. Chadwick, cond.; Symphony Hall, Boston ("Jubilee" and "Noel" only).

W19i. 11 November 1922; New York Philharmonic, Josef Stransky, cond.; Carnegie Hall, New York City ("Jubilee" only).

W19j. 17 February 1924; People's Symphony Orchestra, All-Chadwick program, G. W. Chadwick, cond.; St. James Theatre, Boston ("Jubilee," "Noel," and "Vagrom Ballad" only).

W19k. 23 May 1924; New England Conservatory Orchestra, Wallace Goodrich, cond.; Museum of Fine Arts, Boston, ("Noel" only).

W19l. 18 May 1928; New England Conservatory Orchestra, G. W. Chadwick, cond.; Jordan Hall, Boston ("Jubilee" only).

W19m. 6 March 1930; "American Composers Series"; Eastman-Rochester Orchestra, Howard Hanson, cond.; Kilbourn Hall, Rochester, New York.

W19n. 21 April 1931; Boston Symphony Orchestra, Serge Koussevitzky, cond.; Symphony Hall, Boston ("Noel" only).

W19o. 13 August 1931; New York Philharmonic, Hans Lange, cond.; Lewisohn Stadium, New York City ("Jubilee" and "Noel" only).

W19p. 11/15 December 1931; New England Conservatory Orchestra, Francis Findlay, cond.; Jordan Hall, Boston, ("Noel" only).

W19q. 7 January 1933; New York Philharmonic, "Concert for Children and Young People" (Series I/Concert IV), Ernest Schelling, cond.; Carnegie Hall, New York City ("Jubilee" only).

W19r. 24 December 1933; New York Philharmonic, Hans Lange, cond.; Carnegie Hall, New York City ("Noel" only).

W19s. 14 March 1934; New England Conservatory Orchestra, Wallace Goodrich, cond.; Jordan Hall, Boston ("A Vagrom Ballad" only).

W19t. 18 December 1935; New England Conservatory Orchestra, Wallace Goodrich, cond.; Jordan Hall, Boston.

W19u. 18 December 1937; New York Philharmonic, "Youths' Concert," John Barbirolli, cond.; Carnegie Hall, New York City ("Jubilee" only).

W19v. 4/5 March 1938; Cincinnati Symphony Orchestra, "Josef Hofmann Jubilee Concert," Eugene Goossens, cond.; Music Hall, Cincinnati, Ohio ("Jubilee" only).

W19w. 4 January 1939; CBS Radio Broadcast to Europe and South America; Indianapolis Symphony Orchestra, Fabien Sevitzky, cond.

W19x. 14 March 1939; New England Conservatory Orchestra, Wallace Goodrich, cond.; Jordan Hall, Boston ("Jubilee" only).

W19y. 12 January 1941; Baltimore Symphony Orchestra, Howard Barlow, cond.; Lyric Theatre, Baltimore, Maryland ("Jubilee" only).

W19z. 5/7 December 1941; Pittsburgh Symphony Orchestra, Fritz Reiner, cond.; Pittsburgh, Pennsylvania.

W19aa. 12/13 November 1942; New York Philharmonic, Howard Barlow, cond.; Carnegie Hall, New York City ("Jubilee" only).

W19bb. 21/22 December 1950; Cincinnati Symphony Orchestra, Thor Johnson, cond.; Music Hall, Cincinnati, Ohio ("Noel" only).

W19cc. 11/12 January 1952; Cincinnati Symphony Orchestra, Thor Johnson, cond.; Music Hall, Cincinnati, Ohio ("Jubilee" only).

W19dd. 5 February 1952; Baltimore Symphony Orchestra, Don Gillis, cond.; Lyric Theatre, Baltimore, Maryland ("Jubilee" only).

W19ee. 19/20 December 1952; Cincinnati Symphony Orchestra, Thor

Johnson, cond.; Music Hall, Cincinnati, Ohio ("Noel" only).

W19ff. 23 February 1955; New England Conservatory Orchestra,
Richard Burgin, cond.; Jordan Hall, Boston ("Jubilee" only).

W19gg. 16 February 1957; New York Philharmonic, "Young People's
Concert," Wilfrid Pelletier, cond.; Carnegie Hall, New York
City ("Jubilee" only).

W19hh. 22 December 1959; Cincinnati Symphony Orchestra, Max
Rudolf, cond.; Music Hall, Cincinnati, Ohio ("Noel" only).

W19ii. 16 September 1976; Indianapolis Symphony Orchestra, Oleg
Kovalenko, cond.; Indiana National Bank Plaza, Indianapolis,
Indiana ("Jubilee" only).

W19jj. 12-14 September 1991; National Symphony Orchestra,
Mstislav Rostropovich, cond.; John F. Kennedy Center for the
Performing Arts, Washington, D. C. ("Jubilee" only).

W19kk. 23 April 1992; Detroit Symphony Orchestra, Neeme Jarvi,
cond.; Orchestra Hall, Detroit, Michigan ("Jubilee" only).

W19ll. 15 April 1993; Detroit Symphony Orchestra, Neeme Jarvi,
cond.; Orchestra Hall, Detroit, Michigan ("Noel" only).

W19mm. 7 January 1994; Detroit Symphony Orchestra, Neeme Jarvi,
cond.; Orchestra Hall, Detroit, Michigan ("Hobgoblin" and "A
Vagrom Ballad" only).

W19nn. 23 June 1994; Boston Pops Esplanade Orchestra, Evans Haile,
cond.; Boston ("Jubilee" only).

W19oo. 27-28 October 1995; Boulder (Colorado) Philharmonic, Harvey
Felder, cond.; Mackey Auditorium, Colorado University,
Boulder, Colorado ("Jubilee" only).

W19pp. 9 March 1996; Longwood Symphony Orchestra, Francisco
Noya, cond.; Jordan Hall, Boston ("Jubilee" only).

W19qq. 3-4 July 1996; Baltimore Symphony Orchestra, David Loebel,
cond.; Oregon Ridge State Park, Cockeysville, Maryland
("Jubilee" only).

W19rr. 11 July 1996; United States Marine Band ("The President's Own"), Col. John Bourgeois, cond.; Daughters of the American Revolution Constitution Hall, Washington, D.C.

W19ss. 5 October 1996; Plymouth Philharmonic, Steven Karidoyanes, cond.; Memorial Hall, Plymouth, Massachusetts ("Jubilee" only).

W19tt. 31 January 1997; Oakland East Bay Symphony, Michael Morgan, cond.; Paramount Theatre, Oakland, California ("Jubilee" only).

Bibliography

WB130. R. R. G. "Jordan Hall: Mr. Chadwick's Concert." *Boston Evening Transcript* November 22, 1904: 15. Review of the November 21, 1904 performance in Boston. This review does not specifically consider *Symphonic Sketches* (referred to here as the "Suite in A"), but says of the event: "To turn to last night's concert, it must at once be set down as a success." (See: W19a)

WB131. "Musical Matters -- Chadwick Suite Played at the Symphony." *Boston Globe* February 9, 1908: 30. Review of the Boston performance of February 7, 1908. "In every instance Prof. Chadwick has developed his ideas skilfully, and although utilizing modern methods and expressing the motifs by a modern orchestra, he is lucid and melodic in his forms, and his music is good to hear, for it is music that the average ear finds pleasing." (See: W19b)

WB132. H. T. P. [Henry Taylor Parker]. "Music and Drama -- Mr. Chadwick as a True American Composer." *Boston Evening Transcript* February 10, 1908: 11. Review of the Boston performance of February 7, 1908. " . . . the music shouts because it cannot help it, and sings because it cannot help it, and each as only Americans would shout and sing . . . ." (See: W19b)

WB133. Hale, Philip. "Symphony in 18th Concert -- Long Applause for Chadwick Sketches." *Boston Herald* March 23, 1918: 16. Review of the Boston Symphony Orchestra performance of March 22, 1918. "Mr. Chadwick's sketches . . . may justly be called American music. Not because the two [Hale is referring to "Jubilee" and "Vagrom Ballad"] are derived in any way from Congo, Indian, Creole, or Cowboy themes; not because they strive to illustrate in tones an episode in American history or to portray some prominent American; but because the music has characteristics, rhythmic, melodic, that we believe to be distinctively American . . . ." (See: W19g)

WB134. Aldrich, Richard. "Music -- The Philharmonic Concert." *New York Times* November 12, 1922: I/6. Review of the New York Philharmonic performance, November 11, 1922. On "Jubilee": " . . . a capitol piece deserving, with the whole suite, of more frequent hearing than it gets." (See: W19i)

WB135. H. T. P. [Henry Taylor Parker]. "Week-End Round Over Bostonian Concert-Giving." *Boston Evening Transcript* February 18, 1924: 8. Review of the People's Symphony presentation, February 17, 1924. " . . . the assembled pieces bore witness to the range of his musical mind and imagination." (See: W19j)

WB136. Warner, A. J. "Chadwick Music in Kilburn [*sic*] Hall." *Rochester Times-Union* March 7, 1930. Review of the March 6, 1930 performance in Rochester, New York. (See: W19m)

WB137. Downes, Olin. "A Program of Native Works." *New York Times* August 9, 1931: 8/6. Preview of the New York Philharmonic performance, August 13, 1931. "After MacDowell, Chadwick did the most to give the American composer international standing, and his range of expression was wider than MacDowell's, if his feeling was not so mystical and poetic." Also, Chadwick's " . . . technical equipment was such as to command the highest respect on both sides of the Atlantic." (See: W19o)

WB138. "Activities of Musicians Here and Afield." *New York Times* August 9, 1931: 8/6. Announcement of the New York Philharmonic performance, August 13, 1931. (See: W19o)

WB139. "Native Music Tommorrow." *New York Times* August 12, 1931: 17. Announcement of New York Philharmonic performance, August 13, 1931. (See: W19o)

WB140. H. T. "American Music at the Stadium." *New York Times* August 14, 1931: 21. Review of the New York Philharmonic performance, August 13, 1931. "Jubilee" and "Noël" " . . . were played in memory of Mr. Chadwick, who died last April 4 . . . . It is unfortunate that many in the audience chose to leave before and during the playing of the Chadwick sketches, which are the work of a great American composer. Noel is a moving piece, joyful, dignified, devout. And the Jubilee is alive, sure, and strong." (See: W19o)

WB141. H. H. "Yule Music Given by Philharmonic." *New York Times* December 25, 1933: 28. Review of the New York Philharmonic concert, December 24, 1933. This concert was also broadcast on WABC radio. "Noel" was considered " . . . pleasant [and] meditative . . . ." (See: W19r)

WB142. G. G. "Barbirolli Gives Youth's Concert." *New York Times* December 19, 1937: II/3. Review of the New York Philharmonic performance, December 18, 1937. No specific mention of "Jubilee," but on the overall event: "While there was some squirming in seats, there were very few yawns and no cat calls." (See: W19u)

WB143. Downes, Olin. "U. S. Music Offered by Philharmonic." *New York Times* November 13, 1942: 27. Review of the New York Philharmonic concert, November 12, 1942. "It is brisk and melodious music in the stock German manner, though Chadwick's sentiment and laughter were too genuine with him. Why not have played a far more original movement -- the Vagrom Ballad which is the last and most characteristic and fantastic of the series [?]" (See: W19aa)

WB144. "Philharmonic Fortnight -- More Native Novelties." *Musical America* November 25, 1942: 10. Review of the New York Philharmonic performances of November 12/13, 1942. "'Jubilee' reminded us that Chadwick wrote better music than most people give him credit for nowadays. A revival of his sound and melodious music is long overdue." (See: W19aa)

WB145. Guinn, John. "Familiar Repertoire is Jarvi's Strength." *Detroit Free Press* April 24, 1992: 4C. Review of the April 23, 1992 performance. "It's jolly, it's well-scored, it's well-meant. But it sounded like a reject for the background music for 'The Waltons'." (See: W1kk)

WB146. Guinn, John. "Midori's is a Major Talent." *Detroit Free*

Press April 16, 1993: 11E. Review of the April 15, 1993 performance. Commenting on Chadwick's "Noel" and George Walker's "Sinfonia No. 2": "Both are academically correct; neither proved very interesting." (See: W19ll)

WB147. Guinn, John. "Violinist's Warmth Compensates for a Few Quirks." *Detroit Free Press* January 9, 1994: 3G. Review of the January 7, 1994 performance. The writer states that "Hobgoblin" and "A Vagrom Ballad" " . . . are examples of competent craftsmanship." (See: W19mm)

WB148. Dyer, Richard. "Energetic Haile Directs with Humor." *Boston Globe* June 24, 1994: 51. Review of the June 23, 1994 performance. "Jubilee" is " . . . an exceptionally attractive piece of neglected Americana . . . ." (See: W19nn)

WB149. Blomster, Wes. "Phil Finalist Fulfills Role of Maestro." *Daily Camera* (Boulder, Colorado) October 24, 1995: 6B. Preview of the October 27-28, 1995 concert. Notes conductor Harvey Felder's desire to replace a Mendelssohn work with "Jubilee." Felder states: "Chadwick -- forgotten today -- was once *the* American composer." (See: W19oo)

WB150. Page, Tim. "Marine Band Marks Change of Command." *Washington Post* July 12, 1996: F1. Review of the July 11, 1996 performance in Washington, D. C. Notes that Chadwick's music is played at the retirement concert for Col. John Bourgeois. (See: W19rr)

W20. SYMPHONY [NO. 1] IN C MAJOR, OP. 5 (Begun 1877 in Leipzig; completed in November 23, 1881, in Boston)

Dedication: To Chadwick's stepmother [Susan Collins Chadwick]
Holograph score and parts: MBCM
Unpublished
For: 2. 2. 2. 2./4. 2. 3. 0./timp. strings.

Movements:	Lento: Allegro molto e sostenuto (C)
	Allegro molto vivace (c)
	Adagio molto espressivo (A-flat)
	Finale: Allegro moderato (C)

Premiere

W20a. 23 February 1882; Harvard Musical Association concert, G. W. Chadwick, cond.; Boston Museum, Boston.

Bibliography

WB151. "Chadwick." *Musical Record* 154 (October 8, 1881): 30. Announcement of the premiere. "Glad to see a little more encouragement to home talent." (See: W20a)

WB152. "Theatres and Concerts -- Harvard Musical Association." *Boston Evening Transcript* October 12, 1881: 1. Announcement of the Harvard Musical Association premiere. Notes that the 17th season of the Harvard Musical Association will feature 60 orchestral musicians and the premiere of Chadwick's First Symphony. (See: W20a)

WB153. "Correspondence -- Boston." *Church's Musical Visitor* 11/2 (November 1881): 43. Announcement of the premiere. Notes that Bernhard Listemann will be the violin leader. (See: W20a)

WB154. "Musical Matters -- Mr. George W. Chadwick's First Symphony." *Sunday Herald* (Boston) February 19, 1882: 3. This lengthy preview, discussion, and analysis (which includes six musical examples) is our best source of information regarding the history of the First Symphony. " . . . this composer has created very general interest in his work by the success which has attended the presentation of all the compositions he has made public since he became a resident musician upon his return from Leipzig a few years ago." (See: W20a)

WB155. "Theatres and Concerts -- Harvard Musical Association." *Boston Evening Transcript* February 24, 1882: 1. Review of the premiere. "The themes are modest and graceful, and the orchestral treatment is refined and discreet. The color is used with careful judgment . . . ." (See: W20a)

WB156. "Music and the Stage." *Daily Evening Traveller* (Boston) February 24, 1882: 4. Review of the premiere. ". . . the symphony commanded the closest attention and interest of one of the most exacting audiences that ever filled a music house in Boston; and that it [the composition] was cordially endorsed by them in the main." (See: W20a)

WB157. "Musical Matters." *Boston Herald* February 24, 1882: 1. Review of the premiere. "While there are evidences of a tendency to over-elaborate the motifs of several movements and some lack of finish in the effort, there are many other and far more numerous evidences of a rare genius for this class of composition . . . ." (See: W20a)

WB158. Proteus [Louis Charles Elson]. "Music in Boston -- The Harvard Symphony Concerts." *Church's Musical Visitor* (April, 1882): 187. Review of the premiere. "It is a symmetrical, well written work, earnest, and in some parts [it is] of striking originality. . . . when we think that Mr. Chadwick is a very young man, and that Professor Paine, the leading American composer, in my eyes, had not achieved as much at his age, we find that there is great hope and promise in the already prominent composer." (See: W20a)

W21. SYMPHONY NO. 2 IN B-FLAT MAJOR, OP. 21
(Composed 1883 to 1885 in Boston)

Dedication: "Meinem Lebensfreunde A. T. Scott"
Holograph: DLC (score); MBCM (parts)
Published: Schmidt, 1888 (publ. plate no. 1559); reprint, Schmidt
      1916 [miniature score]; reprint, Earlier American Music, vol.
      4. With a new introduction by H. Wiley Hitchcock. New
      York: Da Capo, 1972
Availability: Fleisher cat. no. 5511
Duration: 35 minutes
For: 2. 2. 2. 2./4. 2. 3. 0./timp. strings.

Movements: Andante non troppo: Allegro con brio (B-flat)
                    Allegretto scherzando (F)
                    Largo e maestoso (d)
                    Allegro molto animato (B-flat)

(See also: WR14)

Premieres

W21a1. 7/8 March 1884; Boston Symphony Orchestra, George Henschel, cond.; Music Hall, Boston (movement no. 2 only).

W21a2. 29 April 1885 [repeated 4 May 1885]; Apollo Club concert, G. W. Chadwick, cond.; Music Hall, Boston (movement no. 1 only).

W21a3. 10/11 December 1886; Boston Symphony Orchestra, G. W. Chadwick, cond.; Music Hall, Boston (First complete performance).

Other Selected Performances

W21b. 6/7 February 1891; Boston Symphony Orchestra, Arthur Nikisch, cond.; Music Hall, Boston.

W21c. 23 May 1893; World's Columbian Exposition, "American Programme," (Series No. 10), The Exposition Orchestra, Theodore Thomas, cond.; Music Hall, Chicago, Illinois.

W21d. 17 February 1924; People's Symphony Orchestra, All-Chadwick program, G. W. Chadwick, cond.; St. James Theatre, Boston (movement no. 2 only).

W21e. 7 February 1926; People's Symphony Orchestra, Stuart Mason, cond.; Hollis Street Theatre, Boston.

W21f. 14 December 1928; New England Conservatory Orchestra, Wallace Goodrich, cond.; Jordan Hall, Boston (movement no. 2 only).

W21g. 26 December 1929; Los Angeles Philharmonic, "Sixth Radio Concert" broadcast, Artur Rodzinski, cond.

W21h. 23 January 1932; New York Philharmonic, "Concert for Youth and Young People" (series 2/concert 4), Ernest Schelling, cond.; Carnegie Hall, New York City (movement no. 2 only).

W21i. 10-12 February 1981; National Symphony Orchestra, "America's Romantic Heritage," Mstislav Rostropovich, cond.; John F. Kennedy Center for the Performing Arts, Washington, D. C.

W21j. 25 March 1994; Detroit Symphony Orchestra, Neeme Järvi, cond.; Orchestra Hall, Detroit, Michigan.

Bibliography

WB159. "Theatres and Concerts." *Boston Evening Transcript* March 10, 1884: 1. Review of the premiere of the second movement, March 7, 1910. "The working up of the movement sounds clear and coherent, even at first hearing; the piquant charm of the whole is irresistible. The orchestration is that of a master, and is full of delicious bits of color . . . ." (See: W21a1)

WB160. Proteus [Louis Charles Elson]. "Music in Boston." *The Musical Visitor* April 1, 1884: 97. Review of the premiere of movement no. 2, March 7-8, 1884. The composition is " . . . full of sprightliness, bright and quaint in its themes (one of them has an Irish flavor), adequate in its treatment and symmetrical in its form." (See: W21a1)

WB161. "Music and the Drama." *Boston Daily Advertiser* April 30, 1885: 4. Review of the premiere of movement no. 1, April 29, 1885. "It was highly interesting, full of freshness, originality, and charm, and in fact seemed more than worthy to belong to the same composition with the scherzo, which has already excited so much admiration." (See: W21a2)

WB162. Proteus [Louis Charles Elson]. "Music in Boston." *The Musical Visitor* 14/6 (June 1885): 153. Review of the premiere of movement no. 1, April 29, 1885. "The symmetry is commendable, the scoring full of rich effects, particularly in the introduction which has some points in the style of Weber, and the development, if not yet very spontaneous, is more flowing and natural than that of the first or last movement of his first symphony." (See: W21a2)

WB163. "Musical Matters -- Mr. Chadwick's Second Symphony Heard." *Sunday Herald* (Boston) December 12, 1886: 17. Review of the first complete performance, December 10, 1886. "Mr. Chadwick has certainly made a great advance in his second symphony, and the work is a credit to this conscientious musician and composer. No more satisfactory effort in this line of writing has as yet been put before the public by a native born citizen . . . ." (See: W21a3)

WB164. "Music and the Drama." *Boston Daily Advertiser* December 13, 1886: 4. Review of the first complete performance, December 10, 1886. ". . . the instrumentation is modified for

power or for fancy in many different ways. The symphony
gave a remarkably strong and agreeable impression." (See:
W21a3)

WB165. "Theatres and Concerts -- Boston Symphony Orchestra."
Boston Evening Transcript December 13, 1886: 1. Review of
the first complete performance, December 10, 1886. " . . . the
composition shows genuine talent, but it seems as though the
composer had not yet sufficiently drilled his powers to cope
with so severe a task as a symphony." (See: W21a3)

WB166. "The Eighth Symphony Concert." *Boston Post* December 13,
1886: 5. Review of the first complete performance, December
10, 1886. "Mr. Chadwick, who is capable of better things,
has sacrificed artistic truth to a desire to please and to produce
brilliant effects; and he will come to grief if he persists in
writing symphonies, at any rate, in this vein. The applause
and enthusiasm were, for a Boston audience, almost un-
bounded . . . ." (See: W21a3)

WB167. "Theatres and Concerts -- Boston Symphony Orchestra."
Boston Evening Transcript February 9, 1891: 3. Review of
the Boston performance of February 6, 1891. "It had every
advantage of skilled performance and artistic rendering. It
shows throughout the art of handling the orchestra; it shows
musical ideas with good skill in working them. Most of the
work is interesting." (See: W21b)

WB168. Proteus [Louis Charles Elson]. "Music in Boston." *The
Musical Visitor* (March 1891): 67. Review of the Boston
performance of February 6, 1891. Elson writes that Chadwick
" . . . won a double triumph, both as composer and conductor. . . . The skill with which he led the orchestra was a
surprise to me, and it may be that in Mr. Chadwick we shall
yet find what we really need at present--a native conductor."
(See: W21b)

WB169. "Works by American Composers." *Chicago Tribune* May 24,
1893: 2. Review of the May 23, 1893 performance at the
World's Columbian Exposition. "The Chadwick composition,
like that of Foote [his Serenade, op. 25, was also on the
program], is unduly long, but, aside from this characteristically American fault, seems to contain much that is meritorious
and worthy of commendation. The faulty acoustics of the hall

render an estimate more definite than 'seems' impossible."
(See: W21c)

WB170. Roberts, A. Cookman. "American Music at the Exposition."
The Musical Herald of the United States 14/9 (July 1893): 1-3.
Commentary about the May 23, 1893 performance at the
World's Columbian Exposition. Roberts discusses the role of
American music at the Exposition with special reference to
Chadwick's Second Symphony: " . . . it vindicated entirely the
right of Mr. Chadwick to a place among the most elevated of
our young American composers, but [is it] unique? Character-
istic in respect of nationality? Not at all." (See: W21c)

WB171. Mathews, W. S. B. [William Smythe Babcock]. "Music at
the Fair" *Music* 4 (1893): 226. Review of the World's
Columbian Exposition performance, May 23, 1893. "There
were clever bits of writing, and there was an earnestness and
manly mood throughout; but after all there was more hard
work than the music seemed to warrant . . . . One would need
to hear the work again, and perhaps under better circumstances." (See: W21c)

WB172. H. T. P. [Henry Taylor Parker]. "Week-End Round Over
Bostonian Concert-Giving." *Boston Evening Transcript*
February 18, 1924: 8. Review of the People's Symphony
presentation, February 17, 1924. " . . . the assembled pieces
bore witness to the range of his musical mind and
imagination." (See: W21d)

WB173. "Boston Week Brings Orchestral and Recital Programs of
Notable Interest." *Musical America* 43/18 (February 20,
1926): 27. Review of the People's Symphony Orchestra
program of February 7, 1926. The conductor ". . . gave an
effective reading of the Chadwick Symphony." (See: W21e)

WB174. Guinn, John. "DSO Scores with American Composers."
Detroit Free Press March 25, 1994: 7C. Announces that the
DSO is involved in recording sessions with the Second
Symphony, and that the work will be performed today for the
public. (See: W21j)

W22. SYMPHONY IN F (NO. 3) (1893-1894)

Dedication: Theodore Thomas

Holograph score and parts: not located
Published: Schmidt, 1896 (publ. plate no. 3765)
Availability: Fleisher cat. no. 5262; Luck's cat. no. 06943
Duration: 35 minutes
For: 2. 2. 2. 2./4. 2. 3. 1./timp. strings.

Movements: Allegro sostenuto (F)
                  Andante cantabile (B-flat)
                  Vivace non troppo (d)
                  Finale: Allegro molto energico (F)

This work was awarded 1st Prize in the second annual composition competition sponsored by the National Conservatory (New York, 1894), Antonin Dvorak, director.

Premiere

W22a.   19/20 October 1894; Boston Symphony Orchestra, G. W. Chadwick, cond.; Music Hall, Boston.

Other Selected Performances

W22b.   8/9 January 1897; Chicago Symphony Orchestra, Theodore Thomas, cond.; Chicago, Illinois.

W22c.   21 November 1904; All-Chadwick concert; [Members of the Boston Symphony Orchestra], G. W. Chadwick, cond.; Jordan Hall, Boston.

W22d.   November 1905 [precise date unknown]; Concordia Choral Society concert in honor of Chadwick; G. W. Chadwick, cond.; [precise location undetermined], Leipzig.

W22e.   13/14 March 1914; Boston Symphony Orchestra, Karl Muck, cond.; Symphony Hall, Boston.

W22f.   19 March 1914; Boston Symphony Orchestra, Karl Muck, cond.; Carnegie Hall, New York City.

W22g.   12 April 1918; New England Conservatory Orchestra, Wallace Goodrich, cond.; Jordan Hall, Boston.

W22h.   3/4 January 1919; Chicago Symphony Orchestra, "Theodore

Thomas Memorial Concert," G. W. Chadwick, cond.; Chicago, Illinois.

W22i. 14 May 1926; New England Conservatory Orchestra, G. W. Chadwick, cond.; Jordan Hall, Boston.

W22j. 31 January 1930; New England Conservatory Orchestra, Wallace Goodrich, cond.; Jordan Hall, Boston.

W22k. 6 May 1930; New England Conservatory Orchestra, Wallace Goodrich, cond.; Jordan Hall, Boston (movement nos. 2 and 4 only).

W22l. 23 November 1936; New England Conservatory Orchestra, Wallace Goodrich, cond.; Jordan Hall, Boston (movement no. 2 only).

W22m. 22-24 April 1993; Detroit Symphony Orchestra, Neeme Jarvi, cond.; Orchestra Hall, Detroit, Michigan.

W22n. 21 August 1993; Bard Music Festival "Rediscoveries" series; American Symphony Orchestra, Leon Botstein, cond.; Festival Tent, Bard College, Annandale-on-Hudson, New York.

Bibliography

WB175. "Chadwick's Symphony Wins the Prize." *American Art Journal* April 21, 1894: 25. This article comprises an open letter to Chadwick from Antonin Dvorak, then Director of the National Conservatory of Music: "I take pleasure in announcing to you that your Symphony offered for [the] second annual competition of the National Conservatory of Music has obtained the prize. In view of your desire to produce it without delay, we have decided to waive our right."

WB176. "Music and Musicians." *The Musical Visitor* 23/6 (June 1894): 153. Announcement that Chadwick won a prize from the National Conservatory. "Mr. Chadwick is one of our foremost American musicians . . . ."

WB177. "Music -- Symphony Concerts." *Saturday Evening Gazette* (Boston) October 20, 1894: 2. Review of the premiere. "While listening to the work, the intellect receives greater pleasure than the imagination . . . . Yet, uninspired as it is,

Mr. Chadwick's Symphony is the finest product that American musical art has produced." (See: W22a)

WB178. "Symphony Girls." *Boston Post* October 21, 1894: 6. Review of the premiere. "The themes are melodious and the working out [of them] brilliant and masterful, yet there seems to be something lacking. The music suggests ideas that are never realized . . . ." (See: W22a)

WB179. Elson, Louis C. "The Symphony: Mr. Chadwick's Ambitious Work Heard." *Boston Daily Advertiser* October 22, 1894: 4. Review of the premiere. "It is a symphony in which the composer has exerted all his ingenuity and studied from the manuscript it must contain many points of profound interest. . . . All in all, one finds much to praise in this work, but at the end one must confess that the great American symphony is not yet written." (See: W22a)

WB180. "Theatres and Concerts -- Music Hall: Boston Symphony Orchestra." *Boston Evening Transcript* October 22, 1894: 4. Review of the premiere. " . . . the symphony is strictly regular and orthodox; and one finds this regularity of form all the more admirable, and in no wise open to the charge of mere scholasticism, in that it plainly springs from the way in which Mr. Chadwick has here confined himself to the coherent and musically logical development and working-out of his thematic subject matter. . . ." (See: W22a)

WB181. Hale, Philip. "Music in Boston." *Musical Courier* 29/17 (October 24, 1894): 18. Review of the premiere. ". . . this symphony was a disappointment. Everywhere there is evidence of labor, thoughtfulness, sincerity and nobility of aim. I do not find, however, the spontaneity, the warm and sensuous coloring, the homogeneity that characterize his best work even when it is of small proportions." (See: W22a)

WB182. "Music Finds a Climax." *Chicago Tribune* January 9, 1897: 3. Review of the January 8, 1897 performance in Chicago. ". . . the Chadwick symphony is popular in appeal in the generally accepted sense. . . . The work was played with notable care in detail and finish, the reading throughout indicating strong sympathy on the part of Mr. Thomas." (See: W22b)

WB183. "Leipsic [sic] Discovers a Boston Composer." *Boston Globe* December 29, 1905. Includes comments about the November 1905 performance in Leipzig. "As he [Chadwick] had only an orchestra from one of the regimental bands of the garrison, the performance must have proceeded under some difficulties. . . ." On the Third Symphony, the Globe reporter quotes a German reviewer at length: "I declare that I consider this symphony the best of all that have been written since Brahms. It is extraordinarily rich in tone color and masterly in construction and instrumentation. It is hard to say what most strongly seizes the listener--the joyous energy of the first movement, the original humor of the third, or the sturdy manliness of the last, which closes in such splendid romp." (See: W22d)

WB184. Vaill, J. H., compiler. *Litchfield County Choral Union*, vol. 1. Norfolk, Connecticut: Litchfield County University Club, 1912: 226. Contains a translation of the famous and oft-repeated passage by critic Paul Zschorlich of the *Leipzig Tageblatt* which reads: "From this symphony, I hold George W. Chadwick to be the most important living Anglo-American composer--Edward Elgar not excepted." (See: W22f)

WB185. "American Music by Boston Symphony." *New York Tribune* March 20, 1914: 9. Review of the Boston Symphony Orchestra's performance in New York, March 19, 1914. "It is a modest, sincere, straightforward piece of music, which contains not a few genuine musical ideas, which are worked out pleasingly and never with a deviation from the path of beauty. If it is not a masterwork, it is at least a finely conceived and finely executed composition and one which should hold its place in the symphonic world . . . ." (See: W22f)

WB186. "The Boston Orchestra." *New York Times* March 20, 1914: 6. Review of the Boston Symphony Orchestra's performance in New York, March 19, 1914. "Mr. Chadwick's symphony is not deficient in frank melody, often of a distinguished sort and his harmonic treatment is rich and expressive, even though it has few of the significant features that are considered 'modern' to-day [sic]." This review also notes Chadwick's presence in the audience. (See: W22f)

WB187. Donaghey, Frederick. "Orchestra Tribute to Thomas." *Chicago Tribune* January 4, 1919: 11. Review of the January

3, 1919 performance in Chicago honoring the 14th anniversary of the death of Theodore Thomas. Chadwick is noted as "a benificent and penetrating influence in spreading love for and knowledge of music . . . ." Also, "[Chadwick] conducted it as if he believed in it . . . ." (See: W22h)

WB188. Parker, W. J. "Give Chadwick Symphony." *Musical America* 44/6 (May 29, 1926): 21. Notice that the performance of May 14, 1926 had occurred. (See: W22i)

W23. TABASCO MARCH (1894)

Dedication: none
Holograph score: not located; printed parts at MBCM
Published: Wood, 1894
Duration: 3 minutes
For: 1. 1. 2. 1./1. 1. 1. 0./perc. strings

This work was published in numerous instrumental and vocal versions as *The New Hail Columbia* march or marching song [when accompanied by a text]. Musical arrangements were prepared for baritone solo and chorus, mixed voices, male chorus, school chorus, small orchestra, full orchestra, and military band by Hans Semper, with words by W. Murdoch Lind (Boston: Wood, 1917). In addition, a German orchestral edition [including piano] was prepared and published (Berlin: Otto Wernthal, 1899).

(See also: W74, WR4, WR7 and WR15)

Premiere

W23a.   29 January 1894; Tremont Theatre, Boston (as part of the premiere of Chadwick's burlesque opera, *Tabasco*; See also W74a).

Other Selected Performances

W23b.   9 April 1894; Thomas Q. Seabrooke Opera Company, Boston Museum (as part of a performance of Chadwick's burlesque opera, *Tabasco*; See also: W74b).

W23c.   19 June 1897; Promenade concert of music by American composers; [Orchestra unidentified]; Schulz [only name listed], cond.; Music Hall, Boston.

Bibliography

WB189. "In the Music World." *Boston Evening Transcript* June 19,
1897: I/8. Announcement of the June 19, 1897 performance.
A work by Sousa opened the concert; *Tabasco March* closed it.
(See: W24c)

W24. TAM O'SHANTER, Symphonic Ballad (Begun September 29,
1914; completed January 23, 1915)

Dedication: Horatio Parker
Pencil holograph: DLC (score); MBCM (parts)
Published: Boston Music Company, 1917
Availability: Fleisher cat. no. 5304; Luck's cat. no. 06138
Duration: 20 minutes
For: 3 (3rd doubles picc). 2. eh. 3 (1 cl. in D, 2 cl. in B-flat).
    bass clar. 2./
    4. 3. 2. 1./
    timp. 8 perc. harp. strings.

Suggested by the poem *Alloway Kirk, or Tam O'Shanter: A Tale*
(1795) by Robert Burns (1759-1796). Chadwick prefaced his printed
score with a lengthy explanation of the music's relationship to Burns's
poem.

(See also: WR16)

Premiere

W24a. 3 June 1915; Norfolk Festival Orchestra, G. W. Chadwick,
cond.; Music Shed, Norfolk, Connecticut.

Other Selected Performances

W24b. 14 January 1916; Minneapolis Symphony Orchestra, G. W.
Chadwick, cond.; The Auditorium, Minneapolis, Minnesota.

W24c. 21/22 January 1916; Chicago Symphony Orchestra, G. W.
Chadwick, cond.; Chicago, Illinois.

W24d. 28/29 April 1916; Boston Symphony Orchestra, G. W.
Chadwick, cond.; Symphony Hall, Boston.

W24e. 12/13 October 1917; Chicago Symphony Orchestra, Frederick

Stock, cond.; Chicago, Illinois.

W24f. 16 November 1917; Minneapolis Symphony Orchestra, Emil Oberhoffer, cond.; The Auditorium, Minneapolis, Minnesota.

W24g. 19 November 1917; Chicago Symphony Orchestra, Frederick Stock, cond.; Milwaukee, Wisconsin.

W24h. 22/23 November 1917; New York Philharmonic, Josef Stransky, cond.; Carnegie Hall, New York City.

W24i. 30 November/1 December 1917; Saint Louis Symphony Orchestra, Max Zach, cond.; Saint Louis, Missouri.

W24j. 9 December 1917; New York Philharmonic, Josef Stransky, cond.; Brooklyn Academy of Music, Brooklyn, New York.

W24k. 20 December 1917; New York Philharmonic, Josef Stransky, cond.; Cleveland, Ohio.

W24l. 16 March 1918; New York Philharmonic, "Programme of American Composers," Josef Stransky, cond.; Carnegie Hall, New York City.

W24m. 22 March 1918; Minneapolis Symphony Orchestra, [Young People's Concert entitled "Master Composers," featured works by Chadwick and Henry Hadley only], Emil Oberhoffer, cond.; The Auditorium, Minneapolis, Minnesota.

W24n. 1 March 1919; New York Philharmonic, Josef Stransky, cond.; Carnegie Hall, New York City.

W24o. 21 March 1919; New York Philharmonic, Josef Stransky, cond.; Columbus, Ohio.

W24p. 10 October 1919; Worcester Festival Orchestra, Thaddeus Rich, cond.; Mechanics Hall, Worcester, Massachusetts.

W24q. 14/15 November 1919; Chicago Symphony Orchestra, Frederick Stock, cond.; Chicago, Illinois.

W24r. 13/14 February 1920; Cincinnati Symphony Orchestra, Eugene Ysaye, cond.; Music Hall, Cincinnati, Ohio.

W24s.   3/4 March 1922; Chicago Symphony Orchestra, Frederick Stock, cond.; Chicago, Illinois.

W24t.   3 January 1926; Cincinnati Symphony Orchestra, Ralph Lyford, cond.; Music Hall, Cincinnati, Ohio.

W24u.   18/20 March 1926; Cleveland Orchestra, Nikolai Sokoloff, cond.; Masonic Hall, Cleveland, Ohio.

W24v.   30/31 December 1927; Chicago Symphony Orchestra, Frederick Stock, cond.; Chicago, Illinois.

W24w. 8 December 1929; Manhattan Symphony, Henry Hadley, cond.; Mecca Auditorium, New York City.

W24x.   25 February 1930; Chicago Symphony Orchestra, Eric De Lamarter, cond.; Chicago, Illinois.

W24y.   6 March 1930; Eastman-Rochester Orchestra, Howard Hanson, cond.; "American Composers Series"; Kilbourn Hall, Rochester, New York.

W24z.   10 April 1930; Chicago Symphony Orchestra, Frederick Stock, cond.; Orchestra Hall, Chicago.

W24aa. 8/9 February 1940; Chicago Symphony Orchestra, Hans Lange, cond.; Chicago, Illinois.

W24bb. 13 March 1945; Chicago Symphony Orchestra, Desire Defauw, cond.; American composers' concert; Chicago, Illinois.

Bibliography

WB190. G. W. J. [George W. Judson] "Final Concert in Three Distinct Respects Touched High Water Mark." *Winsted Evening Citizen* (Connecticut) June 4, 1915: 1. Review of the premiere. " . . . Mr. Chadwick's theme was an oversea [*sic*] distinctively Scotch subject, nothing less than the musical interpretation of Burns's famous ballad . . . . The audience went fairly wild at its close and a great tumult of applause acclaimed the triumph of Chadwick's achievement." (See: W24a)

WB191. G. W. J. [George W. Judson] "Norfolk Festival Music Notes." *Winsted Evening Citizen* (Connecticut) June 4, 1915: 1 [Same issue as above]. Review of the premiere. "Tam O'Shanter combines in music so many of the human elements from the comic to the grave and solemn and is easily understood." (See: W24a)

WB192. "Generosity of George W. Chadwick." In *Report of the Litchfield County Choral Union* [annual meeting minutes], December 10, 1915: 12. Notes that prior to the planning of the 1915 festival, Chadwick asked that *Tam O'Shanter* " . . . be accepted as a gift from him in appreciation of the work which is being done by [the] organization."

WB193. De Lamarter, Eric. "Chadwick Conducts Chicago Symphony." *Chicago Tribune* January 22, 1916: 15. Review of the January 21, 1916 performance in Chicago. "Tam O'Shanter is a sturdy, fascinating creation. It stands on its own as absolute music, as descriptive music, and as a sort of sardonic humor. It is [a] tribute to the mastery of its composer." (See: W24c)

WB194. "Conservatory Composers' Works in the Middle West." *New England Conservatory Magazine-Review* 6/3 (March-April, 1916): 76-78. Reports comments by the local Chicago press on the January 21/22, 1916 performances. Also includes comments by the conservatory writer: "Considering . . . the heavy grind of administrative and teaching duties, it is rather surprising that Mr. Chadwick and his associates are able to accomplish as much creative work as they do." (See: W24c)

WB195. "The Symphony Concert." *Boston Evening Transcript* April 29, 1916: II/7. Review of the April 28, 1916 Boston Symphony Orchestra performance. Although a sub-headline reads "The Contrasts of Mr. Chadwick's Ingenious and Amusing Ballad -- His Humor Again," there is no mention of the composition in the body of the article. (See: W24d)

WB196. Hale, Philip. "Play Chadwick Ballade Under Composer's Baton." *Boston Herald* April 29, 1916: 11. Review of the April 28, 1916 Boston Symphony Orchestra performance. "This ballade must be ranked with Mr. Chadwick's more original and most characteristic compositions." (See: W24d)

WB197. Elson, Louis C. "Brilliant New Work by Chadwick." *Boston Daily Advertiser* April 29, 1916: 3. Review of the April 28, 1916 Boston Symphony Orchestra performance. "The work is the most truly picturesque and dramatic that we can recall in the American repertoire. . . . Tam O'Shanter is undoubtedly one of the very best of American works and can hold its own with the best European symphonic poems." (See: W24d)

WB198. "Mr. Stock Will Put Native Music in All Orchestra Programs." *Chicago Tribune* September 26, 1917: 15. Announces that *Tam O'Shanter* will be included on the Chicago Symphony Orchestra's programs of October 12-13, 1917. (See: W24e)

WB199. Donaghey, Frederick. "The Orchestra Starts its Season." *Chicago Tribune* October 13, 1917: sec. 2, p. 13. Review of the Chicago Symphony Orchestra performance of October 12, 1917. *Tam O'Shanter* ". . . has a bounce and freshness discernible in nothing of his more recent than the operetta of [*sic*] 'Tabasco,' an achievement not likely to find its way into the orchestra repertoire. This 'Tam O'Shanter' is entirely credible in respect to Burns' verse." (See: W24e)

WB200. "Music -- 'Tam O'Shanter' is Played for the First Time at the Philharmonic Concert." *New York Tribune* November 23, 1917: 9. Review of the New York Philharmonic performance of November 22, 1917. "It is an agreeably frank and transparent piece of programme music, simply conceived and resourcefully written, flavored strongly with Scotch folksong." (See: W24h)

WB201. "Audience in Festive Mood at Final Concert Program." *Worcester Telegram* (Massachusetts) October 11, 1919. Review of the Worcester Festival concert of October 10, 1919. "Thus far, the most remarkable orchestral piece yet heard at the festival. Mr. Chadwick's composition is a real, inspired, gorgeous masterpiece of orchestral writing . . . . There was never a lagging moment, nor an enigmatical turn in the whole score. A paramount joy and a monumental tribute to the genius of the composer." (See: W24p)

WB202. Hubbard, W. L. [William Lines]. "The Symphony." *Chicago Tribune* November 15, 1919: 19. Review of the Chicago Symphony Orchestra performance of November 14, 1919.

"Chadwick's rollicking 'Tam O'Shanter,' one of the best descriptive pieces of writing American talent has produced, completed the first half of the program." (See: W24q)

WB203. "'Tam O'Shanter' is Cincinnati Novelty." *Musical America* 43/13 (January 16, 1926): 11. Review of the concert of January 3, 1926 in Cincinnati. "The only number [on the program] not well known was the 'Tam O'Shanter' of Chadwick which was played with all the wry humor of the poem." (See: W24t)

WB204. "The Orchestras -- Maazel, with Hadley Forces." *Musical America* 49/24 (December 25, 1929): 6. Review of the December 8, 1929 performance by the Manhattan Symphony. "The Chadwick piece, which by the bye contains some passages of genuine beauty, would have benefitted by more rehearsal." (See: W24w)

WB205. Warner, A. J. "Chadwick Music in Kilburn [*sic*] Hall." *Rochester Times-Union* March 7, 1930. Review of the March 6, 1930 concert in Rochester, New York. (See: W24y)

WB206. Moore, Edward. "Yankee Music Played as Stock Leads Orchestra." *Chicago Tribune* April 11, 1930: 45. Review of the Chicago Symphony Orchestra performance of April 10, 1930. Brief mention of *Tam O'Shanter* on a program that included works by Henry Hadley, Edward MacDowell, Leo Sowerby, and Charles S. Skilton. (See: W24z)

W25. THALIA, OP. 10, Overture (Subtitled "Overture to an Imaginary Comedy"; completed November 5, 1882, in Boston)

Dedication: Ross Sterling Turner
Ink holograph score and parts: MBCM
Published [?]: Schmidt, 1883 [reported, but copy not located]
For: 2 (2nd doubles picc). 2. 2. 2./4. 2. 3. 1./timp. 3 perc. strings.

Titled after the Greek muse of Comedy. The title is transliterated from the original Greek which appears on the holograph.

Premiere

W25a.   12/13 January 1883; Boston Symphony Orchestra, G. W. Chadwick, cond.; Music Hall, Boston.

Other Selected Performances

W25b.   3 May 1883; Handel and Haydn Society Orchestra (Sixth Triennial Festival), G. W. Chadwick, cond.; Music Hall, Boston.

W25c.   1 May 1986; Boston Composers Orchestra, Gunther Schuller, cond.; Symphony Hall, Boston.

Bibliography

WB207. "Theatres and Concerts." *Boston Evening Transcript* January 15, 1883: 1. Review of the premiere performance. "Mr. Chadwick's new overture took all hearts by storm. Judging merely from first impressions, we have nothing but admiration to express. The tuneful, melodious character of the themes, the ingenuity with which one brilliant effect is made to follow close upon the heels of another, the sharply drawn, but never exagerrated, contrasts of coloring, and, above all, the genial, Hellenic cheerfulness of the whole fill the listener with delight." (See: W25a)

WB208. "Review of Recent Concerts." *The Musical Herald* February 1883: 53. Review of the premiere. "It is brilliant and graphic enough to call up a comedy before the imagination . . . . It is a fine work, and we are glad to learn that both orchestral and piano score are likely to be published in this country soon." (See: W25a)

WB209. Proteus [Louis Charles Elson]. "Correspondence--Boston." *The Musical Visitor* (February 1, 1883): 41-42. Review of the premiere. "It is full of melody, and also of skillful, contrapuntal work . . . . If he succeeds in making composers in America like himself he will do well . . . . Mr. Chadwick, who conducted, was recalled after the work with great enthusiasm, and received a laurel wreath." (See: W25a)

WB210. "Music and the Drama -- The Triennial Festival." *Boston Daily Advertiser* May 4, 1883: 4. Review of the Handel and Haydn Society performance, May 3, 1883. "The composer conducted his work, which renewed and materially strengthened the very favorable impression it made when first produced." (See: W25b)

WB211. "Entertainments -- Handel and Haydn Triennial." *Boston Post* May 4, 1883: 1. Review of the Handel and Haydn Society performance, May 3, 1883. *Thalia* " . . . showed a musical artist of whom Boston may be proud." (See: W25b)

WB212. Dyer, Richard. "Director Schuller Announces Boston Composers Debut." *Boston Globe* March 8, 1986: 25. Announces that a work by Chadwick will be performed by the Boston Composers Orchestra on May 1, 1986. (See: W25c)

WB213. Miller, Margo. "Composers Orchestra to Debut on May Day." *Boston Globe* April 27, 1986: 88. Announces that the new orchestra will debut with Chadwick's *Thalia*, ". . . a piece that probably has not been heard in Boston for 100 years. . . . " (See: W25c)

WB214. Dyer, Richard. "Composers' Orchestra Debuts." *Boston Globe* May 2, 1986: 36. Review of the May 1, 1986 performance. "Thalia sounded like a cheerful piece by some German composer who was a missing link between [Albert] Lortzing and [Franz] Lehar, though its tunes didn't sparkle and spin enough." (See: W25c)

WB215. Kimmelman, Michael. "Redefining the Role of Orchestras." *Philadelphia Inquirer* May 8, 1986: C9. Review of the May 1, 1986 performance in Boston. "The lightweight tunes in Chadwick's overture, Thalia, weren't especially stimulating." (See: W25c)

WB216. Dyer, Richard. "The Critic's Role in Review." *Boston Globe* June 29, 1986: A1. This is Dyer's response to the concert-going public's criticism of his review of the May 1 concert. Dyer admitted that he erred when he stated that all the composers whose music was on the program were present in the audience. Obviously, Chadwick was not in attendance. (See: W25c)

W26. THEME, VARIATIONS AND FUGUE (Completed August 13, 1908, at West Chop)

Dedication: Wallace Goodrich
Ink Holograph: DLC (score); MBCM (copy of score and parts)
Published: Boston Music Company, 1923 (organ solo arrangement)
(publ. plate no. 6708, BMC Edition No. 90)

For: 2. 2. eh. 2. 2./4. 2. 3. 0./timp. strings. organ solo.

Includes six variations.

Wallace Goodrich, the work's dedicatee and Chadwick's longtime student, friend, and colleague, arranged and published a version of this composition for solo organ (Boston: Boston Music Company, 1923).

Premiere

W26a. 13 November 1908; New England Conservatory Orchestra, Wallace Goodrich, organ, G. W. Chadwick, cond.; Jordan Hall, Boston.

Other Selected Performances

W26b. 8/10 April 1909; Boston Symphony Orchestra, Wallace Goodrich, organ, Max Fiedler, cond.; Symphony Hall, Boston.

W26c. 22 June 1909; New England Conservatory Commencement Ceremony; Charles Henry Doersam, organ; New England Conservatory Orchestra, G. W. Chadwick, cond.; Jordan Hall, Boston.

W26d. 3 June 1921; New England Conservatory Orchestra, Earl P. Morgan, organ, Wallace Goodrich, cond.; Jordan Hall, Boston.

W26e. 30/31 December 1921; Boston Symphony Orchestra, Albert W. Snow, organ, Pierre Monteux, cond.; Symphony Hall, Boston.

Bibliography

WB217. E. B. H. [Edward Burlingame Hill]. "Musical News." *Boston Evening Transcript* November 16, 1908: 11. Review of premiere. " . . . excellent music though it be, the attention of the listener is involuntarily attracted first of all by his [Chadwick's] unusual dexterity and skill in combining the various groups of the orchestra with the organ." (See: W26a)

WB218. E. B. H. [Edward Burlingame Hill]. "Music and Drama." *Boston Evening Transcript* April 9, 1909: 12. Review of the April 8, 1909 performance. " . . . the effect of the whole is so genial in invention, so clear-cut and ingenious at every turn that it is difficult to recall a work in which Mr. Chadwick has seemed so unostentatiously in command of his forces." (See: W26b)

W27. TRE PEZZI (First movement composed July 10-July 28, 1916, then orchestrated January to March, 1923; other movements unknown)

Dedication: none
Ink holograph: DLC (score); MBCM (copy of score and parts)
Unpublished
Availability: Fleisher cat. no. 6461 (under the title "Three Pieces for Orchestra")
Duration: 15 minutes
For: 3 (3rd doubles picc.). 3. 2. 2/
4. 3. 3. 1/
timp. 2 perc. harp (ad lib.). strings.

Movements: *Ouverture mignon*: Allegro molto vivace (F)
Canzone vecchia: Andantino e semplice (B-flat)
Fuga giocosa: Molto vivace (F)

Ouverture mignon was originally intended to stand alone under the title, *Arcadia*. The holograph score clearly shows an attempted erasure of *Arcadia*, replaced by the new title. Further, in his *Journal* Chadwick notes that he started the sketch for *Arcadia* on July 10, 1916, and completed it on July 28, 1916. The orchestration, as well as the title change, occurred in early 1923.

Premiere

W27a. 20 March 1931; New England Conservatory Orchestra, Wallace Goodrich, cond.; Jordan Hall, Boston.

Bibliography

WB219. "New Music by Chadwick." *Musical Courier* 102/14 (April 4, 1931): 16. Review of the premiere. The writer finds that the *Ouverture mignon* ". . . contains some rather elaborate orchestration," while the *Canzone vecchia* ". . . has the manner of an old folk song." The *Fuga giocosa* is ". . . a reminder to the composer of the frolic fugues which he used to do when a student at Leipsic [*sic*] more than fifty years ago, these usually

based on decidedly humorous motives." [This review appeared
on the day Chadwick died.] (See: W27a)

CHAMBER MUSIC

W28. EASTER MORN, Reverie (ca. 1914)

For: violin (or cello) and piano (or organ)
Dedication: Eugene Gruenberg
Published: Schmidt, 1914 (both versions); (publ. plate no. 10244-
10245); reprint, Boca Raton, Florida: Music Masters, 1995.
Holograph: chamber version, not located; enlarged version, MBCM
Premiere: unknown

Chadwick later added tutti violins and harp to the organ part to create a
larger ensemble version of the piece. In 1934, Chadwick's former
student and colleague Wallace Goodrich orchestrated it for 2. 2. 2. 2/2.
0. 0. 0./harp. strings (manuscript held at MBCM).

W29. FANFARE (1925)

For: 3 trumpets, 3 trombones, timpani
Dedication: none
Published: Boston: New England Conservatory Press, 1995 [Archival
Manuscripts Edition].
Holograph: MBCM (parts only)

This composition (seven measures in length) was composed for the
unveiling of a John Singer Sargent mural at the Boston Museum of
Fine Art.

Premiere

W29a. 3 November 1925; John Singer Sargent Memorial Exhibition;
Museum of Fine Art, Boston.

Bibliography

WB220. "All of Sargent for All to See." *Boston Evening Transcript*
November 4, 1925: II/3. No specific mention of *Fanfare*, but
the writer notes that an orchestra and "bugles" were present.
(See: W29a)

W30. QUARTET (NO. 1) IN G MINOR, OP. 1 (1878)

For: string quartet
Dedication: Samuel S. Herrmann
Unpublished
Holograph score and parts: MBCM
Duration: 25 minutes

Movements: Allegro con brio (g)
                Adagio: Andante non troppo lento (E flat)
                Menuetto: Poco vivace (c)
                Finale: Allegro ma non troppo (g)

The first two movements were completed by May 1878 in time for the
premiere performance. An annotated program of the premiere, inserted
into Chadwick's *Memoirs* (1877-1880), notes that "There was no time
to work up the last two movements . . ." Those movements were
probably completed shortly after the premiere.

Premiere

W30a.   29 May 1878; Prufungskonzert of the Leipzig Conservatory;
        Student ensemble; Saale des Gewandhauses, Leipzig
        (movement nos. 1 and 2 only).

Bibliography

WB221. "Correspondenzen." *Neue Zeitschrift fur Musik* 74/1 (21 June
        1878): 273. Reprint, Scarsdale, N.Y.: A. Schnase, 1964.
        Review of the premiere. "Nach dem zweiten zu urtheilen
        bezeugt diese Arbeit so ziemlich die Anwendung aller
        Prinzipien, die in harmonischer Hinsicht bei dieser Compo-
        sitionsgattung erfordlich sind. Wenn der Komponist auch
        nicht Originalitat in der Erfindung an den Tag legt, so spricht
        doch in seiner Arbeit sich kundgebende klare Gedankengang
        immerhin zu deren Gunsten." ["The work exhibited a good
        working knowledge of harmonic principles as they apply to
        compositions of this nature, particularly after the second
        phrase. When the composer is not original in his invention it
        is not obvious, and certainly what he has said in this piece
        demonstrates clear thinking."] (See: W30a)

WB222. *Musikaliches Wochenblatt* 9 (7 June 1878): 292. Review of
        the premiere. "Die Form war wohl gewahrt, die Stimm-

furhrung meistens eine quartettgemasse, Klare. . . . Am
besten hat uns in diesem Bezug noch das 2. Thema des 1.
Satzes gefallen. Die Ausfurhrung konnte in den beiden
Mittelstimmen noch etwas glatter gehen." ["The form was
quite pleasing, the voice-leading being clear and mostly in
accordance with quartet style . . . . In this instance, we liked
the second theme of the first movement best. The performance
of the two middle voices could be smoother."] (See: W30a)

W31. QUARTET (NO. 2) IN C MAJOR, OP. 2 (1878)

For: string quartet
Dedication: Salomon Jadassohn
Unpublished
Holograph score and parts: MBCM
Duration: 27 minutes

Movements: Andante: Allegro con brio (C)
                Andante espressivo ma non troppo lento (G)
                Scherzo: Allegro risoluto ma moderato (e)
                Finale: Allegro molto vivace (C)

(See also: W2)

Premiere

W31a.   30 May 1879; Prufungskonzert of the Leipzig Conservatory;
         Student ensemble; Saale des Gewandhauses, Leipzig.

Other Selected Performances

W31b.   5 January 1881; Beethoven Quintet Club (C. N. Allen, violin;
         G. Dannreuther, violin; H. Heindl, viola; W. Fries, cello);
         Euterpe Society concert; The Meionaon, Boston.

W31c.   7 January 1881; Beethoven Quintet Club (C. N. Allen, violin;
         G. Dannreuther, violin; H. Heindl, viola; W. Fries, cello) on a
         Boston Philharmonic Orchestra program, Bernhard Listemann,
         cond.; Music Hall, Boston.

W31d.   30 May 1881; Beethoven Quintet Club (C. N. Allen, violin;
         G. Dannreuther, violin; H. Heindl, viola; W. Fries, cello);
         Music Building Dedication Ceremony; Wellesley College,
         Wellesley, Massachusetts.

W31e.   28 January 1886; Kneisel Quartet; Boston [precise location undetermined]; movement nos. 1 and 4 only.

Bibliography

WB223. *Musikaliches Wochenblatt* 10 (6 June 1879): 290. Review of the premiere. "In diesem Manuscriptwerke fehlt es nicht an interessanten, auf eigenes Empfindungsleben hinweisenden Zugen, z.B. im 1. und 3. Satz. Der musikalisches Auf- und Ausbau des gedanklichen Materials ist nicht ungeschikt, wenn auch nicht mit besonderen polyphonen Kunsten sich beschwerend, und die Form der einzelnen Satze steht nicht in Missverhaltniss zu deren Inhalt, sie ist knapp. Die Ausfuhrung der Composition zeigte sorgsame Vorbereitung." ["In this manuscript work nothing of interest was wanting, and there was a suitable character and sentiment, for example, in the first and third movements. The musical materials of this composition are not unskillfully handled, nor overly burdened with polyphony, and the form of the individual parts is restrained and not disproportionate to its contents. The workmanship of the composition displays careful planning."] (See: W31a)

WB224. B. B. "Correspondenzen." *Neue Zeitschrift fur Musik* 75/1 (20 June 1879): 269. Reprint, Scarsdale, N.Y.: A. Schnase, 1964. Review of the premiere. " . . . im ersten Satz nicht unerheblichen Erfindungskraft, ungeschraubten Emfindung und guten Gestaltungsgabe einen recht guten Eindruck." [". . . in the first movement there was displayed a considerable inventive power, sentiment, and good planning, all of which left a fine impression."] (See: W31a)

WB225. Bernsdorf, G. "Hauptprufungen am Konigl. Consertavorium der Musik zu Leipzig." *Signale fur die Musikalische Welt* 37/41 (June 1879): 642-4. Review of the premiere. "Das Quartett des Herrn Chadwick zeigt neben naturlicher und gesunder Erfindung eine bereits recht anstandige Reife der Factur . . . ." ["Mr. Chadwick's quartet shows, besides natural and resourceful invention, a nicely prepared and graceful execution . . . ."] (See: W31a)

WB226. "Euterpe." *Dwight's Journal of Music* 41/1035 (January 15, 1881): 15. Review of January 5, 1881 performance. " . . . it is fresh and pregnant in its themes and yet free from extravagance, and full of spirit and legitimate effect. It will be welcome to us all again . . . . Being persistently called out, he [Chadwick] stepped upon the platform and modestly bowed his thanks." (See: W31b)

WB227. Clifford [only name supplied]. "Correspondence -- Boston." *Church's Musical Visitor* 10/5 (February 1881): 132-133. Review of the performance of January 5, 1881 in Boston. "The work in question had already been heard in Germany. It is the second work of its kind by the young American composer, and it is certainly a composition of great beauty. At its conclusion, Mr. Chadwick was called to the platform and warmly congratulated by the audience." (See: W31b)

WB228. "Musical." *Boston Evening Transcript* May 31, 1881: 1. Notice of the Wellesley College program, May 30, 1881. (See: W31d)

WB229. "Some Recent American Music." *Boston Evening Transcript* June 24, 1881: 1. Report states that the Second Quartet is " . . . in a concise and admirably rounded form [and] brings material of really great value, and is one of the most promising works that we have known to come from the pen of a young composer."

WB230. Clifford [only name supplied]. "Boston." *Church's Musical Visitor* 10/10 (July 1881): 274-275. This article notes the inclusion of Chadwick's quartet on the concert for the opening of Wellsley College's new music building, May 30, 1881. (See: W31d)

W32. QUARTET (NO. 3) IN D MAJOR (Completed May 25, 1886)

For: string quartet
Dedication: Arthur Foote
Unpublished
Holograph score: MB; manuscript parts at MBCM
Duration: 23 minutes

Movements: Allegro di molto (D)
                  Tema con variazioni (d)
                  Allegretto semplice (G)
                  Finale: Allegro vivace (D)

Premiere

W32a.   9 March 1887; Euterpe Society concert; Musicians: C. N. Allen, violin; T. Human, violin; C. Meisel, viola; W. Fries, cello; Boston [precise location undetermined].

Other Selected Performances

W32b.   22 November 1887; Beethoven String Quartet (Gustave Dannreuther, violin; Ernest Thiele, violin; Otto Schill, viola; Adolf Hartdegen, cello); Chickering Hall, New York City [The fourth in a series of American concerts produced by Frank van der Stucken].

W32c.   23 January 1888; Kneisel Quartet; Boston [presise location undetermined].

Bibliography

WB231. "The American Concerts." *New York Times* November 23, 1887: 5. Review of the November 22, 1887 concert. "Mr. Chadwick's quartet has three good movements, the last being somewhat trifling in character. The first on the other hand, is well conceived and skillfully treated. The second is a pretty andante, and the third a very neat, if somewhat brief, scherzo." (See: W32b)

WB232. Krehbiel, Henry E. *Review of the New York Musical Season, 1887-1888.* New York: Novello, Ewer & Co., 1888 (p. 36). Review of the November 22, 1887 concert. "Mr. Chadwick, in this quartet at least, stops talking when he has nothing more to say. It is not burdened with remplissage, but is straightforward. . . ." (See: W32b)

W33. QUARTET (NO. 4) IN E MINOR (Completed November 1, 1896, in Boston)

For: string quartet
Dedication: Franz Kneisel
Published: Schirmer, 1902 (parts only; score not published; publ. plate no. 16129); reprint, Boca Raton, Florida: Music Masters, 1992.
Ink holograph score: DLC; manuscript parts not located
Duration: 28 minutes

Movements: Andante: Allegro moderato (e)
                       Andante semplice (A)
                       Giocoso, un poco moderato (C)
                       Finale: Allegro molto risoluto (e)

Premiere

W33a.   21 December 1896; Kneisel Quartet; Association Hall, Boston.

Other Selected Performances

W33b.   30 April 1938; Coolidge String Quartet; concert under the auspices of the Elizabeth Sprague Coolidge Foundation; Coolidge Auditorium, Library of Congress, Washington, D. C. (See also: D53)

W33c.   11 May 1983; American String Quartet; performed for a meeting of the International Association of Music Librarians; Coolidge Auditorium, Library of Congress, Washington, D. C. (See also: D49)

W33d.   25 May 1984; American String Quartet; "Festival of American Chamber Music"; Coolidge Auditorium, Library of Congress, Washington, D. C. (See also: D48)

W33e.   6 November 1993; Brentano String Quartet (Mark Steinberg, violin; Serena Canin, violin; Misha Armory, viola; Michael Kannen, cello); Alice Tully Hall, Lincoln Center, New York.

Bibliography

WB233. "Music and Drama -- Association Hall: Kneisel Quartet." *Boston Evening Transcript* December 22, 1896: 7. Review of the premiere. "Ah! What a pleasure it is to be able heartily to like a new work by a fellow-townsman! . . . . [the quartet is] at once delightful and characteristic of [Chadwick] in his most genial vein." (See: W33a)

W34. QUARTET (NO. 5) IN D MINOR (Completed Thanksgiving Day, 1898; revised ca. 1903)

Dedication: Timothee and Josef Adamowski
Published: Privately published (parts only), 1910

Ink holograph score and parts: MBCM
Duration: 33 minutes

Movements: Allegro moderato (d)
                    Andantino (B-flat)
                    Presto e leggiero (F)
                    Allegro vivace (D)

Premiere

W34a.   9 February 1900; Adamowski Quartet; Harvard Musical Association concert; Boston.

Other Selected Performances

W34b.   12 February 1901; Adamowski Quartet; Chickering Hall, Boston.

W34c.   1 June 1908; Virginia Stickney, cello [student recital; other performers undetermined]; Jordan Hall, Boston.

W34d.   10 March 1909; MacDowell Club performance; Musicians: Lillian Durrell, violin; Maurice Warner, violin; George J. Rouleau, viola; Virginia Stickney, cello; Boston (movements 2 and 3 only). [Although the program indicates that the group performed the "Andante and Scherzo" from the Quartet in B [sic] minor, it is probable that it was in fact the D minor quartet.]

W34e.   27 January 1910; Hess-Schroeder Quartet; Boston [precise location undetermined].

W34f.   5 March 1910; Annie L. Haigh, violin [student recital; other performers undetermined]; Jordan Hall, Boston.

W34g.   15 March 1915; Kneisel Quartet; New England Conservatory, Boston. [Private performance for the students of the conservatory according to Chadwick's *Journal*, 1915.]

W34h.   [ca. November] 1929 [precise date not determined]; New York String Quartet; Bohemian Club concert in honor of Chadwick's 75th birthday [precise location undetermined; probably at Harvard Hall]. (See also: B116)

W34i.   10 May 1985; Tremont String Quartet; "Festival of American Chamber Music," Coolidge Auditorium, Library of Congress, Washington, D. C.

Bibliography

WB234. W. F. A. [William Foster Apthorp]. "Music and Drama -- Chickering Hall: The Adamowski Quartet." *Boston Evening Transcript* February 13, 1901: 18. Review of the February 12, 1901 performance. "Of Mr. Chadwick's new quartette my first impressions are considerably vague. Although evidently written with a certain fluent mastery, it is not a work which lays its full meaning bare at the first dash . . . ." (See: W34b)

WB235. "George W. Chadwick is Feted by 'Bohemians'." *Musical America* 49/23 (December 10, 1929): 7. Notice that the New York Quartet performance of ca. November 1929 had occurred. Chadwick, in a speech to those gathered, stated that the quartet was ". . . a relic of the Ice Age." (See: W34h)

W35. QUINTET FOR PIANO AND STRINGS (Completed October 28, 1887)

For: piano quintet (two violins, viola, cello, piano)
Dedication: Mr. and Mrs. Gustave Dannreuther
Published: Schmidt, 1890 (publ. plate no. 2569)
Ink holograph score: DLC
Duration: 34 minutes

Movements: Allegro sostenuto (E-flat)
                  Andante cantabile (A-flat)
                  Intermezzo: Allegretto un poco risoluto (c)
                  Finale: Molto energico (E-flat)

Premiere

W35a.   23 January 1888; Kneisel Quartet with G. W. Chadwick, piano; Chickering Hall, Boston.

Other Selected Performances

W35b.   24 February 1890; Kneisel Quartet with Arthur Whiting, piano; Union Hall, Boston.

W35c.   24 May 1893; Kneisel Quartet with Arthur Whiting, piano; World's Columbian Exposition, Recital Hall (series no. 3), Chicago.

W35d.   9 February 1900; Adamowski Quartet with G. W. Chadwick, piano; Harvard Musical Association concert, Boston.

W35e.   2 December 1901; Kneisel Quartet with Ernest Hutcheson, piano; Chickering Hall, Boston.

W35f.   21 April 1930; "Concert of Compositions of George W. Chadwick"; New England Conservatory, Jordan Hall, Boston.

W35g.   3 April 1932; Durrell Quartet, (Memorial performance in observance of the first anniversary of Chadwick's death); The Art Club, Boston.

W35h.   18 March 1984; Portland String Quartet with Virginia Eskin, piano; Isabella Stewart Gardner Museum, Boston.

Bibliography

WB236. "Theatres and Concerts." *Boston Evening Transcript* January 21, 1888: 1. Announcement of the premiere. (See: W35a)

WB237. "Theatres and Concerts -- The Kneisel Quartet." *Boston Evening Transcript* February 25, 1890: 1. Review of the February 24, 1890 concert. " . . . some of the thematic material in the quintet is as light-hearted as need be; but the treatment is always dignified and earnest in musical purpose." (See: W35a)

WB238. Weld, Arthur. "Music -- Fourth Kneisel Quartette Concert." *Boston Post* February 25, 1890: 2. Review of the February 24, 1890 performance. " . . . it is always constructed in a most masterly manner. There are very few young musicians so prolific in fine ideas as Mr. Chadwick." (See: W35b)

WB239. Proteus [Louis Charles Elson]. "Music in Boston." *The Musical Visitor* (April 1890): 94. Review of the February 24, 1890 performance. "The rock on which most of the American composers split in the sonata is the development. Mr. Chadwick seems to have attained the difficult art. . . . The quintet is more advanced in the classical sonata-form than

anything I have yet heard from this most talented composer."
(See: W35b)

WB240. "Apollo Club Renders 'Elijah'." *Chicago Tribune* May 25,
1893: 2. Brief mention that the May 24, 1893 recital included
Chadwick's quintet. [This article does not review the music.]
(See: W35b)

WB241. R. R. G. "Music and Drama -- Chickering Hall: Kneisel
Quartet." *Boston Evening Transcript* December 3, 1901: 13.
Review of the December 2, 1901 concert. "The whole quartet
is a notable example of effective writing for strings and
pianoforte, but the introduction . . . to the andante, is written
with nothing short of amazing skill." (See: W35e)

WB242. H. T. P. [Henry Taylor Parker]. "Two Bostonians, Bloch and
Toch." *Boston Evening Transcript* April 4, 1932: 8. Review
of April 3, 1932 performance. This performance ". . . recalled
his ease with classic forms . . . his fertility and warmth of
melody . . . . Lacking only was the American quality that
usually seeped into his chamber, as well as his symphonic,
pieces." (See: W35g)

W36. ROMANZE (ca. 1883)

For: cello and piano
Dedication: Josef Adamowski
Holograph score and parts: not located
Published: Schmidt, 1911 (publ. plate no. 9208)

Selected Performance

W36a. 3 January 1884; Arlington Club concert; Josef Adamowski,
cello; W. I. Honnell, piano; YMCA, Boston.

Bibliography

WB243. "Correspondence -- Boston Correspondence." *Musical Courier*
8/1 (January 2, 1884): 22. Notes that a "Romanza" [*sic*]
was played by Adamowski at an Arlington Club concert.
Chadwick was the director/conductor of the club at the time.
(See: W36a)

W37. TRIO IN C MINOR (Composed in the summer of 1877 at Olivet, Michigan, and Lawrence, Massachusetts)

For: strings (probably violin, viola, and cello)
Dedication: Charles Saunders
Holograph score and parts: not located

MUSIC FOR PIANO

W38. APHRODITE (1910-1911)

For: two pianos
Holograph: MBCM
Unpublished
(See also: W5)

W39. THE ASPEN

For: solo piano
Holograph: MBCM
Published: In "Progressive Series Compositions" (Catalog No. 816).
St. Louis, Missouri: Art Publication Society of America,
1924.
(See also: B103)

W40. CHANSON ORIENTALE

For: solo piano
Holograph: DLC
Published: Millet, 1895

W41. DIDDLE DIDDLE DUMPLING

For: solo piano
Holograph: MBCM
Published: In *A Second Book of Piano Pieces*. Boston: New England
Conservatory, 1928.

W42. DREI WALZER FUR DAS PIANOFORTE (f, E, A)

For: solo piano
Dedication: Mrs. E. M. Marsh
Holograph: DLC

Published: Schmidt, 1890 (publ. plate nos. 2582-2584)

Movements: [no indication]; Grazioso; Lento non troppo

No. 1 is headed by the statement: "Motive by B. J. L." [Chadwick's colleague and sometime critic, B. J. Lang]

W43. FIVE PIECES FOR PIANOFORTE

For: solo piano
Dedications: 1. Arthur Foote; 2. Arthur Whiting; 3. and 5. Helen
        Hopekirk; 4. Timothee Adamowski
Holograph: DLC (Nos. 1 and 3); NRU-Mus (Nos. 2, 4, and 5)
Published: Schirmer, 1905 (publ. plate nos. 17846-17850)

Movements: 1. *Prelude joyeux* [prelude]; 2. *Dans le canot* (In the
        Canoe) [barcarolle]; 3. *Le ruisseau* (The Rill) [etude]; 4. *Le
        crepuscule* (The Gloaming) [romance]; 5. *Les grenouilles* (The
        Frogs) [humoresque].

Selected Performances

W43a.   11 November 1907; George Proctor, pianist (student recital);
        New England Conservatory, Boston (no. 3 only).

W43b.   9 October 1908; Mabel Metcalf Holmes, pianist (student
        recital); New England Conservatory, Boston (no. 3 only).

W43c.   10 March 1909; MacDowell Club concert, Mabel Metcalf
        Holmes, pianist; Boston (nos. 1, 3, and 4 only).

W44. THE FOOTLIGHT FAIRY

For: solo piano
Ink holograph: MBCM (incomplete)
Unpublished; date of composition unknown

W45. MELPOMENE (1887)

For: piano four hands
Dedication: Wilhelm Gericke
Holograph: MBCM
Published: Schmidt, 1891 (publ. plate no. 2795)
(See also: W11)

W46. NOCTURNE

For: solo piano
Holograph: not located
Published: Millet, 1895

Selected Performance

W46a. 28 May 1887; Anna B. Whiting, organ (student recital); New
England Conservatory, Boston.

Bibliography

WB244. "Concerts." *The Musical Herald* 8/7 (July 1887): 224. Post-
concert announcement of the May 28, 1887 performance.
(See: W46a)

W47. NOVELETTE II

For: solo piano
Ink manuscript: MBCM (not in Chadwick's hand)
Unpublished; date of composition unknown

The title of this work suggests that there may be another work titled
"Novelette," but, if it exists, it has not been located.

W48. PRELUDE AND FUGUE (a)

For: solo piano
Holograph: MBCM (copy)
Unpublished; date of composition unknown

W49. PRELUDE AND FUGUE (c)

For: solo piano
Holograph: MBCM
Unpublished; date of composition unknown

W50. PRELUDE AND FUGUE A LA HORNPIPE (G)

For: solo piano
Holograph: MBCM (copy)
Unpublished; date of composition unknown

W51. RIP VAN WINKLE

For: four hands
Holograph: not located
Unpublished

In his *Memoirs* (1877-1880), Chadwick states that he scored his orchestral version from this four-hand piano arrangement. (See also: W14)

W52. SIX CHARACTERISTIC PIECES, OP. 7

For: solo piano
Dedications: 1. Frank Fay Marshal; 2. Marie Chadwick; 3. none; 4. A. Preston; 5. W. McEwen; 6. Gustave Heubach
Holograph: DLC (Nos. 1-5); NRU-Mus (No. 6)
Published: Schmidt, 1882 (publ. plate nos. 511-516); "Scherzino" (no. 3); reprinted in John Gillespie, *Nineteenth Century American Piano Music.* New York: Dover, 1978.

Movements: 1. *Congratulations*; 2. *Please Do*; 3. *Scherzino*; 4. *Reminiscence* [mazurka]; 5. *Irish Melody*; 6. *Etude*.

According to his *Memoirs* (1877-1880), *Reminiscence* (no. 4) was inspired by Chadwick's visit to the grave of Chopin in 1880.

Selected Performance

W52a.   15 March 1887; Arthur Foote, piano; Chickering Hall, Boston (no. 3 only).

Bibliography

WB245. L. C. E. [Louis C. Elson]. "Review of New Music." *The Musical Herald* 3/12 (December 1882): 336. Review of the publication. "The entire set is a very worthy one, and will be welcome to advanced pianists."

WB246. "Theatres and Concerts." *Boston Evening Transcript* March 16, 1887: 1. Review of the March 15, 1887 concert. Only brief mention of Chadwick and his music. (See: W52a)

W53. TABASCO MARCH: MARCH OF THE PASHA'S GUARD

For: solo piano
Holograph: unknown
Published: Wood, 1894 (publ. plate no. 103EL)
(See also: W23 and W74)

W54. TEN LITTLE TUNES FOR TEN LITTLE FRIENDS

For: solo piano
Holograph: DLC
Published: Wood, 1903 (publ. plate nos. 1558-1567)

Movements: 1. *Pitty Itty Sing*; 2. *Now I Lay Me*; 3. *Sis Tempy's Story*; 4. *Making Kitty Dance*; 5. *Little School Bell* ["for Thid"]; 6. *The Cricket and the Bumble Bee*; 7. *Spoiled Darling* (mazurka); 8. *The Merry Go-Round*; 9. *The King of Orinktum Jing*; 10. *In Grandma's Gown*.

The Cricket and the Bumble-Bee was arranged for two pianos, four hands by Esther Dickie (Boston: Wood, 1935).

W55. TWO CAPRICES FOR PIANOFORTE (C, g)

For: solo piano
Dedication: "To Mollie"
Holograph: DLC
Published: Schmidt, 1888; no. 2 reprinted in John Gillespie, *Nineteenth Century American Piano Music*. New York: Dover, 1978.

Premiere

W55a.   27 February 1891; Mrs. H. H. A. Beach, piano; Tremont Temple, Boston (no. 2 only).

W56. YE ROBIN

For: solo piano
Holograph: MBCM
Published: In *A Second Book of Piano Pieces*. Boston: New England Conservatory, 1928.

MUSIC FOR ORGAN

W57. CANZONETTA (G)

Dedication: none
Holograph: MB
Published: Millet, 1895 (In Dudley Buck, ed., *Vox Organi: A*
Collection of New Music for the Organ Written for this Work
by Eminent Composers of Europe and America. Boston: J. B.
Millet, 1895. Vol. 3, pp. 345-351; reprinted, Barbara Owen,
compiler, *The Victorian Collection.* Miami: Belwin Mills,
1978, pp. 54-58.)

W58. ELEGY

Dedication: "In memoriam Horatio Parker" [d. December 18, 1919]
Holograph: not located
Published: Boston Music Company, 1920 (In *American Organ*
Monthly, 1/3 [May 1920]: 29-33).

This work was probably first performed at a memorial service held for
Parker at Boston's Trinity Church on February 1, 1920.

(See also: W7)

W59. FOUR CANONS FOR THE ORGAN (OP. 16)

Dedication: Eugene Thayer
Holograph: not located
Published: In *Organist's Quarterly Journal and Review* 3/2 (July
1876): 20-22 (no. 1 [E-flat Major] only); reprint, *19th*
Century American Periodicals. Guilford, Connecticut: Opus
Publications [microfilm; n.d.].

Canons 2-4 have not been located.

Selected Performance

W59a. 6 November 1876; G. W. Chadwick, organist; Michigan
Conservatory of Music at Olivet College, Olivet, Michigan.

W60. IN TADAUSSAC CHURCH (1735)

Dedication: Charles H. Doersam

Holograph: not located
Published: Gray, 1926 (St. Cecilia Series, No. 399)

Chadwick's visit to Tadaussac Church in the Province of Quebec on July 18, 1919, inspired this composition.

W61. INTRODUCTION AND THEME FOR ORGAN (E-flat)

Dedication: none
Holograph: MB
Published: Millet, 1895 (In Dudley Buck, ed., *Vox Organi: A Collection of New Music for the Organ Written for this Work by Eminent Composers of Europe and America.* Boston; J. B. Millet, 1895. Vol. 2, pp. 200-202.)

W62. PASTORALE

Dedication: none
Holograph: MB
Published: Millet, 1895 (In Dudley Buck, ed., *Vox Organi: A Collection of New Music for the Organ Written for this Work by Eminent Composers of Europe and America.* Boston; J. B. Millet, 1895. Vol. 1, pp. 6-8; reprinted, Washington, D.C.: Library of Congress, 1980.)

Selected Performance

W62a.   Easter Sunday, 1911; Frank Otis Nash, organ; First Congregational Church; Jamaica Plains, Massachusetts.

W63. PROGRESSIVE PEDAL STUDIES (PEDAL ETUDEN)

Dedication: E. M. Bowman
Holograph: DLC
Published: Schmidt, 1890; reprint, 1918

Movements: 1. *Prelude*; 2. *Postlude*; 3. *Offertory*; 4. *Response*; 5. *Postlude*; 6. *Prelude*; 7. *Prelude*; 8. *Offertory*; 9. *Postlude*; 10. *March.*

W64. REQUIEM

Dedication: none
Holograph: MB

Published: Millet, 1895 (In Dudley Buck, ed., *Vox Organi: A
Collection of New Music for the Organ Written for this Work
by Eminent Composers of Europe and America*. Boston: J. B.
Millet, 1895. Vol. 3, pp. 272-275.)

W65. SUITE IN VARIATION FORM FOR ORGAN

Dedication: Homer Humphrey
Holograph: not located
Published: Gray, 1923

Movements: 1. *Prelude*; 2. *Recitative*; 3. *Cipher* (Pastorale);
4. *Romance*; 5. *Tema*; 6. *Finale* (Fuga)

Selected Performance

W65a. 21 April 1930; Albert W. Snow, organ; "Concert of
Compositions of George W. Chadwick"; New England
Conservatory, Jordan Hall, Boston.

W66. 10 CANONIC STUDIES FOR ORGAN, OP. 12

Dedication: Henry M. Dunham
Holograph: DLC
Published: Schmidt, 1885; reprint, Minneapolis, Minnesota: Augsburg
Publishing House, 1976. Foreword by Robert Kendall.

W67. THREE COMPOSITIONS FOR ORGAN

Dedication: none
Holograph: No. 2 in MBCM; nos. 1 and 3 not located
Published: Schmidt 1890; reprint, 1907

Movements: 1. *Prelude*; 2. *Response*; 3. *March*

MUSIC FOR THE STAGE

W68. EVERYWOMAN: HER PILGRIMAGE IN QUEST OF LOVE (Incidental Music; 5 Canticles [acts]) (1910)

Text by: Walter Browne
Dedication: none
Published: Harms, 1911 (piano-vocal score)

Holograph and orchestra parts: not located; one holograph chorus
       part at MBCM
For: Soloists, chorus, pit orchestra

(See also: W9, W25, and W72)

Premiere

W68a.   9 February 1911; Parsons Theatre, Hartford, Connecticut;
Cast: Laura Nelson Hall, Everywoman; H. Cooper Cliff,
Nobody; Sarah Cowell LeMoyne, Truth; Frederick de
Belleville, Wealth; Patricia Collinge, Youth; Virginia
Hammond, Beauty; Stella Hammerstein, Vice; Edward
MacKay, King Love the First; John L. Shine, Stuff; Henry
Wenman, Bluff; Juliett Day, Modesty; Wilda Bennett,
Conscience; Hugo Frey, Music Director.

Other Selected Performances

W68b.   27 February 1911; Herald Square Theatre, New York City.
Cast: Laura Nelson Hall, Everywoman; H. Cooper Cliff,
Nobody; Sarah Cowell LeMoyne, Truth; Frederick de
Belleville, Wealth; Patricia Collinge, Youth; Virginia
Hammond, Beauty; Stella Hammerstein, Vice; Edward
MacKay, King Love the First; John L. Shine, Stuff; Henry
Wenman, Bluff; Juliett Day, Modesty; Wilda Bennett,
Conscience; Hugo Frey, Music Director.

W68c.   4 September 1911; Lyric Theatre, New York City.
Cast: Laura Nelson Hall, Everywoman; H. Cooper Cliff,
Nobody; Sarah Cowell LeMoyne, Truth; Frederick de
Belleville, Wealth; Patricia Collinge, Youth; Aurora Piatt,
Beauty; Stella Hammerstein, Vice; Edward MacKay, King
Love the First; John L. Shine, Stuff; Henry Wenman, Bluff;
Juliett Day, Modesty; Wilda Bennett, Conscience; Hugo
Frey, Music Director.

W68d.   13 November 1911; Majestic Theatre, Boston. Cast: Laura
Nelson Hall, Everywoman; H. Cooper Cliff, Nobody; Sarah
Cowell LeMoyne, Truth; Frederick de Belleville, Wealth;
Patricia Collinge, Youth; Aurora Piatti, Beauty; Stella
Hammerstein, Vice; Edward MacKay, King Love the First;
John L. Shine, Stuff; Henry Wenman, Bluff; Juliett Day,

Modesty; Wilda Bennett, Conscience; Hugo Frey, Music Director.

W68e.   12 September 1912; Drury Lane Theatre, London. Cast: Alexandra Carlisle, Everywoman; Fred Lewis, Wealth; Jessie Winter, Modesty; H. B. Irving, Nobody; W. H. Denny, Stuff; Harry Wenman, Bluff; Austin Melford, Flattery; Clara Beck, Vice; Birtie White, Witless; Patricia Collinge, Youth; Wilda Bennett, Conscience; Vera Beringer, Self; Mary Brough, Greed; Gladys Cooper, Beauty; Howard Russell, Time; E. W. Royce, Age; Ion Swinley, King Love the First; John Tresahar, Puff; Wilfrid Douthitt, Passion; Arthur Collins, producer; James Glover, conductor.

Bibliography

WB247. "Everywoman on the Stage." *New York Times* February 10, 1911: 9. Review of the premiere. "The production is wholly of to-day [*sic*], and while there is more than a touch of allegory in the story and action, the dominant note of the drama is realism." (See: W68a)

WB248. "Novelties for Playgoers." *New York Times* February 26, 1911: VII/2. Preview of the Herald Square performance, February 27, 1911. Brief outline of the play is included with a photo of Laura Nelson Hall. (See: W68b)

WB249. A. W. "The Drama -- 'Everywoman,' Her Pilgrimage in Quest of Love; by Walter Browne." *New York Daily Tribune* February 28, 1911: 7. Review of the New York premiere, February 27, 1911. "Mr. [Henry] Savage has done all he could to make it a notable production, even going so far as to commission Mr. George Whitefield Chadwick to compose the overture, entr'act and incidental music." A. W. states that the music "... charms and instructs the ear." (See: W68b)

WB250. "Modern Morality at Herald Square." *New York Times* February 28, 1911: 8. Review of the New York premiere, February 27, 1911. "But the total result, when all is said and done, is about a three-hour exposition of various platitudinous statements about life without any especial originality in the form of driving the lesson home ...." The dialogue is not helped "... by the obtrusive music, conducted by a director, who, if possible, is even more obtrusive." (See: W68b)

WB251. "Scenes from Everywoman at the Herald Square." *New York Times* March 5, 1911: I/2 (picture section). Photo layout of the Herald Square production. (See: W68b)

WB252. "About Everywoman -- Henry W. Savage Discusses his Latest Production." *New York Daily Tribune* March 5, 1911: V/6. Answering whether all the music is by Chadwick, producer Savage states: "Yes. Mr. Browne read his play to Mr. Chadwick and Mr. Chadwick became very interested. He wanted to write the music as a labor of love, but I could not accept such a sacrifice. Mr. Chadwick's music was finished at Christmas time. It wonderfully enhances the value of the play and does not interrupt the action." (See: W68b)

WB253. Advertisement. *New York Times* September 3, 1911: VII/9. Ad for Lyric Theatre presentation reads: "Exactly as presented last season . . . ." (See: W68c)

WB254. "Lyric Re-opens with Everywoman." *New York Times* September 5, 1911: 7. Announcement of the New York revival with "no changes of personnel of the important characters . . . ." (See: W68c)

WB255. "This Week at the Theatres -- 'Everywoman' Coming to the Majestic." *Sunday Herald* (Boston) November 12, 1911: 24. Preview of the Boston performance, November 13, 1911. Describes the plot; no mention of Chadwick. (See: W68d)

WB256. Hale, Philip. "Everywoman at the Majestic." *Sunday Herald* (Boston) November 14, 1911: 10. Lengthy review of the Boston performance, November 13, 1911. "While it is called a morality play, it is in fact a spectacle with music, with a pleasing dash of musical comedy." Hale further states that "Mr. Chadwick's music is of real value to the production." (See: W68d)

WB257. H. T. P. [Henry Taylor Parker]. "A Queer Entertainment." *Boston Evening Transcript* November 14, 1911: 11. Review of the Boston performance, November 13, 1911. "Mr. Chadwick has written excellent incidental music for it that often accompanies declamation and occasionally songs and dances. It is effective music heigthening [*sic*] text and action, taking color from the scene . . . ." (See: W68d)

WB258. "Plays and Players." *Sunday Times* (London) September 8, 1912: 4. Announcement and preview of the London performance, September 12, 1912. "The incidental music is of an important character, and is from the pen of George W. Chadwick, the well-known Bostonian composer." (See: W68e)

WB259. Grein, J. T. "The Dramatic World -- The Week's Premieres." *Sunday Times* (London) September 15, 1912: 4. Review of the London performance, September 12, 1912. Notes that the text for this performance had been revised by Stephen Phillips. ". . . a fascinating mixture of an allegory and decoration with a little moral appended to it for the benefit of the masses." [No mention of music; the score is considered in another column in the same issue.] (See: W68e)

WB260. "Music and Musicians." *Sunday Times* (London) September 15, 1912: 4. Review of the London performance, September 12, 1912. "[Chadwick's] prelude is a spirited enough affair, with orchestration that is clever and stirring rhythms, but it hardly suggests a morality, however modern. His entr'actes are just a trifle colourless. The chords with which he accentuates the more important speeches prove rather tiresome in the process of time. . . ." (See: W68e)

W69. **JUDITH,** Lyric Drama (3 Acts) (Begun May, 1899; completed December 12, 1900)

Text by: Rev. William Chauncy Langdon, after a scenario by G. W. Chadwick
Dedication: none
Published: Schirmer, 1901 (piano-vocal); (publ. plate no. 15555); copyright renewed, Boston: New England Conservatory, 1928; reprinted in Earlier American Music, vol. 3. Introduction by H. Wiley Hitchcock. New York: Da Capo, 1972.
Holograph: DLC (including piano-vocal score); MBCM (copy of score and parts, and a pencil holograph of Act 1); DLC also holds original typescript libretto (17 pp.)
For: Mezzo soprano, tenor, baritone, and bass soloists
SATB chorus
2. 2 (2nd doubles eh). 2. bass clar. 2./4. 3. 3. 1./
timp. side drum. bass drum. cymbals. triangle. harp. strings.
Duration: 1 hour, 45 minutes

New York Public Library holds a copy of the piano-vocal score which includes autographs of the composer, the librettist, and singers who took part in the premiere performance.

The title page of the holograph piano-vocal score reads "Judith and Holofernes" with the last two words struck.

(See also: W116, W131 [nos. 14-15], W161, and W199)

Premiere

W69a. 26 September 1901; Worcester Festival. Cast: Gertrude May Stein, Judith; David Bispham, Holofernes; Mr. Carl E. Dufft, Ozias; Mr. Towne, Achior; The Worcester Festival Chorus [400 voices] and Orchestra, G. W. Chadwick, cond.; Mechanics Hall, Worcester, Massachusetts.

Other Selected Performances

W69b. 26 January 1902; Symphony Hall, Boston. Cast: Gertrude May Stein, Judith; A. Janpowlski, Holofernes; Herbert Witherspoon, Ozias; C. B. Shirley, Achior; the choruses of the Cecilia Club, the Apollo Club, and the New England Conservatory, G. W. Chadwick, cond.

W69c. 30 September 1902; Worcester Festival; Cast: Gertrude May Stein, Judith; G. Campanari, Holofernes; Mr. Van Yorx, Achior; Herbert Witherspoon, Ozias; The Worcester Festival Chorus [400 voices] and Orchestra, Wallace Goodrich, cond.; Mechanics Hall, Worcester, Massachusetts.

W69d. 20 December 1907; Jessie Swartz, vocalist; New England Conservatory Orchestra, G. W. Chadwick, cond.; Jordan Hall, Boston ("Prayer" only).

W69e. 16 March 1910; Florence Jepperson, vocalist; New England Conservatory Orchestra, Wallace Goodrich, cond.; Jordan Hall, Boston ("Prayer" only).

W69f. 26 April 1911; Strawbridge and Clothier Chorus and members of the Philadelphia Orchestra; Cast: Mrs. Russell King Miller, Judith; Reinald Werrenrath, Holofernes; Franklin Lawson, Achior; Frederic Martin, Ozias; Herbert J. Tily, cond.; Academy of Music, Philadelphia.

W69g. 8 October 1919; Worcester Festival; Cast: Louise Homer, Judith; Reinald Werrenrath, Holofernes; George Hamlin, Achior; Edgar Schofield; Ozias; Worcester Festival Chorus and the Delphia Orchestra, Arthur Mees, cond.; Mechanics Hall, Worcester, Massachusetts.

W69h. 6 May 1930; New England Conservatory Orchestra and Choral Class. Cast: Gladys Miller, Judith; David Blair McCloskey, Holofernes; Thomas McLaughlin, a sentinel; assisted by The Apollo Club of Boston, Thompson Stone, dir.; Wallace Goodrich, cond.; Jordan Hall, Boston (act 2/scene 5 only).

W69i. 17 and 24 May 1931; WEAF Radio broadcast (two parts, 1 hour each); National Oratorio Society; Georgia Graves, contralto; Harold Branch, tenor; Theodore Webb, baritone; Earl Waldo, bass; Reinald Werrenrath, cond.

W69j. 29 January 1977; Handel Society Chorus and Orchestra; Katharine Johnson, Judith; James Todhunter, Holofernes; James Beams; William Ledbetter; Steven Ledbetter, cond.; Hopkins Center, Spaulding Auditorium, Dartmouth College, Hanover, New Hampshire.

Bibliography

WB261. H. E. K. [Henry E. Krehbiel]. "Mr. Chadwick's 'Judith'." *New York Tribune* September 22, 1901: 2-3 (Illustrated supplement section). Lengthy preview of the premiere with a photo of Chadwick and musical examples. "Mr. Chadwick is both new and old fashioned in his writing. Although he calls the work a lyric drama . . . he drops frankly into the oratorio manner . . . ." (See: W69a)

WB262. R. R. G. "The Worcester Festival." *Boston Evening Transcript* September 27, 1901: 8. A lengthy review of the premiere. "The music suffers from the same failing as the text--lack of distinct purpose," but, " . . . on the whole, a great success." (See: W69a)

WB263. H. E. K. [Henry E. Krehbiel]. "Music -- Mr. Kelley's and Mr. Chadwick's Compositions at Worcester." *New York Daily Tribune* September 27, 1901: 11. Review of the premiere. "I cannot say that the work sounds spontaneous as a whole, but it hangs together and the music keeps pace admirably with the sentiments of the text. . . . There were splendid elasticity, animation and color in his orchestra." (See: W69a)

WB264. "Worcester Music Festival." *New York Times* September 27, 1901: 7. Review of the premiere. "The great event of the day, naturally, was the first production of Judith, in the evening . . . . It is perfectly plain that this work is an opera . . . . It demands more than the imagination is willing to give, and its most intensely dramatic features do not attain their proper effect." (See: W69a)

WB265. Burton, Frederick R. "The New Opera Judith." *New York Times* (magazine supplement) September 29, 1901: 2. Review of the premiere. "Fortunately for the general cause of music, Judith was a success. It aroused no end of discussion among visiting musicians . . . ." (See: W69a)

WB266. R. R. G. "Judith, Lyric Drama." *Boston Evening Transcript* October 28, 1901: 11. Review of the newly published piano-vocal score by Schirmer. "Both book and music suffer from a lack of distinct purpose . . . . It [the music] suffers, to be sure, from the want of unity that mars the whole work, for one-half is pure oratorio and in the other dramatic half there are perhaps half a dozen different styles of opera represented."

WB267. "In the World of Music -- Chadwick's Judith Tonight in Symphony Hall." *Sunday Herald* (Boston) January 26, 1902: 40. Preview of the Boston premiere. " . . . there is every reason to anticipate that the event will take on the nature of an ovation to this Boston musician, whose work has been so generally recognized throughout the country." (See: W69b)

WB268. "Mr. Chadwick's Judith." *Boston Globe* January 27, 1902: 11. Review of the Boston premiere. "Mr. Chadwick's work contains many orchestral beauties, his handling of his instrumental score is very skillful . . . the whole composition is a credit to the scholarly musician." (See: W69b)

WB269. R. R. G. "Music and Drama -- Symphony Hall: Judith." *Boston Evening* Transcript January 27, 1902: 11. Lengthy review of the Boston premiere. "Judith has its faults, and serious ones, but . . . it can make a far deeper impression than it did last night." (See: W69b)

WB270. Elson, Louis C. "New Oratorio of Merit." *Boston Daily Advertiser* January 27, 1902: 5. Review of the Boston premiere. "Although Mr. Chadwick does not keep to the strict Wagnerian road, he is sufficiently modern to use the guiding motive effectively . . . ." Elson also notes that Chadwick ". . . conducted with authority and decision." (See: W69b)

WB271. "Chadwick's Judith." *Boston Post* January 27, 1902: 6. Review of the Boston premiere. The writer states that *Judith* ". . . may be described as a biblical opera. On first hearing the strongest portions seem to be those where the oratorio characteristics are in evidence, as in the choruses." Further, "[Librettist] Mr. Langdon has not added to his literary reputation by his version of Judith." On Chadwick: "Judith may not be the equal of some of the composer's previous efforts in larger choral forms, but it is worth hearing . . . ." (See: W69b)

WB272. "'Judith' Sung to Academy Audience." *Public Ledger* (Philadelphia) April 27, 1911: 3. Review of the 26 April 1911 performance in Philadelphia. " 'Judith' is one of the most notable contributions that have [*sic*] been made to the choral music of America. It is not merely scholarly . . . but it is graphic, dramatic, emotionally expressive and prolific in agreeable melody and delightful harmony." The reviewer also notes that Chadwick was in the audience. (See: W69f)

WB273. "The World of Music -- Various Music Events." *New York Times* October 5, 1919: sec. 10, p. 8. Announcement of the Worcester Festival performance of October 8, 1919. (See: W69g)

WB274. Downes, Olin. "Festival Audience Greets Chadwicks [*sic*] 'Judith' Eagerly." *Worcester Telegram* (Massachusetts) October 9, 1919. Review of the October 8, 1919 performance at the Worcester Festival. "The composer did not feel that he had written a cantata or [an] oratorio. Nor yet had he made a music drama . . . . The second act is operatic music. It would need but a little alteration or extension of transitional passages to be put on in the opera house. The first and third acts are not operatic . . . . It was an unusually interesting performance, of a singularly uneven work, by one of the greatest of American composers." (See: W69g)

WB275. Downes, Olin. "All-American Concerts." *Boston Post* October 12, 1919: 37. Review of the October 8, 1919 performance at the Worcester Festival. After a generally positive review, Downes states: "Hearing this music, written two decades ago, one wonders what Mr. Chadwick would have evolved into if when he grew up there had been opera houses in every city in America where American composers, without having to go to Europe to do it, might have gained knowledge of writing music for the theatre." After noting parallels with Saint-Saens's *Samson et Delilah*, Downes continues: "It is a singular piece of work by the most gifted composer of his generation." (See: W69g)

WB276. "Werrenrath to Present Chadwick Work." *Musical Courier* 102/20 (May 16, 1931): 36. Notice of the radio broadcast, May 17, 1931. (See: W69i)

WB277. "National Oratorio Society Honors Chadwick." *Musical Courier* 102/21 (May 23, 1931): 22. Review of the May 17, 1931 radio performance with a preview of the second half of the broadcast, May 24. "The music is noble and dramatic, and, under Werrenrath's expert direction, orchestra, chorus, and soloists combined in a performance of uniform excellence. This is under stood [*sic*] to be the radio premiere of Mr. Chadwick's opera." (See: W69i)

WB278. M. D. D. "Debuts & Appearances -- Dartmouth College: Judith." *High Fidelity and Musical America* 27/5 (May 1977): MA20-21. Review of the January 29, 1977 performance at Dartmouth College. ". . . Chadwick's admirable workmanship was apparent throughout, although listeners had to contend with a variety of musical styles. Traces of Mendelssohn, Puccini, and Saint-Saens mixed . . . with Eastern evocations, marches (Chadwick's are nearly identical with Sousa's) and anthem-like music." (See: W69j)

W70. LOVE'S SACRIFICE, Pastoral Opera (1 Act) (1916-1917)

Text by: David Kilburn Stevens (1860-1946)
Dedication: none
Published: Birchard, 1917 (piano-vocal score)
Holograph score: MBCM [parts not located]
For: Soloists, mixed chorus or unchanged voices (school chorus)/
          2. 1. 2. 1./2. 2. 2. 0./triangle. harp. strings.

Duration: 30 minutes

According to a former Chadwick student, Allen Lincoln Langley, this work was almost entirely orchestrated from the piano-vocal score by students in Chadwick's orchestration class at New England Conservatory. (See: B142)

Premiere

W70a. 5 May 1922; New England Conservatory production; Cast: Muriel LaFrance, Daphne; Elizabeth Bingham, Myrtil; Mary Hobson, Laura; Antoinette Perner, Esta; Martha Atwell, Celia; Katherine O'Brien, an acolyte; members of the New England Conservatory vocal department and dramatic interpretation classes; New England Conservatory Orchestra, Wallace Goodrich, cond.; Jordan Hall, Boston.

Other Selected Performance

W70b. 1 February 1923; Chicago Playhouse, Chicago, Illinois. Cast: Ellen Young; Floyd Jones; Lillian Knowles; Bertha Caspar; Dorothy Greathouse; Charlotte Holt. Produced by Chicago's Opera in Our Language Foundation, Inc.

Bibliography

WB279. Moore, Edward. " 'Opera in Our Language' Again Fails." *Chicago Tribune* February 2, 1923: 2/21. Review of the February 1, 1923 performance. "Much pleasure had been evinced at the performance of the Chadwick work, though the number of hearers was limited. The opera, in one act, is written in terms of suave, pleasant, and not too complex melody and was mounted and costumed with much color." [Chadwick's work was the Foundation's final production.] (See: W70b)

W71. **THE PADRONE,** Opera (2 Acts) (Conceived in 1911; score completed June 15, 1913)

Text by: David Kilburn Stevens (1860-1946), after a scenario by G. W. Chadwick
Dedication: none
Published: Boston: New England Conservatory Press, 1995
Ink holograph and parts: MBCM (original piano-vocal rehearsal score

lost; a new piano-vocal reduction has been prepared by The Waterbury Symphony Orchestra); two versions of the libretto are held at MBCM

For: Soprano, mezzo soprano, contralto, tenor, baritone
SATB chorus
2 (2nd doubles picc). 2 (2nd doubles eh). 2. bass clar. 2./ 4. 3. 2. 1./timp. bass drum. cymbals. glock. triangle. tamb. xylo. bells. celesta. harp. strings.

Premiere
(Concert performance)

W71a.   29 September 1995; Thomaston (Connecticut) Opera House. Cast: Thomas Woodman, Catani; Alexandra Gruber-Malkin, Marietta; Jacqueline Pierce, Francesca; Barton Green, Marco; Chad Shelton, Dino; Concora Chorus, Richard Coffey, Artistic Director and Conductor; Members of the Connecticut Choral Society, Waterbury Chorale, and Naugatuck Valley College Chorus; and The Waterbury Symphony Orchestra, Leif Bjaland, Musical Director and Conductor. (See also: B262)

Premiere
(Fully-staged performances)

W71b.   10-13 April 1997; New England Conservatory Opera Theatre performance at Blackman Theater, Northeastern University, Boston; Cast: Keith Phares and Curtis Olds, Catani; Kara Shay Thomson, Marietta; Rachel Satanoff and Suzanne Ryan, Francesca; Stewart Howe and Theodore Green, Marco; Robert Havens, Dino; Yvonne Field, Marta's mother; Damian Savarino, immigration officer; John Hellyer, the messenger; Marc Astafan, director; John Moriarty, cond. [This performance featured a revised text by John Moriarty.]

Other Selected Performance
(Excerpt)

W71c.   6 December 1961; Virginia Babikian, Marelena Kleinman, Louise Parker, and Don Yule, vocalists; Orchestra of America, Richard Korn, cond.; Carnegie Hall, New York [Quartet from Act II only].

Bibliography

WB280. Parmenter, Ross. "Music: Modern Works." *New York Times* December 7, 1961: 53. Review of the Carnegie Hall performance, December 6, 1961. "Chadwick was represented by a quartet from The Padrone, an opera about Italian immigrants in Boston that has never been performed. It was winning enough to arouse curiosity for a little more of the opera." (See: W71c)

WB281. Dyer, Richard. "Classical Notes: Chadwick Found Tragedy in the North End." *Boston Globe* April 4, 1997. Announcement and preview of the upcoming New England Conservatory Opera Theatre performance, with a brief outline of the plot. (See: W71b)

WB282. Dyer, Richard. "Passionate Padrone Gets Delayed Premiere." *Boston Globe* April 12, 1997: C4. Review of the fully-staged performances of 10-13 April 1997. ". . .a very effective piece, and if it had been performed [during Chadwick's day], it might have changed the history of opera in a country that would have to wait another 30 years for anything composed with comparable skill. . . ." (See: W71b)

W72. THE PEER AND THE PAUPER, Comic Operetta (2 Acts) (1884)

Text by: Robert Grant (1852-1940)
Dedication: none
Unpublished
Holograph: full score not located; ink piano-vocal score [with
        numerous corrections and pasteovers] and manuscript voice
        parts at MBCM; the libretto has not been located
For: soloists, orchestra
Premiere: unperformed

Victor Yellin has noted that this composition uses ideas from the composer's own *Schon Munchen* (See: W15), and that parts of this composition were later used in *Tabasco* (See: W74) and *Everywoman* (See: W68). For further details consult B240 [p. 52].

Bibliography

WB283. "Major and Minor." *Musical Record* 269 (June 1884): 9.

Notice that a new opera by Chadwick is ". . . in the course of composition."

W73. A QUIET LODGING, Operetta (2 acts) (1892)

Text by: Arlo Bates (1850-1918)
Dedication: none
Unpublished
Holograph score and parts: lost, except No. 5, "The First Man I
        Married" (held in the private collection of Victor Fell Yellin);
        libretto at MBCM [marked: "first prompter's book"]
For: soloists, orchestra

The whereabouts of the score was known as late as 1916, when the work may have been under consideration for another performance. An entry in Chadwick's *Journal* (December 4, 1916) states: "Left Quiet Lodging at Tavern [Club] for Stanley Parker. John Codman had it last." Parker and Codman were principals in the 1914 performances.

Premiere

W73a.   1 April 1892; The Tavern Club, Boston (private performance). Cast: Sullivan Armory Sargent, Christopher Higginbottom; Eliot Hubbard, Ariminta Blowbellow. [Program not located for this performance, but the 1914 program states that the above-listed actors originated their respective characters in the 1892 production.]

Other Selected Performances

W73b.   10 and 17 December 1914; The Tavern Club, Boston (private performance). Cast: John Sturgis Codman, Professor Erasmus Blowbellow; William Stanley Parker, Signor Yayelli; Sullivan Armory Sargent, Christopher Higginbottom; Eliot Hubbard, Ariminta Blowbellow; Richard Clipston Sturgis, Mrs. Maria Smutchbread; Wallace Goodrich, conductor. [A program for these performances, located in Chadwick's *Journal* (1914), reads as follows: "This operetta was first performed by the Tavern Club in 1892. Since then both the music and the words have been partially re-written." It is also noted that the repeat performance of 17 December is given "for the edification of the ladies."]

W74. TABASCO, Burlesque Opera (2 Acts) (1893-1894)

Text by: Robert Ayres Barnet (1850?-1933)
Dedication: none
Published: Wood, 1894 (piano-vocal score; publ. plate no. BFW12)
Ink holograph score, manuscript parts, and copyist's piano-vocal score
      (incomplete) are held at MBCM
For: Soloists, chorus
      1. 1. 2. 1./1. 1. 1. 0./perc./strings

Critic Philip Hale reports that *Tabasco* was orchestrated by Chadwick's
pupil, Lucien Hosmer (1870-1935). (See: WB296)

(See also: W23, W53, W158, W162, W207, W231, W246, W247,
     W253, W271; and WR4, WR7 and WR15)

Premiere

W74a. 29 January 1894; Tremont Theatre, Boston; First Corps
     Cadets (amateur production); Cast: T. E. Stutco, Hot-Hed-
     Ham-Pasha; B. P. Cheney, Jr., Francois; Jason G. White,
     Marco; Robert A. Barnet, Ben-Hid-Den; C. B. Tucker, Sid-
     Has-Sem; W. N. Lockwood, Hahomelet; George P. Davis,
     Lola; L. C. Burton, Has-Been-A; Rodney Thayer, Matina.

Other Selected Performances

W74b. 9 April 1894 [Printed program reads 30 April, but reviews
     appear on the 10th]; Boston Musuem; Thomas Q. Seabrooke
     Comic Opera Company (first professional production); Cast:
     Thomas Q. Seabrooke, Francois; Walter Allen, Hot-Hed-
     Ham-Pasha; Joseph F. Sheehan, Marco; Otis Harlan, Ben-
     Hid-Den; Robert E. Bell, Exhausted Hawkins; Edgar Smith,
     Dusty Rhodes; George W. Thomas, A-Sel; G. Bardini,
     General Mahomed; H. C. Davis, Major-General Mahomed;
     Arthur Concors, Lieutenant-General Mahomed; Walter
     Abling, Adjutant-General Mahomed; D. S. Loeb,
     Ambassador; John Crane, Attendant; William S. Lavine,
     Ben-Abed-Ab-Der U-Hassem; Catharine Linyard, Fatima;
     Rosa Cooke, Has-Been-A; Grace Vaughn, Saa-Dee-Hassem;
     Elvia Crox, Lola. Paul Steindorff, Conductor; C. D. Marius,
     Director.

W74c. 14 May 1894; Broadway Theatre, New York; Thomas Q.

Seabrooke Opera Company. Cast: Thomas Q. Seabrooke, Francois; Walter Allen, Hot-Hed-Ham-Pasha; Joseph F. Sheehan, Marco; Otis Harlan, Ben-Hid-Den; Robert E. Bell, Exhausted Hawkins; Edgar Smith, Dusty Rhodes; George W. Thomas, A-Sel; G. Bardini, General Mahomed; H. C. Davis, Major-General Mahomed; Arthur Concors, Lieutenant-General Mahomed; Walter Abling, Adjutant-General Mahomed; D. S. Loeb, Ambassador; John Crane, Attendant; William S. Lavine, Ben-Abed-Ab-Der U-Hassem; Catharine Linyard, Fatima; Rosa Cooke, Has-Been-A; Grace Vaughn, Saa-Dee-Hassem; Elvia Crox, Lola; Paul Steindorff, Conductor; C. D. Marius, Director.

Bibliography

WB284. Hale, Philip. "Music in Boston." *Musical Courier* January 24, 1894: 8. Announcement of the premiere. (See: W74a)

WB285. "Stage and Concert Hall -- The Story of Tabasco." *Boston Evening Transcript* January 20, 1894: 7. Preview of the premiere with detailed plot. (See: W74a)

WB286. "At the Theatres." *Boston Daily Advertiser* January 27, 1894: 4. Preview of the premiere. "It is described as being remarkably bright and witty, and possessing musical features of the highest order." (See: W74a)

WB287. "Stage and Concert Hall." *Boston Evening Transcript* January 27, 1894: 7. Preview of the premiere. "A great success is confidently anticipated for Tabasco . . . ." (See: W74a)

WB288. "Musical Matters -- Tabasco at Tremont." *Sunday Herald* (Boston) January 28, 1894: 13. Preview of the premiere. The music and the libretto " . . . combined to render Tabasco a subject of universal discussion in amusement circles." (See: W74a)

WB289. "The Dramatic Night -- Tabasco." *Boston Post* January 30, 1894: 4. Review of the premiere. ". . . altogether the most praiseworthy piece the Cadets have given to the public . . . . Songs there are in abundance." (See: W74a)

WB290. "Piquant Tabasco." *Boston Daily Advertiser* January 30, 1894: 4. Review of the premiere. This lengthy article features a thorough plot description. The writer notes that fun ". . . infected composer Chadwick's music more than once." (See: W74a)

WB291. "Music and Drama -- Tremont Theatre: Tabasco." *Boston Evening Transcript* January 30, 1894: 5. Review of the premiere. "Mr. Chadwick's [music] shows rare ingenuity. Here are tunes that have nothing remarkable about them . . . but which, heard in their full estate, have a certain distinction." (See: W74a)

WB292. "Tabasco." *Boston Post* January 30, 1894. Discusses the social spectacle occasioned by the premiere of *Tabasco*. The event brought out Boston's most important people in lavish dress. (See: W74a)

WB293. "Brimful of Pleasing Tunes -- Burlesque Opera at the Tremont Theatre a Great Success." *Boston Herald* January 30, 1894: 1. Review of the premiere. "Of Mr. Chadwick's music, much was expected and much more was realized . . . as a whole, the music of Tabasco calls for the highest commendation." (See: W74a)

WB294. "Drama and Music -- Amusement Notes." *Boston Globe* February 1, 1894: 6. Two notices on this page regard the Tremont Theatre performances. "Barnet and Chadwick's jolly burlesque Tabasco is drawing phenomenal audiences at the Tremont Theatre." And, regarding "Military Night" at the theatre: "In honor of the occasion the naval battalion band . . . will play in the lobby before the performance. Among the selections to be given is the Tabasco march which has been scored for full band by E. N. Lafricain, the director, from advance sheets, by courtesy of G. W. Chadwick, the composer." (See: W74a and WR15)

WB295. "Drama." *Saturday Evening Gazette* (Boston) February 3, 1894: 2. Review of the premiere. "It [the music] is never on stilts, its melodies flow easily and gracefully, and a popular level has been reached without the sacrifice of artistic dignity . . . . The success of the undertaking was complete . . . ." (See: W74a)

WB296. Hale, Philip. "Music in Boston." *Musical Courier* February 7, 1894: 18. Review of the premiere. After resoundingly praising Chadwick, Hale writes: "It is only fair to Mr. Chadwick to reserve in a measure judgement until his work receives a more adequate performance." Hale also writes: "The instrumentation of the work was done by Mr. Lucien Hosmer, a pupil of Mr. Chadwick's, after the sketches of the composer." (See: W74a)

WB297. "Notes of the Stage." *New York Times* April 8, 1894: 12. Announcement of the Boston opening by the Seabrooke Company, April 9, 1894. (See: W74b)

WB298. "Theatres and Concerts -- Boston Museum: Tabasco." *Boston Evening Transcript* April 10, 1894: 4. Review of the Seabrooke Company premiere, April 9, 1894. Reports that there has been a great deal of alteration in the dialogue since the premiere. "So far as the music is concerned there is little change and the vocal portions gain in effectiveness by the addition of female voices." (See: W74b)

WB299. "Stage and Concert Hall." *Boston Evening Transcript* April 14, 1894: 7. Review of the Seabrooke Company premiere, April 9, 1894. ". . . The fun of the text and the catching quality of the music are as pronounced as ever . . . ." (See: W74b)

WB300. "At the Theatres -- Tabasco." *Boston Journal* April 24, 1894: 7. Review of the Seabrooke Company premiere, April 9, 1894. ". . . tuneful music, catchy songs, its costumes, its mirth, is nightly enjoyed by large audiences. There is no intimation of its withdrawal . . . ." (See: W74b)

WB301. "The Week at the Theatre -- New Bills of the Week." *New York Times* May 13, 1894: 12. Notice that *Tabasco* will begin at four-week run at New York's Broadway Theatre on May 14. (See: W74c)

WB302. "New Bills at the Theatres -- Tabasco at the Broadway." *New York Times* May 15, 1894: 5. Review of the May 14, 1894 Broadway Theatre performance. "It may as well be said at once that Mr. Chadwick's music does him no credit whatever. A composer of his standing should have sought his models elsewhere than in the farces of Mr. [Edward] Harrigan." (See: W74c)

WB303. "Music -- The Drama." *New York Daily Tribune* May 15, 1894: 7. Review of the May 14, 1894 Broadway Theatre performance. "The music . . . was in general superior to the book. It was simple and melodious, and much good use was made of the orchestra in helping out the spirit of the farce. Hubbard Smith and Ludwig Englander were credited with the composition of one song each." (See: W74c)

MUSIC FOR CHORUS WITH ORCHESTRA

W75. COMMEMORATION ODE (ca. 1927-1928)

Text by: James Russell Lowell (1819-1891)
Dedication: none
Published: Ditson, 1928 (piano-vocal score; publ. plate no. 76251)
Holograph score and parts: MBCM; piano-vocal score holograph at
      DLC
Premiere: unknown
For: SATB chorus
      2. 2. 2. 2./4. 2. 3. 0./timp. harp. strings

This work, from Lowell's *Ode Recited at the Commemoration of the Living and the Dead Soldiers of Harvard University, July 21, 1865*, commemorates the 10th anniversary of the end of The Great War.

(See also: W119)

W76. DEDICATION ODE, OP. 15 (Completed March 18, 1883)

Text by: Rev. Henry Bernard Carpenter
Dedication: Rev. Henry Bernard Carpenter
Published: Schmidt, 1886 (piano/organ-vocal score; Octavo Edition, 1st
      Series, No. 7)
Holograph score and parts: MBCM
For: SATB soloists and SATB chorus
      2. 2. 2. 2./2. 2. 0. 0./timp. strings

(See also: W120)

Premiere

W76a.   1883; Dedication ceremonies of the Hollis Street Church, Boston [precise details not discerned].

Bibliography

WB304. "Review of New Music." *Musical Herald* 7/5 (May 1886):
159. In this review of the piano-vocal score publication the
writer remarks that the ode " . . . requires good singers to do it
justice."

W77. ECCE JAM NOCTIS (1897)

Text by: St. Gregory of Tours (538-604); In Latin with English
translation by Isabella G. Parker
Composed for the commencement exercises of Yale University, 1897
Published: Schmidt, 1897 (piano-vocal score)
Ink holograph score: DLC; chorus ms. parts at CtY; MBCM (copy of
score and parts)
For: TTBB chorus
2. 2. 2. 2./4 (3 and 4 ad lib.). 3. 3. 0./timp. organ. strings.

Chadwick received an honorary M.A. degree at the ceremony for which
this work was composed.

(See also: W122)

Premiere

W77a.   30 June 1897; Yale University commencement ceremony;
New Haven, Connecticut.

Other Selected Performances

W77b.   November 1905 [precise date unknown]; Concordia Choral
Society concert in honor of Chadwick; G. W. Chadwick,
cond.; [precise location undetermined], Leipzig.

W77c.   2 May 1924; New England Conservatory Orchestra, assisted
by the Sinfonia Glee Club and the Harvard Alumni Chorus, G.
W. Chadwick, cond.; Jordan Hall, Boston.

W77d.   21 April 1930; "Concert of Compositions of George W.
Chadwick," New England Conservatory Orchestra and Glee
Club, Francis Findlay, cond.; Jordan Hall, Boston.

W77e.   6 May 1930; New England Conservatory Orchestra, assisted
by the Apollo Club of Boston, Thompson Stone, dir., Wallace

Goodrich, cond.; Jordan Hall, Boston.

W77f.   19 May 1931; "George Whitefield Chadwick Memorial
Concert," New England Conservatory Orchestra and the Apollo
Club of Boston, Wallace Goodrich, cond.; Jordan Hall,
Boston.

Bibliography

WB305. "Leipsic [*sic*] Discovers a Boston Composer." *Boston Globe*
December 29, 1905. Includes comments about the November
1905 performance in Leipzig. "As he [Chadwick] had only an
orchestra from one of the regimental bands of the garrison, the
performance must have proceeded under some difficulties. . . ."
(See: W77b)

W78. ELFIN SONG (1913)

Text by: Joseph Rodman Drake (1795-1820); from the poem *The
Culprit Fay* (1859)
Dedication: S. L. Herrmann and the Treble Clef Club of Philadelphia
Published: Schmidt, 1910 (piano-vocal score)
Holograph score and parts: MBCM
For: SSAA chorus
2. 1. 2. 1./2. 0. 0. 0./harp. triangle. strings.

(See also: W123)

Selected Performances

W78a.   19 December 1913; New England Conservatory Orchestra and
Chorus, G. W. Chadwick, cond.; Jordan Hall, Boston.

W78b.   6 April 1921; MacDowell Club concert, Georges Longy,
cond.; Jordan Hall, Boston.

W78c.   7 April 1926; MacDowell Club concert, Clement Lenom,
cond.; Jordan Hall, Boston.

W79. FATHERS OF THE FREE (ca. 1927)

Text by: Elmer Ellsworth Brown (1861-1934)
Dedication: "Written and composed for the Hall of Fame"
Published: Gray, 1927 (piano-vocal score)

Holograph score: not located; copyist's score (incomplete; ink and
pencil) and parts at MBCM
For: SATB chorus
2. 2. 2. 2./4. 3. 3. 0./timpani. strings.

According to New York University's Office of University Archives,
Chadwick's music was used for the university's Hall of Fame for Great
Americans processional ceremonies annually until 1941. The author of
the text, Elmer Ellsworth Brown, was the University's Chancellor at
the time the work was composed.

(See also: W124)

Premiere

W79a. 5 May 1927; Hall of Fame for Great Americans, Dedication
Ceremony; New York University (University Heights
campus), the Bronx, New York.

Bibliography

WB306. "Six Busts Unveiled at the Hall of Fame." *New York Times*
May 6, 1927: 6. This article chronicles the events which
occurred at New York University's Hall of Fame Dedication
Ceremony, although there is no mention of Chadwick or his
music. (See: W79a)

W80. THE FIGHTING MEN (ca. 1918)

Text by: Mark A. DeWolfe Howe (1864-1960)
Dedication: none
Published: Birchard, 1918 (piano-vocal score)
Pencil holograph score and parts: MBCM
For: unison chorus
picc. 2. 2. 2. 2./4 (3rd and 4th ad lib.). 2. 3. 1 (ad lib.)./
timp. 4 perc. strings.

(See also: W125)

W81. JEHOVAH REIGNS IN MAJESTY (ca. 1916)

Text: Psalm 99
Dedication: Harry B. Jepson
Published: Ditson, 1916 (organ-vocal score)

Holograph score: not located; parts at MBCM
For: TTBB chorus
      brass sextet: 2. 2. 2. 0./organ

(See also: W137)

W82. JOSHUA (MARCH) (Alternate title: Jericho March) (ca. 1919)

Text by: Richard Darwin Ware (1869-1931)
Dedication: none
Published: Ditson, 1919 (in solo song and TTBB with piano versions)
Pencil holograph score and parts: MBCM
For: TTBB chorus
      picc. 2. 2. 2. 2./4. 2. 3. 0./
      timp. snare drum. bass drum. cymbals. strings.

This work, a chorus with orchestra version of the song *Joshua*, was originally titled *Jericho March*; the title was later changed to *Joshua*.

(See also: W10, W100, W138, W234)

W83. LAND OF OUR HEARTS, Patriotic Hymn (Completed July 26, 1917)

Text by: John Hall Ingham
Dedication: Mr. and Mrs. Carl Stoeckel
Published: Church, 1918 (piano-vocal score)
Ink holograph score: DLC
For: SATB chorus
      2. 2. 2. 2./4. 2. 3. 0./timp. strings. organ (ad lib.).

(See also: W142)

Premiere

W83a. 4 June 1918; Norfolk Festival; G. W. Chadwick, cond.; Music Shed, Norfolk, Connecticut.

Other Selected Performances

W83b. 30/31 December 1918; "Celebrating the Close of the Year of Victory," Boston Symphony Orchestra, Henri Rabaud, cond.; Symphony Hall, Boston.

W83c. 28 February 1923; New England Conservatory Orchestra and Chorus, G. W. Chadwick, cond.; Jordan Hall, Boston.

W83d. 1926 [precise date and details undetermined]; performance in celebration of the City of Lowell's 100th anniversary; Harold Schwab, organ; Francis Findlay, cond.; Lowell, Massachusetts.

W83e. 29 April 1927; New England Conservatory Orchestra and Chorus, Harold Schwab; organ, Francis Findlay, cond.; Jordan Hall, Boston.

W83f. 25 February 1939; National Symphony Orchestra, "Final Student's Concert," with Washington Inter-High School Chorus; Washington, D. C.

W83g. 13 April 1980; Westfield State College Chorale, Theodore C. Davidovich, cond., Beth Rattman, accompanist; Springfield City Library, Springfield, Massachusetts (piano-vocal version).

Bibliography

WB307. *Report of the Music Committee, Litchfield County Choral Union* (Norfolk, Connecticut), December 14, 1917: 6-7. Announcing that he is presenting his work to the Norfolk Festival for the coming season, Chadwick states, "I had rather have my new work [which he refers to as a "patriotic ode"] born at Norfolk than at any other place on the planet."

WB308. H. T. P. [Henry Taylor Parker] "Symphony Concert -- Record of a Disillusionizing Afternoon." *Boston Evening Transcript* December 31, 1918: II/8. Review of the December 30, 1918 performance in Boston. "Mr. Chadwick's 'hymn' sounded neither better nor worse than the 'potboiler' of a practiced composer . . . . a frank piece d'occasion designed for general usage, with little imagination, with no distinction." (See: W83b)

WB309. Parker, W. J. "Boston Composers Represented on Conservatory Program." *Musical America* 46/3 (May 7, 1927): 23. Reports on the performance of April 29, 1927 at New England Conservatory, and also mentions the performance of 1926 in Lowell, Massachusetts [further details of the latter performance not located]. (See: W83e)

W84. THE LILY NYMPH, Dramatic Cantata (7 scenes and an epilogue); (Orchestration begun November 5, 1894; completed July 21, 1895 at West Chop)

Text by: Arlo Bates (1850-1918)
Dedication: Philharmonic Society of Montreal
Published: Schmidt, 1895 (piano-vocal score; publ. plate no. 3829)
Ink holograph score: DLC; MBCM (copy of score; manuscript parts);
       DLC also holds the holograph of the condensed score, dated
       1893
Duration: 35 minutes
For: STTB soloists and SATB chorus
       2. 2. eh. 2. 2./4. 2. 3. 0.
       timp. triangle. glock. cymbals. bass drum. harp. strings.

(See also: W144)

Premiere

W84a.   7 December 1895; New York Musical Society; Cast:
       Clementine de Vere-Sapio, soprano; William H. Rieger, tenor;
       H. Evan Williams, tenor; Archie Crawford, bass; Frank G.
       Dossert, cond.; Carnegie Hall, New York.

Other Selected Performances

W84b.   2 April 1896; Montreal Festival, Montreal, Canada; Cast:
       Emma Juch; Giuseppe Campanari; Barron Berthald; Phil-
       harmonic Society of Montreal, G. W. Chadwick, cond.

W84c.   6 May 1896; Springfield Festival, Springfield, Massa-
       chusetts; Cast: Emma Juch; Giuseppe Campanari; Barron
       Berthald; G. W. Chadwick, cond.

W84d.   28 September 1898; Worcester Festival, Mechanics Hall,
       Worcester, Massachusetts; Cast: Johanna Gadski, soprano;
       H. Evan Williams and Dudley Buck, Jr., tenors; Gwilym
       Miles, bass; The Worcester Festival Chorus and Orchestra, G.
       W. Chadwick, cond.

W84e.   27 September 1899; Worcester Festival, Mechanics Hall,

Worcester, Massachusetts; Cast: Louise B. Voigt, soprano; George Hamlin and W. Theodore Van Yorx, tenors; Gwilym Miles, bass; The Worcester Festival Chorus and Orchestra, G. W. Chadwick, cond.

Bibliography

WB310. Krehbiel, Henry E. Program notes for the premiere performance at Carnegie Hall, December 7, 1895. "In the music Mr. Chadwick has been eclectic, as the loose form of the poem permitted him to be." (See: W84a)

WB311. "A Week's Musical Topics -- Notes of Music -- The Musical Society." *New York Times* November 3, 1895: 13. This article notes the postponement of the originally scheduled concert of the New York Musical Society at which *The Lily Nymph* was to be performed because of the difficulty of retaining "first class orchestral artists."

WB312. "A Week's Musical Topics -- Notes of Music." *New York Times* December 1, 1895: 13. Announcement of the first performance. (See: W84a)

WB313. "A New Choral Society." *New York Daily Tribune* December 9, 1895: 4. Review of the premiere. The writer believes that the composition ". . . is full of good music--the kind of music that all patriotic lovers of the art are glad to hear, ingenious, original, well conceived, well carried out . . . ." (See: W84a)

WB314. "New York Musical Society." *New York Times* December 9, 1895: 4. Review of the premiere. "It is a pretty, sad story, suitable for the good young ladies and gentlemen of the typical provincial singing school. But Mr. Chadwick has made the music a little too difficult for such organizations. It is very sweet and fluent music without a single harsh or discordant phrase." (See: W84a)

WB315. "Festival Opens Brilliantly." *Springfield Daily Republican* (Massachusetts) May 7, 1896: 7. Review of the Springfield Festival performance, May 6, 1896. " . . . it is a beautiful and charming composition; full of delicious orchestration and showing skill in the handling of musical material. It is a real midsummer night's [*sic*] dream . . . ." (See: W84c)

WB316. Hale, Philip. "Worcester and Boston." *The Musical Record* 454 (November 1, 1899): 488-490. Review of the September 27, 1899, performance at Worcester, Massachusetts. "Mr. Chadwick's Lily Nymph, which was poorly performed last year, had evidently been rehearsed with special loving care, for the chorus appeared to better advantage than in the preceding concert . . . ." (See: W84e)

W85. LOVELY ROSABELLE, Ballad (Completed March 7, 1889 in Brookline, Massachusetts)

Text by: Sir Walter Scott (1771-1832)
Dedication: Orchestra and Chorus of the Boston Orchestral Club
Published: Schmidt, 1889 (piano-vocal; publ. plate no. 448/2516);
　　　reprint, Huntsville, Texas: Recital Publications, 1994
Pencil holograph score: DLC; ink holograph score and parts at MBCM
Duration: 10 minutes
For:　S and T soloists and SATB chorus
　　　2. 2. 2. 2./4. 2. 3. 0./timp. harp. strings.

Based on Scott's *The Lay of the Last Minstrel*, Canto Sixth, verse 23.

(See also: W147)

Premiere

W85a.　10 December 1889; Boston Orchestral Club, G. W. Chadwick, cond.; Association Hall, Boston.

Bibliography

WB317. "Music--The Boston Orchestral Club." *Boston Post* December 11, 1889: 4. Review of the premiere. "The Lovely Rosabelle is melodious and clean-cut, sweet in motive and charming in harmony. It is worthy of a further hearing." (See: W85a)

WB318. "Theatres and Concerts -- Association Hall: Orchestral Club." *Boston Evening Transcript* December 12, 1889. Review of the premiere. "The writing for both voices and instruments is thematically interesting, put in original and expressive form, and with much richness of color. The performance left something to be desired . . . ." (See: W85a)

W86. LULLABY (ca. 1889)

Text by: unknown
Dedication: none
Published: Schmidt, 1889 (piano-vocal score)
Holograph score: not located; parts at MBCM
For: SSAA chorus
        string orchestra

(See also: W148)

W87. MEXICAN SERENADE (1920)

Text by: Arthur Guiterman (1871-1943)
Dedication: none
Published: Silver Burdett, 1921 (piano-vocal score)
Holograph score and parts: MBCM
For: SATB chorus
        2. 1. 2. 2./2. 0. 0. 0./triangle. guitar. mandolin. strings.

(See also: W112 [no. 3])

W88. NOEL (A CHRISTMAS PASTORAL) (Begun January 7, 1908; completed 1908)

Texts compiled by: Ida May Chadwick
Dedication: To Carl Stoeckel and composed for the Litchfield County
        University Club
Published: Gray, 1909 (piano/organ-vocal score)
Holograph score: DLC; copy of score and manuscript parts at MBCM
For: SATB soloists and SSAATTBB chorus
        3 (3rd dbls. picc). 2 (2nd dbls. eh). 2. 2. contrabsn. (ad lib.)/
        4. 2. 3. 1/
        timp. harp. organ. strings.

The cover page reads: "The words compiled from various sources."

(See also: W115, W156, W164, W195, and W221)

Premiere

W88a. 2 June 1909; Norfolk Festival; Singers: Marie Rappold,
        soprano; Louise Homer, alto; George Hamlin, tenor; Herbert

Witherspoon, bass; G. W. Chadwick, cond.; Music Shed, Norfolk, Connecticut.

Other Selected Performances

W88b.   19 December 1913; New England Conservatory Orchestra and Chorus, G. W. Chadwick, cond.; Jordan Hall, Boston ("Parvum quando cerno Deum" [for chorus] only).

W88c.   29-31 December 1916; Baltimore Symphony Orchestra with Baltimore Choral Society, Gustave Strube, cond.; Lyric Theatre, Baltimore, Maryland.

W88d.   17 December 1920; New England Conservatory; Cast: Hildred Polly and Norma Jean Erdmann, sopranos; Mildred Mitton and Lela B. Johnstone, altos; Owen Hewitt and Charles Stratton, tenors; Earl Oliver, bass; New England Conservatory Orchestra and Chorus, Alfred Hamer, organ, G. W. Chadwick, cond.; Jordan Hall, Boston.

W88e.   9 December 1921; New England Conservatory; Cast: Norma Jean Erdman, soprano; Mildred Mitten and Antoinette Perner, altos; Owen Hewitt, tenor; Charles Bennett, bass; Harold F. Schwab, organ; New England Conservatory Orchestra and Chorus, G. W. Chadwick, cond.; Jordan Hall, Boston.

W88f.   23 December 1923; Members of the New England Conservatory Chorus, Mr. Zeuch, organist, G. W. Chadwick, cond.; South Congregational Church, Boston.

W88g.   12 February 1924; Katherine Hemmeter and David Blair McCloskey, vocalists; New England Conservatory Orchestra, Wallace Goodrich, cond.; Jordan Hall, Boston ("Hark, A Voice from Yonder Manger," Ms. Hemmeter, and; "I was a Foe to God," Mr. McCloskey, only).

W88h.   14 January 1927; New England Conservatory; Cast: Myrtle Sooy, soprano; Helen Grant, contralto; Maurine Palmer, contralto; Rulon Y. Robison, tenor; David Blair McCloskey, bass; The Choirs of the Church of Redemption (Boston) and the Choral Art Society of Boston University; Thomas Lander, organ; New England Conservatory Orchestra, G. W. Chadwick, cond.; Jordan Hall, Boston.

W88i.   6 March 1930; Chadwick Choral Club of Rochester, Eva
         Wannamaker, dir.; Eastman-Rochester Orchestra, Howard
         Hanson, cond.; "American Composers Series"; Kilbourn Hall,
         Rochester, New York ("Parvum Quando cerno deum" [part 1,
         mvt. 4] only).

W88j.   17 December 1941; New England Conservatory; Cast:
         Gertrude McKinley and Elaine Patee, sopranos; Olive
         Strickland, alto; Clarence F. Mosher, Jr., tenor; Bernard
         Barbeau, bass; Dowell McNeill, organ; New England
         Conservatory Orchestra and Chorus, G. W. Chadwick, cond.;
         Jordan Hall, Boston (incomplete performance; excerpts not
         specified in program).

Bibliography

WB319. "Report of the Music Committee, 1908." Reprinted in J. H.
       Vaill, editor, *Litchfield County Choral Union.* Norfolk,
       Connecticut, 1912: 191-193. Regarding plans for the 1909
       festival: "The program committee, having been accorded the
       privilege of examining the manuscript, believes the work to be
       one of great merit."

WB320. Wilson, Arthur B. "Community Work in Music -- George W.
       Chadwick's Cantata -- Part II." *The Musician* 14/5 (May
       1909): 251. Preview of the premiere. "Mr. Chadwick
       beautifully characterizes the Christmas spirit as the most
       sublime expression of the maternal instinct . . . ." (See:
       W88a)

WB321. Judson, George W. "Noel, Under the Direction of Its
       Composer, Mr. Chadwick, Delighted." *Winsted Evening
       Citizen* (Connecticut) June 3, 1909: 1. Review of the
       premiere. " . . . one of the striking features of last night's
       concert was the universal approval with which Noel was
       greeted by musical critics, not a dissenting voice being heard
       . . . . Mr. Chadwick was presented with a wreath of laurel and
       Mrs. Chadwick a bunch of lilies of the valley in recognition of
       her work, as she arranged the words in Noel." (See: W88a)

WB322. "Community Work in Music." *Winsted Evening Citizen*
       (Connecticut) June 8, 1908. Discussion of *Noel* includes
       information about its genesis and structure. "It is eclectic
       rather than formal in its structure. The work has not the

logical sequence of action which characterizes the drama, yet it observes a steady progress in the development of the theme, which . . . depicts the sweetness and joy of the Christmas spirit . . . ."

WB323. "Mr. Chadwick at Baltimore." *New England Conservatory Magazine-Review* 7/3 (March-April 1917): 84-85. Reports on the Baltimore performances, December 29-31, 1916. " . . . the composer returned from Baltimore greatly impressed, as he stated, by the perfection of the [guest] arrangements and the high musical quality of the work done by the entertaining associations." (See: W88c)

WB324. Warner, A. J. "Chadwick Music in Kilburn [*sic*] Hall." *Rochester Times-Union* March 7, 1930. Review of the March 6, 1930 performance in Rochester, New York. (See: W88i)

W89. ODE FOR THE OPENING OF THE WORLD'S FAIR HELD AT CHICAGO, 1892 (Also known as *Columbian Ode* or *Columbia*); (Begun May 17, 1892; completed July 10, 1892 in Hingham, Massachusetts; rewritten February 1907)

Text by: Harriet Monroe (1860-1936)
Dedication: none
Published: Church, 1892 (piano/organ-vocal score; pub. plate no. 8873)
Ink holograph score: DLC (under the title, *Columbia*); manuscript parts
    at MBCM
Duration: 20 minutes
For: Soprano and tenor soli; double SATB chorus
        Orchestra: 3 (3rd doubles picc). 3. eh (ad lib.). 3. contrabssn./
            4. 3. 3. 1./timp. 4 perc. harp. strings
        Military Band No. 1 (to the north): 1. 2. 4 (one in E-flat). 2./
            4. 3. 3. 1. and 1 euphonium. 1 baritone. basses
        Military Band No. 2 (to the south): SATB saxophone quartet
        Military Band No. 3 (to the east): 3 trumpets. 3 trombones.
            tuba. snare drum

Mvts.: I. "Over the Wide Unknown" (chorus) (C)
        II. "Columbia, Men Beheld Thee Rise" (soli, chorus) (A-flat)
        III. "Lo, Clan on Clan, the World's Great Nations Gather to
            be One" (chorus, instrumentalists) (C)

(See also: W163)

Premiere

W89a. 21 October 1892; World's Columbian Exposition, Chicago,
Illinois; Chicago Columbian Chorus and Exposition
Orchestra, William L. Tomlins, chorus director, Theodore
Thomas, cond.; Festival Hall Series No. 15 (movement nos. I
and III only.)

Other Selected Performances

W89b. October 1892 [precise date undetermined]; According to
"Notes," *Boston Journal* October 31, 1892: 7, the *Columbian
Ode* was performed by a double quartet ". . . at Dr. [Edward
Everett] Hale's Church [South Congregational Church,
Boston]."

W89c. 26 April 1929; New England Conservatory Orchestra and
Chorus, Wallace Goodrich, cond.; Jordan Hall, Boston.

W89d. 6 May 1930; New England Conservatory Orchestra and Choral
Class, assisted by The Apollo Club of Boston, Thompson
Stone, dir., Wallace Goodrich, cond.; Jordan Hall, Boston.

Bibliography

WB325. "Notes." *Boston Journal* March 7, 1892: 5. Announcement
of music selection for the Dedication Ceremonies at the
World's Columbian Exhibition, Chicago.

WB326. "World's Fair Notes." *The Musical Visitor* (April 1892): 103.
Discussion of music for the Dedication Ceremonies. "The
march [by J. K. Paine] and the music to the ode are to be
written especially for the occasion."

WB327. "Drama and Music." *Boston Journal* August 6, 1892: 7.
Notes that Chadwick's *Columbian Ode* has been completed.
"The composer has used for this [composition] three bands of
trumpets, trombones, and military drums to be stationed about
two hundred feet apart . . . ."

WB328. [Editorial column]. *The Musical Visitor* (September 1892):
248-249. This preview article mentions that the composition
is ". . . now on the press," and provides a full description.
"The composer has used for this [the finale] three bands of

trumpets, trombones and military drums, to be stationed about two hundred feet apart in the north, south, and east, respectively (a la Berlioz)."

WB329. "To Sing at the Fair -- Five Thousand Voices Asked for the Dedication." *Chicago Tribune* September 4, 1892: 27. The writer discusses plans for the music at the dedication and lists participating choruses. The program is erroneously given as: Chadwick's "Dedication Ode" [*sic*] and John Knowles Paine's "Columbian Ode" [*sic*]. ". . . many singers have been rehearsing for a year or more . . . ."

WB330. "Music for the Ode -- George W. Chadwick's Work for the Fair Dedication." *Chicago Tribune* September 18, 1892: sec. 5, p. 37. Announcement of the publication of the piano-vocal score, with an assessment of the composition based on the writer's attendance at a rehearsal in which the piano-vocal score was utilized. "Mr. Chadwick's composition has the great merit of conciseness, there being at no time evident a tendency to over elaborate or unduly develop a theme or subject. The ideas, almost without exception, are pleasing without being pedantic. There is no striving for bizarre effects in harmonization, no strained, questionable modulations and transitions, yet harmonic richness and variety are at no time lacking, and skill in invention is clearly shown."

WB331. "Dedication--Music Pleasing and Effective." Chicago *Tribune* October 22, 1892: sec. 1, p. 3. Review of the premiere. "Only the first and third parts of Mr. Chadwick's ode were performed, the lyrical, more delicate part being wisely omitted. It would have proven entirely ineffective in such a [large] hall. The two parts given but deepened the favorable impression made by a study of the pianoforte and vocal score . . . ." (See: W89a)

WB332. "Of Social Interest." *Springfield Graphic* (Massachusetts) October 29, 1892: 16. Announcement of upcoming Hampden Musical Association [Springfield Festival] rehearsals: "Conductor Chadwick is liable to bring a new stick along, and will come with the consciousness that his own was the ode sung at Chicago . . . even if no one could hear a note or distinguish a word of it in the great building." [No performance of the Ode is associated with this article.]

WB333. Jenks, Francis H. "World's Columbian Exposition: The Dedication, October 21, 1892." *Musical Herald of the U. S.* 14/1 (November 1892): 1, 13-17. Report on the premiere performance. Includes four pages of discussion about the World's Columbian Exposition performances and photos of the event. On the *Ode*: "Here are lines that are by turn descriptive, didactic, reflective, and prophetic . . . . Mr. Chadwick is a master of technique, which he knows how to employ as a means--and there stands the artist." (See: W89a)

WB334. Mathews, W. S. B. [William Smythe Babcock]. "The Case of American Composers." *The Musical Record* January 1893: 12. Mathews discusses the general lack of respect given the American composer and uses the poor conditions under which Chadwick's *Ode* was performed as an example: "It was rendered and paid for; but when the time of performance came it was almost entirely left out [the second movement was omitted], so that I doubt whether the composer himself got much information as to the success or non-success of his work from witnessing the performance."

W90. PHOENIX EXPIRANS, Cantata (Begun August 10, 1891; completed the same month in Oxford, New Hampshire)

Text by: Latin Hymn (also in English translation by John Lord Hayes)
Dedication: Hampden County Musical Association (on holograph);
     Springfield Festival, 1892 (on piano-vocal score)
Published: Schmidt, 1892 (piano/organ-vocal; publ. plate no. 2386-56)
Pencil holograph score: DLC; MBCM (manuscript parts and copy of
     score); ink holograph of piano-vocal score is located at MS
Duration: 30 minutes
For: SATB soloists and SATB chorus
      2. 2.(2nd doubles eh.). 2. 2./4. 2. 3. 0./timp. organ. strings.

The text for this work is derived from: Richard Chevenix Trench, *Sacred Latin Poetry*. London: John W. Parker, 1849 (pp. 232-233, "Phoenix Inter Flammas Exspirans [*sic*]," attributed to William Alard).

Premiere

W90a.   5 May 1892; Springfield Festival; City Hall, Springfield, Massachusetts; Singers: Mrs. Lawson, soprano; Mrs. Wyman, alto; Mr. Mockridge, tenor; Mr. [Max] Heinrich, baritone; Boston Festival Orchestra, G. W. Chadwick, cond.

[The premiere featured the Latin version of the text.]

(See also: W166)

Other Selected Performances

W90b. 15 December 1892; Church of Zion and St. Timothy, New York. Singers: Mrs. Theodore Toedt, soprano; Mrs. Hattie Clapper Morris, alto; Charles H. Morse, tenor; Francis Fisher Powers, baritone; Horatio Parker, organ; "chorus of 100"; Richard Henry Warren, cond.

W90c. 5 February 1893; Handel & Haydn Society, Music Hall, Boston. Singers: Lillian Nordica, soprano; Clara Poole, alto; Italo Campanini, tenor; Emil Fischer, bass; B. J. Lang, organ; members of the Boston Symphony Orchestra, Carl Zerrahn, cond.

W90d. 9 February 1913; Handel and Haydn Society, Symphony Hall, Boston. Singers: Caroline Hudson-Alexander, soprano; Ernestine Schumann-Heink and Adelaide Griggs, altos; Paul Althouse, tenor; Frederic Martin, bass; Boston Festival Orchestra, Emil Mollenhauer, cond.

W90e. 9 May 1913; Springfield Festival, Springfield Auditorium, Springfield, Massachusetts. Singers: Marie Sundelius, soprano; Mildred Potter, alto; Mr. Pagdin, tenor; Howard White, bass; Boston Festival Orchestra, Emil Mollenhauer, cond.

W90f. 29 July 1915; San Francisco Eisteddfod [choral competition] featuring the Oakland [California] Chorus, Alexander Stewart, director; and the Haydn Choir of Chicago, Hugh Owen, director; San Francisco Civic Auditorium [Only the final two choruses of the piano-vocal version were featured].

W90g. 13 April 1980; Westfield State College Chorale, Theodore C. Davidovich, cond., Beth Rattman, accompanist; Springfield City Library, Springfield, Massachusetts (excerpts).

Bibliography

WB335. "Of Social Interest." *Springfield Graphic* (Massachusetts)

January 23, 1892: 8. Notice that rehearsals of *Phoenix Expirans* had begun in preparation for the premiere performance. (See: W90a)

WB336. "Of Social Interest." *Springfield Graphic* (Massachusetts) April 23, 1892: 5. After listening to the music at a rehearsal in preparation for the premiere, the writer states: "In listening to the grand choruses of Chadwick's 'Dying Phoenix' one does not wonder that this composer should have been invited to write the Columbian ode for the World's fair." (See: W90a)

WB337. "Chadwick's Phoenix Expirans." *Springfield Daily Republican* (Massachusetts) May 6, 1892: 5. Review of the premiere. "This is a work of the first order in its class; marked by dignity and symmetry of conception, largeness of plan and depth of sentiment; the composer has absorbed the devotional feeling of the Christian poet, and expressed it with a comprehensive knowledge of both voices and instruments, so that the work is unified in his strong inspiration, and no effect is blurred, but it captivates the hearer and bears him on up into lofty realms of thought on divine strains of noble harmony." (See: W90a)

WB338. Hale, Philip. "At Springfield -- The First Performance of Phoenix Expirans." *Boston Journal* May 6, 1892: 5. Review of the premiere. "Mr. Chadwick's contrapuntal technique is not exhibited at the expense of his melodic expression. His harmonies are often exceedingly happy, and here and there a return to Gregorian tonality lends churchly dignity." Further, "The hymn was enthusiastically received by an audience of 1,500 . . . . it deserves the serious attention of any choral society of pretension." (See: W90a)

WB339. "The Church Choral Society." *New York Times* December 16, 1892: 4. Review of the New York performance, December 15, 1892. "It is not a work of marked originality, but it is one of genuine musical dignity and expressiveness. It is written in the modern adaptation of old-established ecclesiastical style, but without any attempt at large elaboration of pure church counterpoint." (See: W90b)

WB340. "Music and Musicians." *The Musical Visitor* 22/1 (January 1893): 10. Preview of the Handel and Haydn Society performance, February 5, 1893. "The music is said to be most excellent in every respect." (See: W90c)

WB341. Regal, Francis E. "The Music Festival in Springfield."
Western New England Magazine 3/6 (June 1913): 233-237.
Review of the May 9, 1913 performance. " . . . one of the
best of the American choral works." The author also notes
that Chadwick was present at the performance. (See: W90e)

WB342. Mason, Redfern. "$10,000 Prize is Sung For by Choruses."
San Francisco Examiner July 30, 1915: 6. Review of the July
29, 1915 performance in San Francisco. "The two choruses
from Chadwick's magnificent setting of the medieval hymn
. . . to my disappointment, was given in English . . . ." (See:
W90f)

W91. THE PILGRIMS (ca. 1890)

Composed: unknown
Text by: Felicia Dorothea Browne Hemans (1793-1835)
Dedication: Arthur P. Schmidt
Published: Schmidt, 1890 (piano-vocal); reprint, Schmidt, 1918 (publ.
plate no. 2703); reprint, Huntsville, Texas: Recital
Publications, 1994
Holograph score: not located; MBCM (copyist's score and parts)
For: SATB chorus
2. 1. 1. 1/1. 4. 1. 1./timp./strings

From Hemans's poem "The Landing of the Pilgrim Father's in New
England," in: *Records of Woman: With Other Poems.* Edinburgh:
William Blackwood, 1828: pp. 261-263.

(See also: W167)

Premiere

W91a.   2 April 1891; Cecilia Society concert; Singers: Gertrude
Edmands; William Ludwig; George J. Parker; Joshua Phippen;
G. W. Chadwick, cond.; Music Hall, Boston.

Other Selected Performances

W91b.   19 February 1914; Concord, New Hampshire, Mr. Conant,
cond. [A program for this performance, incomplete and dated
by hand, is located in Chadwick's 1914 *Journal*]

W91c.   18 February 1917; Handel & Haydn Society; Singers: Geneva Jeffords, soprano; William W. Hicks, tenor; G. Roberts Lunger, bass; Boston Festival Orchestra, Emil Mollenhauer, cond.; Jordan Hall, Boston.

W91d.   13 April 1980; Westfield State College Chorale, Theodore C. Davidovich, cond., Beth Rattman, accompanist; Springfield City Library, Springfield, Massachusetts (piano-vocal version).

Bibliography

WB343. "Theatres, Concerts, Lectures -- The Cecilia Concert." *Boston Evening Transcript* April 3, 1891: 2. Review of the premiere. " . . . it is dignified, sweet, and inspiring. Its movement is smooth, melodious, and free; it follows the words in a natural manner, and goes straight through without undue dwelling at any point." (See: W91a)

W92. SILENTLY SWAYING ON THE WATER'S QUIET BREAST (ca. 1916)

Text by: Victor von Scheffel (trans. by Isabella G. Parker)
Dedication: Eurydice Club of Philadelphia
Published: Ditson, 1916 (piano-vocal score)
Holograph score and parts: MBCM
For: SSAA chorus/harp. strings.

(See also: W175)

Selected Performance

W92a.   6 March 1930; Chadwick Choral Club of Rochester, Eva Wannamaker, dir.; Eastman-Rochester Orchestra, Howard Hanson, cond.; "American Composers Series"; Kilbourn Hall, Rochester, New York.

Bibliography

WB344. Warner, A. J. "Chadwick Music in Kilburn [*sic*] Hall." *Rochester Times-Union* March 7, 1930. Review of the March 6, 1930 concert in Rochester, New York. (See: W92a)

W93. THE SONG OF THE VIKING (1882; orchestrated 1914)

Text by: Louisa T. Craigin
Dedication: Concordia Singing Society, Leipzig
Published: Schmidt, 1882 (piano-vocal score)
Holograph full score, piano-vocal score, and parts: MBCM
For: TTBB chorus
      picc. 2. 2. 2. 2./4. 2. 3. 0./timp. bass drum. cymbals. strings.

This 1914 orchestrated version was prepared in German and dedicated "dem Gesang-Verein Concordia in Leipzig bruderschaftlich gewidmet." According to Chadwick's *Memoirs* (1877-1880), he sang second bass in the Concordia Singing Society while a student at the Leipzig Conservatory.

(See also: W176)

Premiere

W93a.   ?1882-1883 concert season; The Mozart Society of Boston [other details not located]. (See: WB345)

Selected Performances

W93b.   10 February 1886; Apollo Club concert, Music Hall, Boston [version for chorus and piano].

W93c.   21 April 1930; "Concert of Compositions of George W. Chadwick," New England Conservatory Orchestra and Glee Club, Francis Findlay, cond.; Jordan Hall, Boston.

Bibliography

WB345. "Our Musical Hopper." *Church's Musical Visitor* 11/12 (September 1882): 328. "Mr. G. W. Chadwick, the young and talented composer and conductor, has written music to "The Song of the Viking," which is to be produced by the Mozart Society of Boston the coming season." [Further information not discerned.] (See: W93a)

WB346. "Theatres and Concerts -- The Apollo Concert." *Boston Evening Transcript* February 11, 1886: 1. Review of the February 10, 1886 performance by the Apollo Club. "Though the music has not much that is strikingly original, it has a certain strength, which was well expressed by the club." (See: W93b)

W94. THESE TO THE FRONT (1918)

Text by: Mark A. DeWolfe Howe (1864-1960)
Dedication: none
Published: Ditson, 1918 (piano-vocal score)
Holograph score: not located; holograph instrumental parts at MBCM
For: TTBB chorus
        1. 0. 4 (1 e-flat, 3 b-flat). 1./
        4. 4 (1 solo). 0. 3 baritones. 2./drums

(See also: W184)

W95. THE VIKING'S LAST VOYAGE (Completed March, 1881)

Text by: Sylvester Baxter (1850-1927)
Dedication: A. Parker Browne
Published: Schmidt, 1881 (piano-vocal score; reprinted 1909)
Ink holograph score: MBCM; holograph parts not located
Duration: 15 minutes
For: Baritone soloist, TTBB chorus
        2. 2. 2. 2./4. 2. 3. 0./timp. strings.

(See also: W193)

Premiere

W95a.   22 and 26 April 1881; Apollo Club concert; C. E. Hay, baritone, G. W. Chadwick, cond.; Boston.

Bibliography

WB347. "Musical." *Boston Evening Transcript* April 23, 1881: 3. Review of the premiere. The work ". . . deals cleverly in descriptive effects of instrumentation in the orchestral accompaniment, . . . has an easy flow of graceful melody, and rises into a superb climax . . . ." (See: W95a)

WB348. "Here and There." *Church's Musical Visitor* 10/8 (May 1881): 218. Announcement of the premiere. "Mr. Chadwick's latest work, a dramatic composition for male chorus, called 'The Viking's Last Voyage,' will be produced at the next concert of the Apollo Club. The composer regards it as his strongest work." (See: W95a)

WB349. "Recent Concerts -- Apollo Club." *Dwight's Journal of Music* 41/1045 (May 7, 1881): 76. Review of the premiere. "The young composer, who was warmly welcomed, conducted the performance. The cantata, almost unavoidably, seemed somewhat in the vein of Max Bruch's *Frithjof* music, heroic, gloomy, wild, tempestuous, now mournful, now exulting, nor does it lag far behind that for vivid graphic power, felicitous invention, or mastery of the art of thematic development and instrumental coloring." (See: W95a)

WB350. "Boston's Musical Clubs." *The Musical Record* 161 (October 29, 1881): 65-66. In this inventory of Boston's music club activities, the writer notes that a presumably recent performance of *The Viking's Last Voyage* by the Apollo Club ". . . was very favorably received." [Further details of this performance have not been located.]

MUSIC FOR SOLO VOICE
WITH ORCHESTRA

W96. **AGHADOE** Irish Ballad (Completed July 8, 1910 at West Chop)

Text by: John Todhunter
Dedication: Lilla Ormond
Published: Schmidt, 1911 (piano-vocal score)
Pencil holograph score and parts: DLC; MBCM (copy of score)
For: Alto solo
      picc. 2. 2. 2. 2./4. 2. 3. 0./timp. tamb. cymbals. harp. strings.

Regarding the title, a note on the published music states: "Pronounced approximately like the German 'Ach-du.' "

(See also: W200)

Selected Performances

W96a. 14 May 1914; Mima Montgomery, alto; New England Conservatory Orchestra, G. W. Chadwick, cond.; Jordan Hall, Boston.

W96b. 16 April 1915; Dorothy Cook, alto; New England Conservatory Orchestra, G. W. Chadwick, cond.; Jordan Hall, Boston.

W96c. 23 January 1923; Rebecca D. Stoy, alto; New England Conservatory Orchestra, Wallace Goodrich, cond.; Jordan Hall,
Boston.

W97. A BALLAD OF TREES AND THE MASTER (Composed ca.
1899; scored for orchestra at West Chop beginning July 3, 1920)

Text by: Sidney Lanier (1842-1881)
Dedication: D. Ffrangcon-Davies
Unpublished in orchestral version; song version, Ditson, 1899
Holograph score and parts: MBCM
For: Low or medium voice
2. 2. 2. 2./2. 2. 3. 0./timp. strings.

Based on Lanier's poem *A Ballad of Trees and the Master* (1880).

(See also: W108, W205)

Premiere

W97a. 21 November 1904; All-Chadwick concert; Herbert
Witherspoon, baritone; members of the Boston Symphony
Orchestra, G. W. Chadwick, cond.; Jordan Hall, Boston.

Other Selected Performance

W97b. 17 February 1924; All-Chadwick program; Charles Bennett,
soloist; People's Symphony Orchestra, G. W. Chadwick,
cond.; St. James Theatre, Boston.

Bibliography

WB351. R. R. G. "Jordan Hall: Mr. Chadwick's Concert." *Boston
Evening Transcript* November 22, 1904: 15. Review of the
November 21, 1904 performance in Boston. This review does
not specifically consider this composition, but the writer says
of the event: "To turn to last night's concert, it must at once
be set down as a success." (See: W97a.)

W98. THE CURFEW (Composed ca. 1914; scored for orchestra during the
summer of 1920 at West Chop)

Text by: Henry Wadsworth Longfellow (1807-1882)
Dedication: [song version to Marianne Kneisel]
Unpublished in orchestra version; song version, Schmidt, 1914
Holograph score and parts: MBCM
For: Low or medium voice
2. eh. 2. 2./2. 0. 0. 0./harp, strings

(See also: W212)

Selected Performances

W98a. 17 February 1924; All-Chadwick program; Charles Bennett, soloist; People's Symphony Orchestra, G. W. Chadwick, cond.; St. James Theatre, Boston.

W98b. 16 March 1926; Adelaide Viewig, vocalist; New England Conservatory Orchestra, Wallace Goodrich, cond.; Jordan Hall, Boston.

W99. DRAKE'S DRUM (The song version was composed on September 13, 1917; the date of the orchestration is unknown)

Text by: Henry Newbold
Dedication: none for orchestral version
Unpublished in orchestra version; song version, Ditson, 1920
Holograph score and parts: MBCM
For: Low or medium voice
2. 2. 2. 2./2. 2. 3. 0./timp. snare drum. strings.

(See also: W265 [no. 2])

Premiere

W99a. 17 February 1924; All-Chadwick program; Charles Bennett, soloist; People's Symphony Orchestra, G. W. Chadwick, cond.; St. James Theatre, Boston.

W100. JOSHUA (originally titled *Jericho March*; the date of orchestration is unknown)

Text by: Richard Darwin Ware (1869-1931)
Dedication: none
Unpublished in orchestral version; song and chorus versions, Ditson, 1919

Pencil holograph score and parts: MBCM
For: Medium voice
          picc. 2. 2. 2. 2./4. 2. 3. 0./
          timp. snare. bass drum. cymbals. strings.

This work, a vocalist with orchestra version of the song *Joshua*, was originally titled *Jericho March*; the title was later changed to *Joshua*.

(See also: W10, W82, W138, W234)

W101. LOCHINVAR, Ballad (Completed March, 1896)

Text by: Sir Walter Scott (1771-1832)
Dedication: Max Heinrich
Published: Schmidt, 1896 (piano-vocal score)
Pencil holograph score: DLC; copyist's score and manuscript parts at
          MBCM
For: Baritone soloist
          2 (2nd doubles picc). 2. 2. 2./4. 2. 3. 0./timp. harp. strings.

Based on Scott's *Marmion*, Canto Fifth ("The Court"), verse 12 ("Lochinvar").

(See also: W241)

Premiere

W101a. 7 May 1896; Springfield Festival; Max Heinrich, baritone; G. W. Chadwick, cond.; Springfield, Massachusetts.

Other Selected Performances

W101b. 14 January 1900; Recital performance by Stephen Townsend, baritone; Gustave Strube, cond.; Jordan Hall, Boston.

W101c. 21 November 1904; All-Chadwick concert; Herbert Witherspoon, baritone; members of the Boston Symphony Orchestra, G. W. Chadwick, cond.; Jordan Hall, Boston.

W101d. 24/25 May 1907; May Music Festival at the Iowa State Normal School; Herbert Witherspoon, baritone; Theodore Thomas Orchestra, Frederick Stock, cond.; Cedar Rapids, Iowa.

W101e. 16 February 1908; U. S. Kerr, baritone; Minneapolis Symphony Orchestra, Emil Oberhoffer, cond.; The Auditorium, Minneapolis, Minnesota.

W101f. 14 January 1909; Stephen Townsend, baritone; members of the Boston Symphony Orchestra, Gustave Strube, cond.; Jordan Hall, Boston.

W101g. 18 April 1909; American Music Society concert; David Bispham, baritone; People's Symphony Orchestra, G. W. Chadwick, cond.; Carnegie Hall, New York City.

W101h. 28 May 1909; Grand Rapids May Festival; Herbert Witherspoon, baritone; Theodore Thomas Orchestra, Frederick Stock, cond.; Grand Rapids, Michigan.

W101i. 16 February 1910; Herbert Witherspoon, baritone; Theodore Thomas Orchestra, Frederick Stock, cond.; Cleveland, Ohio.

W101j. 14 March 1913; F. Morse Wemple, baritone; New England Conservatory Orchestra, G. W. Chadwick, cond.; Jordan Hall, Boston.

W101k. 11/12 January 1918; Reinald Werrenrath, soloist; Saint Louis Symphony Orchestra, Max Zach, cond.; Saint Louis, Missouri.

W101l. 17 February 1924; All-Chadwick program; Charles Bennett, baritone; People's Symphony Orchestra, G. W. Chadwick, cond.; St. James Theatre, Boston.

W101m. 23 July 1943; Private Glen Darwin, soloist; National Symphony Orchestra [conductor not discerned]; Washington, D. C. [precise location not discerned].

Bibliography

WB352. "Mme. Nordica and Max Heinrich." *Springfield Daily Republican* (Massachusetts) May 8, 1896: 6. Review of the premiere. "Lochinvar is a tempting theme for a composer with the gift of suggestive pictorial music, and while Mr. Chadwick has not pressed realism to extremes, the skirl of the bagpipes, the tread of the dancers, and the racing and chasing of Cannobie Lee are effectively delineated." (See: W101a)

WB353. Elson, Louis C. "Stephen Townsend Gives Orchestral-Vocal Concert." *Boston Daily Advertiser* January 15, 1900: 3. Review of the January 14, 1900 recital. Elson thought *Lochinvar* ". . . the best of the native works given." However, ". . . the ending of Lochinvar is better than the beginning." (See: W101b)

WB354. R. R. G. "Jordan Hall: Mr. Chadwick's Concert." *Boston Evening Transcript* November 22, 1904: 15. Review of the November 21, 1904 performance in Boston. ". . . an effective composition that has been strangely neglected." (See: W101c)

WB355. "Concerts of the Week." *New York Times* April 18, 1909: VI/7. Announcement of the People's Symphony concert, April 18, 1909. (See: W101g)

WB356. "Concert of American Music." *New York Times* April 19, 1909: 2. Review of the People's Symphony concert, April 18, 1909. The concert, organized by David Bispham, was intended ". . . to bring together certain distinctive features of music written by Americans." (See: W101g)

WB357. Krehbiel, Henry E. "Music -- A Concert of American Compositions." *New York Daily Tribune* April 19, 1909: 7. Review of the New York performance of April 18, 1909. "It is a fluent piece of writing, frankly melodious and which in its introduction of Scotch color (the rhythm of the reel and the skirling and drone of the pipes in the episode of the dance) suggested that possibly [Charles Villiers] Stanford's 'Phaudrig Crohoore' [op. 62, 1896] had not been without effective influence." (See: W101g)

WB358. "American Music Society Concert." *Musical Courier* 58/16 (April 21, 1909): 25. Review of the New York performance of April 18, 1909. "Chadwick's ballad was rousingly done by Bispham, and exhibited the solid musicianship and sure expression of a composer who has something to say and knows how to say it." (See: W101g)

WB359. H. T. P. [Henry Taylor Parker]. "Week-End Round Over Bostonian Concert-Giving." *Boston Evening Transcript* February 18, 1924: 8. Review of the People's Symphony presentation, February 17, 1924. " . . . the assembled pieces bore witness to the range of his musical mind and imagination." (See: W101l)

W102. PIRATE SONG (Date of orchestration unknown)

Text by: Arthur Conan Doyle (1859-1930)
Dedication: Charles Bennett [in song version]
Unpublished in orchestral version; solo song version, Ditson, 1920
Holograph score and parts: MBCM
For: Baritone soloist
          picc. 2. 2. 2. 2./2. 2. 3. 0./timp. strings.

(See also: W265 [no. 3])

W103. VOICE OF PHILOMEL (Composed ca. 1914; scored for orchestra during the summer of 1920 at West Chop)

Text by: David Kilburn Stevens (1860-1946)
Dedication: none in this version; Louise Homer in song version
Unpublished in orchestral version; solo song version, Schirmer, 1914
Holograph score and parts: MBCM

For: Low or medium voice
          2. eh. 2. 2./2. 0. 0. 0./strings

(See also: W219 [no. 1])

Premiere

W103a. 17 February 1924; All-Chadwick program; Charles Bennett, baritone; People's Symphony Orchestra, G. W. Chadwick, cond.; St. James Theatre, Boston.

MUSIC FOR CHORUS

W104. ABIDE WITH ME (Sacred)

For: SAT, organ
Hymn text by: Henry F. Lyte
Dedication: O. B. Brown
Holograph: DLC
Published: Schmidt, 1888

W105. ART THOU WEARY (Anthem)

For: SATB, organ
Published: Schmidt, 1890 (Sacred Octavo Series No. 94)

W106. THE AUTUMN WINDS ARE CHILL

For: SSA, piano
Text by: Arlo Bates (1850-1918)
Holograph: DLC
Published: Schmidt, 1890

This is an arrangement of the song from *Songs of Brittany* (See: W258 [no.4])

W107. AWAKE UP MY GLORY (Anthem)

For: SATB
Published: Schmidt, 1895

W108. A BALLAD OF TREES AND THE MASTER (1927)

For: SATB, piano or organ
Text by: Sidney Lanier (1842-1881)
Holograph: DLC
Published: Ditson, 1930

(See also: W97 and W205)

W109. THE BEATITUDES (Sacred)

For: SATB, organ
Text: Gospel according to St. Matthew (chapter 5, verses 3-5, 7-9, 12)
Holograph: DLC
Published: Schmidt, 1895 (publ. plate no. 3761-2); reprint, Fort
        Lauderdale, Florida: Walton Music Corporation, 1996 [Library
        of Congress Choral Series, no. WLC-1004.]

W110. BEHOLD THE WORKS OF THE LORD (Anthem)

For: SATB
Published: Schmidt, 1891

W111. THE BLUEBELLS OF NEW ENGLAND

For: SSA, piano
Text by: Thomas Bailey Aldrich (1836-1907)
Dedication: St. Cecilia Club of New York, Victor Harris, cond.
Published: Ditson, 1917

W112. A BOOK OF CHORUSES FOR HIGH SCHOOLS AND CHORAL SOCIETIES

1. Land of Our Hearts (John Hall Ingham) (SATB) (p. 1) (See also: W83 and W142)
2. Caravan Song (Alfred H. Hyatt) (SATB, piano) (p. 2)
3. Mexican Serenade (Arthur Guiterman) (SATB, piano) (p. 29) (See also: W87)
4. Mister Moon (Bliss Carman) (SSAA, piano) (p. 147)
5. Buie Annajohn (Bliss Carman) (SATB, piano) (p. 189)
6. Chorus of Pilgrim Women (Josephine Peabody) (SSAA, piano) (p. 227)
7. Deep in the Soul of a Rose (Alfred H. Hyatt) (SSA, piano) (p. 247)
8. Little Lac Grenier (Wm. H. Drummond) (SSATTB, piano) (p. 295)

Holographs: MB (nos. 2, 5-7); DLC (nos. 1, 3-4, 8)
Published: Silver-Burdett, 1923; This volume, edited by Chadwick, Osbourne McConathy, Edward Bailey Birge, and W. Otto Miessner, includes the above-listed choruses by Chadwick.

No. 1 is the hymn from the cantata of the same title; No. 6 was "written especially for the Pilgrim Tercentenary Pageant of 1921"; Nos. 2-5 and 7-8 were "composed for this book."

W113. BRIGHTEST AND BEST (Christmas Song)

For: SATB
Text by: R. [Reginald?] Heber
Published: Schmidt, 1888 (in both choral and song versions)

(See also: W208)

W114. BUSY LARK (School Chorus)

For: Children's voices
Text by: Geoffrey Chaucer (1340?-1400)
Published: Birchard, 1912

W115. A CHILD IS BORN IN BETHLEHEM (Carol from NOEL)

For: SATB
Text by: "From the Latin (14th Century)"
Published: Gray, 1909

(See also: W88 and W131 [no. 11])

W116. CHORUS OF HEBREWS (Chorus from JUDITH)

For: SATB, piano
Text by: William Chauncy Langdon (1871-1947)
Published: Schirmer, 1901; Ditson, 1928

(See also: W69 and W131 [no. 14])

W117. A CHRISTMAS GREETING

For: SATB, piano (ad lib.)
Text by: Words from "Life"
Facsimile: DLC
Published: Privately, 1925; reprint, Ditson, 1928

(See also: W131 [no. 12])

W118. COME HITHER YE FAITHFUL (Christmas Anthem)

For: SATB
Published: Schmidt, 1891

W119. COMMEMORATION ODE (ca. 1927-1928)

For: SATB, piano
Text by: James Russell Lowell (1819-1891)
Dedication: none
Published: Ditson, 1928 (publ. plate no. 76251)

(See also: W75)

W120. DEDICATION ODE, OP. 15 (Completed March 18, 1883)

For: SATB soloists and chorus, piano or organ

Text by: Rev. Henry Bernard Carpenter
Dedication: Rev. Henry Bernard Carpenter
Published: Schmidt, 1886 (Octavo Edition, 1st Series, No. 7)

(See also: W76)

W121. DOLLY

For: SSA, piano
Text by: Auston Dobson
Published: Ditson, 1917

Selected Performance

W119a. 1 January 1919; MacDowell Club concert; Renee Longy,
piano, Georges Longy, cond.; Jordan Hall, Boston.

W122. ECCE JAM NOCTIS (1897)

For: TTBB, organ
Text by: St. Gregory of Tours (538-604); in Latin with English
translation by Isabella G. Parker
Composed for the commencement exercises of Yale University, 1897
Holograph: DLC; manuscript chorus parts at CtY
Published: Schmidt, 1897 (publ. plate no. 4407-9)

(See also: W77)

W123. ELFIN SONG

For: SSAA, piano
Text by: Joseph Rodman Drake (1795-1820); from "The Culprit Fay"
(1859)
Dedication: S. L. Herrmann and the Treble Clef Club of Philadelphia
Holograph: DLC
Published: Schmidt, 1910

(See also: W78)

W124. FATHERS OF THE FREE (ca. 1927)

For: SATB, piano
Text by: Elmer Ellsworth Brown (1861-1934)
Dedication: "Written and composed for the Hall of Fame"

Published: Gray, 1927

(See also: W79)

W125. THE FIGHTING MEN (March with Chorus)

For: Unison chorus, piano
Text by: Mark A. DeWolfe Howe (1864-1960)
Holograph: MBCM
Published: Birchard, 1918

(See also: W80)

W126. FOUR PARTSONGS FOR MALE VOICES

1. The Boy and the Owl
2. Serenade
3. Drinking Song
4. When Love was Young

For: TTBB
Text by: John Leslie Breck (nos. 1 and 2); Arlo Bates (nos. 3 and 4)
Dedication: David Loring (nos. 1-4)
Published: Schmidt, 1886

Selected Performance

W126a. 8 March 1893; Apollo Club concert; Music Hall, Boston
(no. 1 only).

Bibliography

WB360. "Theatres and Concerts." *Boston Evening Transcript* March 9,
1893: 5. Review of the March 8, 1893 performance. "The
funny things by Mr. Chadwick and Mr. [Edward] MacDowell
[his "Dance of the Gnomes"] are simply delicious. The club
sang them with its usual perfection." (See: W126a)

WB361. Jenks, Francis H. "Music in Boston -- Other Matters." The
Musical Herald of the U. S. 14/6 (April 1893): 139-140.
Review of the March 8, 1893 performance. "The droll pieces
by Chadwick and [Edward] MacDowell [his "Dance of the
Gnomes"] were the novelties . . . ." (See: W126a)

W127. GOD BE MERCIFUL (Anthem)

>For: SATB, organ
>Text by: Deus misereatur
>Dedication: Rev. George J. Prescott
>Published: Schmidt, 1890

W128. HAIL US DOCTORS OF SONG (SAENGERFEST LIED)

>For: TTBB, piano
>Text by: John Koren
>Published: Boston: The Saengerfest, 1914

W129. HARK! HARK, MY SOUL (Anthem)

>For: Alto solo, SATB, organ
>Text by: Frederick William Faber (1814-1863)
>Holograph: NRU-Mus
>Published: Schirmer, 1903

>(See also: W227)

W130. HERE COMES THE FLAG (School Chorus)

>For: Children's voices
>Text by: Arthur Macy (1842-1904)
>Dedication: "To All American Children Who Love Their Flag"
>Published: Birchard, 1918 ("Songs of Freedom" series)

>(See also: W131 [no. 9])

W131. HOLIDAY SONGS (FOR HIGH SCHOOLS AND CHORAL SOCIETIES BEING SONGS APPROPRIATE FOR PATRIOTIC & POPULAR FESTIVALS)

>1. New Year's Song (G. E. Troutbeck)
>2. A Valentine (Matilda B. Edwards)
>3. The Runaway (Cale Young Rice)
>4. A May Carol (Frank Dempster Sherman)
>5. What Say (Grace F. Norton)
>6. The Immortal (Spring Song) (Cale Young Rice) (See also: W132)
>7. In the Hammock We Swing ("For Mother's Day") (Charles Stuart Pratt)
>8. Concord Hymn ("For Patriots' Day") (Ralph Waldo Emerson)

9. Here Comes the Flag (Independence Day) (Arthur Macy) (See also: W130)
10. Angel of Peace ("For Armistice Day") (Oliver Wendell Holmes)
11. A Child is Born in Bethlehem (Christmas carol) (Latin, 14th century) (See also: W115)
12. A Christmas Greeting (Carol) (Words from "Life") (See also: W117)
13. The Mistletoe Bough (Christmas) (Words from "Life")
14. Chorus of Hebrews (from *Judith*) (William Chauncy Langdon) (See also: W69)
15. Prayer ("O Noblest of Judah's Women" from *Judith*) (William Chauncy Langdon) (See also: W69 and W162)
16. Evening (S. Baring-Gould)

For: SATB (nos. 1-5, 8, 10, 13); SATTBB (no. 16); SSA (no. 7); piano (ad lib. on nos. 1, 10, 13, 16)
Dedication: None
Holographs: DLC
Published: Ditson, 1928 (publ. plate no. 76058)

Selected Performance

W131a. 10 and 14 May 1883; Boylston Club concert, Music Hall, Boston (no. 4 only [reported as "May Song"]).

W132. THE IMMORTAL (Spring Song)

For: SATB, piano
Text by: Cale Young Rice (1872-1943)
Published: Birchard, 1923

(See also: W131 [no. 6])

W133. IN A CHINA SHOP

For: SSAA, piano
Text by: George C. Hellman
Dedication: "To the Three C's of Boston" [A possible reference to the composer's wife and two children, i.e., The Chadwicks.]
Published: Schmidt, 1910

W134. INCONSTANCY

For: SATB or SSAA or TTBB, piano (ad lib.)

Text by: William Shakespeare (1564-1616)
Dedication: S. L. Herrmann and the Treble Clef Club of Philadelphia
Published: Schmidt, 1910

Selected Performances

W134a. 5 April 1911; MacDowell Club concert, Arthur Foote, cond.;
Jordan Hall, Boston.

W134b. 26 March 1912; St. Cecilia Club, Victor Harris, cond.;
Charles Gilbert Spross, pianist; Grand Ballroom, Waldorf-
Astoria Hotel, New York City.

Bibliography

WB362. "St. Cecilia Concert." *New York Times* March 27, 1912: 13.
Review of the March 26, 1912 performance. The critic only
mentions that "incidental music to Shakespeare" was included
on the concert. (See: W134b)

WB363. A. W. K. "St. Cecilia Club a Splendid Chorus." *Musical
America* 15/22 (April 6, 1912): 34. This review of the March
26, 1912, performance does not discuss *Inconstancy* in any
detail. (See: W134b)

W135. IT WAS A LOVER AND HIS LASS

For: SSA, piano; or TTBB, piano (ad lib.)
Text by: William Shakespeare (1564-1616)
Dedication: S. L. Herrmann and the Treble Clef Club of Philadelphia
Published: Schmidt, 1910

W136. JABBERWOCKY (Humorous Song)

For: TTBB
Text by: Lewis Carroll (1832-1898)
Dedication: "To Our Society" [Apollo Club of Boston]
Published: Schmidt, 1886

Premiere

W136a. 23 February 1887; Apollo Club concert; Mr. B. J. Lang,
cond.; Music Hall, Boston.

Other Selected Performances

W136b. 10 December 1887; Apollo Club concert; [conductor not discerned]; Boston [precise location not discerned].

W136c. 20 March 1895; Apollo Club concert; [conductor not discerned]; Boston [precise location not discerned].

Bibliography

WB364. "Theatres and Concerts -- The Apollo Club." *Boston Evening Transcript* February 24, 1887: 1. Review of the premiere. " . . . humorous music set to humorous words. . . . The music is dramatically expressive of the poem throughout, and the grand rhetorical figures of the verses are brought out with redoubled splendor." (See: W136a)

WB365. "Review of Recent Concert." *The Musical Herald* 8/4 (April 1887): 112. Review of the premiere. "The humor of Mr. Chadwick's 'Jabberwocky' cannot be overstated. It is a fine instance of a classical composer at play, and belongs to the healthy English school." (See: W136a)

W137. JEHOVAH REIGNS IN MAJESTY (Anthem)

For: TTBB, organ
Text by: Psalm 99
Dedication: Harry B. Jepson
Holograph: DLC
Published: Ditson, 1916

(See also: W81)

W138. JOSHUA (Humorous Song)

For: TTBB, piano
Text by: Richard Darwin Ware (1869-1931)
Published: Ditson, 1919

(See also: W10, W82, W100, W234)

W139. JUBILATE IN B-FLAT (Sacred)

For: SATB, organ

Text by: Psalm 100
Published: Schmidt, 1895

W140. JUNE

For: SSA, piano
Text by: Justin H. Smith
Published: Ditson, 1918

W141. THE LAMB (School Chorus)

For: Children's voices
Text by: William Blake (1757-1827)
Published: Birchard, 1914

W142. LAND OF OUR HEARTS (Patriotic Hymn)

For: SATB, piano
Text by: John Hall Ingham
Dedication: Mr. and Mrs. Carl Stoeckel
Published: Church, 1918

(See also: W83)

W143. THE LARK THAT SANG WHEN MORNING BROKE

For: SSA, piano
Text by: Arlo Bates (1850-1918)
Published: Schmidt, 1890; reprint, 1914

This is an arrangement of the song from *Songs of Brittany* (See: W258 [no.9])

W144. THE LILY NYMPH (Dramatic Cantata)

For: STTB soloists and SATB chorus, piano
Text by: Arlo Bates (1850-1918)
Dedication: Philharmonic Society of Montreal
Published: Schmidt, 1895 (publ. plate no. 3829)

(See also: W84)

W145. LORD OF ALL POWER AND MIGHT (Anthem)

For: SATB, organ
Text by: unknown
Published: Schmidt, 1895

W146. LOVE IS FLEETING AS THE WIND

For: SSA, piano
Text by: Arlo Bates (1850-1918)
Published: Schmidt, 1890; reprint, 1914

This is an arrangement of the song from *Songs of Brittany* (See: W258 [no.6])

W147. LOVELY ROSABELLE (Ballad)

For: S and T soloists and SATB chorus, piano
Text by: Sir Walter Scott (1771-1832)
Dedication: Orchestra and Chorus of the Boston Orchestral Club
Published: Schmidt, 1889 (publ. plate no. 448/2516); reprint,
        Huntsville, Texas: Recital Publications, 1994

(See also: W85)

W148. LULLABY

For: SSAA, piano
Text by: unknown
Published: Schmidt, 1889

(See also: W86)

W149. A MADRIGAL FOR CHRISTMAS

For: SATB
Text by: G. W. Chadwick (1854-1931)
Published: Privately, ca. 1925 (publ. plate no. 421)

W150. MARGARITA

For: TTBB
Text by: Victor von Scheffel (Texts in German and English)
Published: Schmidt, 1881 (The Arlington [Club] Collection)

Selected Performances

W150a. 7 March 1881; Arlington Club concert; William J. Winch, conductor; assisted by G. W. Chadwick, organ; Tremont Temple, Boston.

W150b. 16 May 1881; Arlington Club concert; William J. Winch, conductor; assisted by G. W. Chadwick, organ; Tremont Temple, Boston.

Bibliography

WB366. "New Music." *Boston Evening Transcript* March 7, 1881: 6. Announcement of publication in the Arlington Club's part-song series.

WB367. Clifford [only name supplied]. "Correspondence -- Boston." *Church's Musical Visitor* 10/7 (April 1881): 188. Notes performance of March 7, 1881. Chadwick served as organist at the concert. "One of the pieces sung was a new and beautiful part song by Mr. Chadwick . . . ." (See: W150a)

WB368. "Musical." *Boston Evening Transcript* May 17, 1881: 4. Review of the May 16, 1881 concert. The music was ". . . well rendered." (See: W150b)

W151. MARY'S LULLABY

For: SSAA, piano (ad lib.)
Text by: Cora Adele Matson Dolson
Dedication: "To the Three C's of Boston" [A possible reference to the composer's wife and two children, i.e., The Chadwicks.]
Holograph: DLC
Published: Schmidt, 1910 (Octavo Series No. 478; publ. plate no. 8819-2); reprint, Fort Lauderdale, Florida: Walton Music Corporation, 1996 [Library of Congress Choral Series, no. WLC-2000].

Selected Performance

W151a. 6 March 1930; Chadwick Choral Club of Rochester, Eva Wannamaker; Eastman-Rochester Orchestra, Howard Hanson, cond.; "American Composers Series"; Kilbourn Hall, Rochester, New York.

Bibliography

WB369. Warner, A. J. "Chadwick Music in Kilburn [*sic*] Hall."
Rochester Times-Union March 7, 1930. Review of the March
6, 1930 performance in Rochester, New York. (See: W151a)

WB370. Isaacs, Kevin Jay. Review of Walton Music Corporation
reprint. In *Choral Journal* 37/2 (September 1996): 74-75.
"This brief but moving work is appropriate for either the
Advent or Lenten season . . . ."

W152. MISS NANCY'S GOWN (Minuet)

For: SSA, piano
Text by: Zitella Cook
Dedication: "To the Three C's of Boston" [A possible reference to the
composer's wife and two children, i.e., The Chadwicks.]
Published: Schmidt, 1910

Selected Performance

W152a. 25 April 1926; Federated Choral Society, George Sawyer
Dunham, conductor; Susan Williams, piano; Copley Theatre,
Boston.

W153. MORN'S ROSEATE HUES (Easter Anthem)

For: Alto and bass soli, SATB chorus, piano or organ
Text from: The Hymnal (1892), nos. 120, 121
Published: Novello, 1903 ("The Church Music Review Supplement,
No. 17"); reprint, Orleans, Massachusetts: Paraclete Press,
1994 (Craig Timberlake, editor).

W154. MY SWEETHEART GAVE A CRIMSON BLOSSOM

For: SSA, piano
Text by: Arlo Bates (1850-1918)
Published: Schmidt, 1890; reprint, 1914

This is an arrangement of the song from *Songs of Brittany* (See: W258
[no.7])

W155. NOBLE'S TRADITIONS (School Song)

>   For: Children's voices, piano
>   Text by: Robert W. Rivers
>   Published: Boston: The Nobleman, 1913

W156. NOEL (A CHRISTMAS PASTORAL) (Begun January 7, 1908; completed 1908)

>   For: SATB soloists and SATB double chorus, piano or organ
>   Texts compiled by: Ida May Chadwick
>   Dedication: To Carl Stoeckel and composed for the Litchfield County
>   University Club
>   Published: Gray, 1909

>   (See also: W88)

W157. O CEASE MY WANDERING SOUL (Sacred)

>   For: SAB, organ
>   Text by: unknown
>   Dedication: O. B. Brown
>   Published: Schmidt, 1888

W158. O DARKIES DON'T YER 'MEMBER (Plantation Ballad from **TABASCO**)

>   For: Tenor soloist, chorus, piano
>   Text by: Robert Ayres Barnet (1850?-1933)
>   Dedication: none
>   Published: Wood, 1894 (publ. plate no. 12)

>   (See also: W74)

W159. O DAY OF REST (Anthem)

>   For: Tenor solo, ATB chorus, organ
>   Hymn text by: Christopher Wordsworth
>   Dedication: O. B. Brown
>   Published: Schmidt, 1888; copyright renewed 1916 by G. W. Chadwick

W160. O HOLY CHILD OF BETHLEHEM (Christmas Anthem)

>   For: Alto solo, SATB, organ

Text by: Phillips Brooks (1835-1893)
Published: Schmidt, 1896

W161. O NOBLEST OF JUDAH'S WOMEN ("Prayer" from JUDITH)

For: SATB, piano
Text by: Bayard Taylor (1825-1878)
Published: Schmidt, 1913; Ditson, 1928

(See also: W69 and W131 [no. 15])

W162. O WIVES IF YOU'D KEEP (Song and Chorus from TABASCO)

Alternate Title: "Greet the Old Man with a Smile"
For: Vocal soloist, SATT chorus, piano
Text by: Robert Ayres Barnet (1850?-1933)
Dedication: none
Published: Wood, 1894 (publ. plate no. 13. E. 892)

(See also: W74)

W163. ODE FOR THE OPENING OF THE WORLD'S FAIR HELD AT CHICAGO, 1892 (Also known as *Columbian Ode* or *Columbia*)

For: Soprano and tenor soli, SSAATTBB chorus, piano or organ
Text by: Harriet Monroe (1860-1936)
Dedication: none
Published: Church, 1892 (pub. plate no. 8873)

(See also: W89)

W164. PARVUM QUANDO CERNO DEUM (Chorus from NOEL)

For: SSAA
Text by: Anonymous
Published: Gray, 1909

(See also: W88)

W165. PEACE AND LIGHT (Anthem)

>For: SATB, organ
>Text by: unknown
>Published: Schmidt, 1895

W166. PHOENIX EXPIRANS (Cantata)

>For: SATB soloists and chorus, piano or organ
>Text by: Latin Hymn (also in English translation by John Lord Hayes)
>Dedication: Hampden County Musical Association (on holograph);
>   Springfield Festival, 1892 (on published edition)
>Published: Schmidt, 1892 (publ. plate no. 2386-56)

(See also: W90)

W167. THE PILGRIMS (ca. 1890)

>For: SATB, piano
>Text by: Felicia Dorothea Browne Hemans (1793-1835)
>Dedication: Arthur P. Schmidt
>Published: Schmidt, 1890; reprint, Schmidt, 1918 (publ. plate no.
>   2703); reprint, Huntsville, Texas: Recital Publications, 1994

(See also: W91)

W168. PRAYER (THOU WHO SENDEST SUN AND RAIN)
(Anthem)

>For: SATB and alto solo
>Text by: Bayard Taylor (1825-1878)
>Dedication: S. Carr, Jr.
>Published: Schmidt, 1889

W169. REITERLIED (TROOPER'S SONG) (1881)

>For: TTBB
>Text by: unknown
>Published: Schmidt, 1881

Selected Performance

W169a. 16 May 1881; Arlington Club concert; William J. Winch, director, assisted by G. W. Chadwick; Tremont Temple, Boston.

Bibliography

WB371. "New Music." *Boston Evening Transcript* March 7, 1881: 6. Announcement of publication in the Arlington Club's part-song series.

WB372. "Musical." *Boston Evening Transcript* May 17, 1881: 4. Review of the May 16, 1881 concert. The music was ". . . well rendered." (See: W169a)

W170. SAINT BOTOLPH

For: TTBB with unspecified soloist, piano
Text by: Arthur Macy (1842-1904)
Dedication: Orpheus Club (Springfield, Massachusetts), John J.
    Bishop, cond.
Published: Ditson, 1929 (publ. plate no. 1386 and 14,316)

Selected Performance

W170a. 21 April 1930; "Concert of Compositions of George W. Chadwick," New England Conservatory Glee Club, Francis Findlay, cond.; Jordan Hall, Boston.

(See also: W250)

W171. SAVIOUR, AGAIN TO THY DEAR NAME (Anthem)

For: Alto, SATB chorus, piano or organ
Text by: Rev. John Ellerton
Published: Novello, 1904 ("The Church Music Supplement, No. 33")

W172. SAVIOUR LIKE A SHEPHERD (Anthem)

For: SATB
Published: Schmidt, 1891

W173. SENTENCES AND RESPONSES (Sacred)

For: SATB, organ
Published: Schmidt, 1895

W174. SHOUT, YE HIGH HEAVENS (Easter Anthem)

For: SATB, organ
Text by: Plaudite coeli (trans. by John Lord Hayes)
Dedication: To the choir of the Trinity Church, Boston
Published: Schmidt, 1897

Selected Performance

W174a. 16 April 1911 [Easter Sunday]; Arthur H. Ryder, organist and
cond.; Immanuel Congregational Church, Boston.

W175. SILENTLY SWAYING ON THE WATER'S QUIET BREAST

For: SSAA, piano
Text by: Victor von Scheffel (trans. by Isabella Parker)
Dedication: Eurydice Club, Boston
Published: Ditson, 1916

(See also: W92)

Selected Performances

W175a. 12 January 1927; MacDowell Club concert; William Ellis
Weston, leader; Jordan Hall, Boston.

W175b. 16 May 1927; MacDowell Club concert; "Contemporary
Living Boston Composers"; William Ellis Weston, leader;
Jordan Hall, Boston.

W175c. 20 January 1932; MacDowell Club concert; William Ellis
Weston, leader; Jordan Hall, Boston.

W176. THE SONG OF THE VIKING

For: TTBB, piano
Text by: Louisa T. Craigin
Dedication: Benjamin L. Knapp
Published: Schmidt, 1882 (Octavo Edition for Men's Voices, No. 51)

Chadwick prepared a German-language version of this composition
("Lied des Viking by Georg W. Chadwick") "Dem Gesang-Verein

Concordia in Leipzig -- bruderschlaftlich gewidmet" in approximately 1904.

(See also: W93)

Premiere

W176a. 10 February 1886; Apollo Club concert; Music Hall, Boston.

Bibliography

WB373. "Theatres and Concerts -- The Apollo Concert." *Boston Evening Transcript* February 11, 1886: 1. Review of the premiere. "Though the music has not much that is strikingly original, it has a certain strength, which was well expressed by the club." (See: W176a)

W177. SONS OF HERMAN (School Chorus)

For: Children's voices
Text by: J. L. Sanford
Published: Ditson, 1914

W178. THE SPRING BEAUTIES

For: SSA, piano
Text by: Helen Gray Cone
Dedication: "To the Eurydice Club of Philadelphia"
Published: Schmidt, 1911

Selected Performance

W178a. 27 April 1911; Eurydice Club concert, G. W. Chadwick, cond.; Philadelphia [This concert is recorded in Chadwick's 1911 *Journal.*]

W179. SPRING SONG, OP. 9

For: SSAA, piano
Text by: Undetermined [possibly G. W. Chadwick]
Dedicated: Ross Sterling Turner
Published: Schmidt, 1882 (publ. plate no. 530)

W180. STORMY EVENING (School Chorus)

>For: Children's voices
>Text by: Robert Louis Stevenson (1850-1894)
>Published: Birchard, 1901

W181. SUN OF MY SOUL (Anthem)

>For: Tenor solo, SATB chorus, organ
>Text by: John Keble
>Published: Novello, 1904 (Octavo Anthems, No. 792)

W182. TEACH ME, O LORD

>For: SATB
>Text: unknown
>Published: Ditson, 1903

W183. THERE WERE SHEPHERDS (Christmas Anthem)

>For: SATB
>Text: Luke 2:8-11, 14
>Dedication: S. A. Ellis
>Published: Schmidt, 1888

W184. THESE TO THE FRONT (Patriotic Song)

>For: TTBB, piano
>Text by: Mark A. DeWolfe Howe (1864-1960)
>Published: Ditson, 1918 ("Patriotic Music, Mens [*sic*] Voices,
>   No. 13,247")

(See also: W94)

W185. THOU, WHO ART DIVINE! (Anthem)

>For: SATB with tenor solo
>Text by: English words adapted by O. B. Brown
>Published: Schmidt, 1895

W186. THREE CHORUSES FOR WOMEN'S VOICES

>1. To Heliodora
>2. At the Bride's Gate

3. Dorcas

For: SSA, piano
Texts by: Meleager (translated from the Greek by Lilla Cabot Perry)
Dedication: The Tuesday Morning Singing Club (New York) and
      Victor Harris, cond.
Published: Schirmer, 1904 (publ. plate nos. 17047-17049; publ. nos.
      4389-4391)

Premiere

W186a. 28 August 1904; Tuesday Morning Singing Club, Victor
      Harris, cond.; New York City.

W187. THREE PART-SONGS FOR MEN'S VOICES

1. Darest Thou Now, O Soul (Walt Whitman)
2. Credo (W. M. Thackeray)
3. Pack, Clouds, Away (Thomas Heywood)

For: TTBB, (piano [ad lib.] on no. 3 only)
Dedication: Orpheus Club of Philadelphia and Horatio Parker, cond.
Published: Schmidt, 1910

W188. THREE SACRED ANTHEMS, OP. 6

1. Praise the Lord (unknown)
2. Blessed Be the Lord (Benedictus)
3. O Thou That Hearest Prayer (John Burton, Jr.)

For: SATB, organ
Published: Schmidt, 1882; copyright renewed [no. 3] by G. W.
      Chadwick, 1910

Selected Performance

W188a. 17 April 1881; Miss Ward, soprano; Mrs. Alden, contralto;
      Mr. Webber, tenor; Mr. Titus, bass; John A. Preston, organist
      and music director; St. Paul's Episcopal Church, Boston (no.
      2 only).

Bibliography

WB374. "Eastertide." *Boston Evening Transcript* April 16, 1881: 3.

Announcement of the April 17, 1881 performance. (See: W188a)

W189. THREE SACRED QUARTETS, OP. 13

1. As the Hart Pants (Psalm 42)
2. God Who Madest Earth and Heaven (unknown)
3. God to Whom We Look up Blindly (Bayard Taylor [1825-1878])

For: SATB, organ
Published: Schmidt, 1885

W190. TWO ANTHEMS FOR MIXED VOICES

1. Come unto Me
2. Thou Shalt Love the Lord Thy God

For: SATB, organ
Texts by: unknown
Holograph: NRU-Mus (No. 1 only)
Published: Schirmer, 1904; reprint, Schirmer [n.d.; no. 1 only]

W191. TWO FOUR-PART CHORUSES FOR WOMEN'S VOICES (1902)

1. Stabat Mater Speciosa (Giacopone da Todi [1230-1306])
2. Thistledown (Arthur Macy [1842-1904])

For: SSAA, piano
Dedication: The Thursday Morning Musical Club (Boston)
Holograph: NRU-Mus
Published: Schirmer, 1902 (publ. plate nos. 16080-16081)

Selected Performances

W191a. 13 March 1903; Choral Arts Society concert; Trinity Church, Boston (no. 1 only).

W191b. 19 May 1909; New England Conservatory Choral Club, G. W. Chadwick, cond.; Jordan Hall, Boston (no. 2 only).

W191c. 26/27 February 1914; St. Cecilia Club, Victor Harris, cond. (*Stabat Mater Speciosa* only was performed *a capella* at this concert of the New York Philharmonic, Josef Stransky, cond.); Carnegie Hall, New York City.

Bibliography

WB375. "Music and Drama -- Sacred Music and the Ritual." *Boston Evening Transcript* March 7, 1903: 26. Preview of the March 13, 1903 performance of *Stabat Mater Speciosa*. "The text of the Stabat Mater is a paraphrase of the ancient Stabat Mater, written by a Franciscan in the early part of the thirteenth century." (See: W191a)

W192. TWO FOUR-PART CHORUSES FOR FEMALE VOICES (1903)

1. Rondel (canon) (James Cameron Grant)
2. Behind The Lattice (Samuel Minturn Peck [1854-1938])

For: SSAA
Dedication: The Thursday Morning Musical Club (Boston)
Holograph: NRU-Mus
Published: Schirmer, 1903 (publ. plate nos. 16601-16602; Octavo
    Edition nos. 4274-4275)

No. 1 is unaccompanied; no. 2 includes accompaniment for rehearsal only.

Selected Performance

W192a. 19 May 1909; New England Conservatory Choral Club, G. W. Chadwick, cond.; Jordan Hall, Boston (no. 2 only).

W193. THE VIKING'S LAST VOYAGE

For: Baritone soloist, TTBB chorus, piano
Text by: Sylvester Baxter (1850-1927)
Dedication: A. Parker Browne
Published: Schmidt 1881; reprinted, 1909

(See also: W95)

W194. WELCOME HAPPY MORN (Anthem)

For: SATB

Published: Schmidt, 1895

W195. WHEN I VIEW THE MOTHER HOLDING (Anthem from NOEL)

For: Women's voices
Published: Gray, 1909

(See: W88)

W196. WHEN THE LORD OF LOVE WAS HERE (Hymn)

For: SATB
Text adapted from the hymn tune "Armstrong"
Published: Schmidt, 1895

W197. WHILE SHEPHERDS WATCHED (Christmas Carol)

For: SATB
Published: Schmidt, 1899

W198. WHILE THEE I SEEK (Anthem)

For: SATB, organ
Published: Schmidt, 1891

SONGS

W199. AFAR ON THE PLAINS OF THE TIGRIS ("Aria of Holofernes" from JUDITH)

Text by: William Chauncy Langdon (1871-1947) (second verse by
        William Dana Orcutt)
Published: Schirmer, 1911

(See also: W69)

W200. AGHADOE

Text by: John Todhunter
Dedication: Lilla Ormond
Pencil holograph: DLC; MBCM (copy)

Published: Schmidt, 1911

(See also: W96)

W201. ALLAH

Text by: Henry Wadsworth Longfellow (1807-1882)
Dedication: Gardner S. Lamson
Published: Schmidt, 1887 (publ. plate no. 1552); reprint, 1915

(See also: W216 [no. 4] and W252 [no. 2])

Selected Performances

W201a. 23 January 1888; All-Chadwick concert; William J. Winch, baritone; G. W. Chadwick, piano; Chickering Hall, Boston.

W201b. 9 May 1888; Boston Orchestral Club; Gardner S. Lamson, vocalist; G. W. Chadwick, cond.; Boston.

W201c. 7 May 1896; Springfield Festival; Max Heinrich, baritone; G. W. Chadwick, piano; Springfield, Massachusetts.

W201d. 30 December 1912-2 January 1913 [the exact date of this particular performance is not given on the program]; 34th Annual Meeting of the Music Teachers National Association; Carrie Bridewell, vocalist; Vassar College, Poughkeepsie, New York.

W202. ARMENIAN LULLABY

Text by: Eugene Field (1850-1895) (from *Lullaby Land: Songs of Childhood* [ca. 1895])
Published: Scribner, 1896

W203. BABY'S LULLABY BOOK: MOTHER SONGS

Text by: Charles Stuart Pratt (b. 1854); Decorative watercolors by W. L. Taylor
Published: Prang, 1888

1. January: The Snowflakes Float down from the Skies
2. February: The Snowbirds That Chirped in the Sun
3. March: Hark, and Hear the March Wind Blowing

4. April: On the Roof the Rain is Dropping
5. May: This Sweet May Day
6. June: On the Red Rose Tree is a Bud
7. July: If I Were a Lily
8. August: In the Hammock We Swing
9. September: O Moon, Round Moon
10. October: Through the Day the Heavenly Father
11. November: Summer Birds Have Taken Wing
12. December: Long Years Ago in the Eastern Heaven

W204. THE BALLAD OF THE FOX AND THE RAVEN

Text by: unknown [probably G. W. Chadwick]
Unpublished; not located

The only reference to this work is in Chadwick's *Journal* (27 April 1916). The entry states that the song was performed that evening by Charles Bennett, bass, for the Composers' Club meeting at the Harvard Musical Association. About the apparently humorous work, Chadwick wrote: "Nobody laughed. One must be careful about joking when real composer's are present."

W205. A BALLAD OF TREES AND THE MASTER

Text by: Sidney Lanier (1842-1881)
Dedication: D. Ffrangcon-Davies [in London edition]
Published: Ditson, 1899 (publ. plate no. 47-61833) and 1927 (publ. plate no. 4-83-63600-4); also published, London: Enoch & Sons, 1899; also published in *Musical Record & Review* [Song Edition] 1/3 (1901).

This composition was awarded First Prize in the song category of the competition sponsored by *The Musical Record & Review*, 1899.

(See also: W97 and W108)

Selected Performances

W205a. 9 February 1900; Harvard Musical Association concert; U. S. Kerr, bass; G. W. Chadwick, piano; Boston.

W205b. 21 November 1904; All-Chadwick concert; Herbert Witherspoon, vocalist; members of the Boston Symphony Orchestra, G. W. Chadwick, cond.; Jordan Hall, Boston.

W205c. 2 March 1909; MacDowell Club recital; Janet Spencer, vocalist; J. A. Colburn, piano; The Tuileries, Boston.

W205d. 22 January 1911; Mme. Hesse-Sprotte, soprano; Mrs. James A. Bliss, piano; Sung at the Twelfth Popular Concert ("American Program") of the Minneapolis Symphony Orchestra, Emil Oberhoffer, cond.; The Auditorium, Minneapolis, Minnesota.

W205e. 18 November 1916; Charles Bennett, bass; Wallace Goodrich, piano; Seventh Annual Joint Meeting of the American Academy of Arts and Letters and the National Institute of Arts and Letters; Jordan Hall, Boston.

Bibliography

WB376. "George W. Chadwick." *The Musical Record* 454 (November, 1899): 495-496. Announcement that Chadwick had won the magazine's competition and a prize of $75. Includes a brief biography. "Mr. Chadwick is perhaps today the most industrious, as he is one of the most effective, of American composers."

W206. BEDOUIN LOVE SONG

Text by: Bayard Taylor (1825-1878)
Dedication: J. F. Winch
Published: Schmidt, 1890

(See also: W252 [no. 1])

Selected Performances

W206a. 22 January 1891; Eliot Hubbard, vocalist; Cecilia Society concert; Boston.

W206b. 9 February 1900; U. S. Kerr, baritone; G. W. Chadwick, piano; Harvard Musical Association concert; Boston.

Bibliography

WB377. *Church's Musical Visitor* 11/9 (June 1882): 233. Bayard Taylor's verses appear in this issue under the title "Bedouin Song."

W207. BOLERO (From TABASCO)

Text by: Robert Ayres Barnet (1850?-1933)
Dedication: none
Published: Wood, 1894 (publ. plate no. 12)

(See also: W74)

W208. BRIGHTEST AND BEST (Christmas song)

Text by: R. [Reginald?] Heber
Published: Schmidt, 1888 (in both choral and song versions)

(See also: W113)

W209. THE BROOK

Text by: Harriet Monroe (1860-1936)
Published: In *Children's Souvenir Song Book.* [Compiled by William
    L. Tomlins, Choral Director of the Columbian Exposition,
    Chicago, 1893.] London and New York: Novello, Ewer &
    Co., 1893 (p. 8).

This song is incorrectly attributed to J. [*sic*] W. Chadwick. Some of
the confusion may have been caused by the inclusion of a song by Mrs.
H. H. A. Beach, "Singing Joyfully" (pp. 50-51), the text for which is
by John White Chadwick.

W210. CHILD'S AMERICAN HYMN

Text by: Julia W. Howe
Published: In *Children's Souvenir Song Book.* [Compiled by William
    L. Tomlins, Choral Director of the Columbian Exposition,
    Chicago, 1893.] London and New York: Novello, Ewer &
    Co., 1893 (p. 114).

W211. A CHRISTMAS LIMERICK

Text by: unknown [probably G. W. Chadwick]
Published: Printed privately as Chadwick's Christmas card, 1927

W212. THE CURFEW

Text by: Henry Wadsworth Longfellow (1807-1882)

Dedication: Marianne Kneisel
Published: Schmidt, 1914

(See also: W98)

W213. THE DAUGHTER OF MENDOZA (Serenade)

Text by: Mirabeau Bonaparte Lamar (1798-1859)
Dedication: Edmont Clement
Published: Schmidt, 1914

W214. FAITH

Sacred song with piano or organ accompaniment
Text by: Arthur Macy (1842-1904)
Published: Church, 1899

Selected Performances

W214a. 9 February 1900; U. S. Kerr, bass; G. W. Chadwick, piano;
Harvard Musical Association concert; Boston.

W214b. 27 January 1907; U. S. Kerr, bass (pianist not listed); sung at
the Fourth Popular Sunday Afternoon Concert of the
Minneapolis Symphony Orchestra, Emil Oberhoffer, cond.;
The Auditorium, Minneapolis, Minnesota.

W215. FAREWELL TO THE FARM

Text by: Robert Louis Stevenson (1850-1894)
Published in: *The Stevenson Songbook: Verses from A Child's Garden*
by Robert Louis Stevenson with music by various
composers. New York: Charles Scribner's Sons, 1898.

W216. FIFTEEN SONGS FOR SOPRANO OR TENOR

1. Nocturne (Thomas Bailey Aldrich) (See: W252 [no. 6] and W270
[no. 1])
2. Song from the Persian (Thomas Bailey Aldrich) (See: W252 [no.
17] and W270 [no. 2])
3. He Loves Me See (Newton MacIntosh) (See: W252 [no. 3] and
W255 [no. 2])
4. Allah (Henry Wadsworth Longfellow) (See: W201 and W252
[no. 2])

5. The Danza (Arlo Bates) (See: W252 [no. 16] and W255 [no. 1])
6. In Bygone Days (John Leslie Breck) (See: W252 [no. 13] and W255 [no. 3])
7. Sweet Wind that Blows (Oscar Leighton) (See: W252 [no. 14] and W255 [no. 5])
8. Lullaby (unknown) (See: W255 [no. 6])
9. Gay Little Dandelion (unknown) (See: W263 [no. 2])
10. Request (Barry Cornwall) (See: W263 [no. 1])
11. Thou Art So Like a Flower (after Heine) (See: W252 [no. 11] and W263 [no. 3])
12. The Lament (Egyptian Song from "Ben Hur") (Lew Wallace) (See: W252 [no. 7] and W238)
13. The Lily (Alessandro Salvini, trans. by T. R. Sullivan) (See: W240)
14. Serenade (Arlo Bates) (See: W264 [no. 2])
15. Before the Dawn (Arlo Bates) (See: W252 [no. 15] and W264 [no. 3])

Dedication: none
Published: Schmidt, ca. 1885-1886 (Edition Schmidt no. 13)

W217. THE FIGHTING MEN

Text by: Mark A. DeWolfe Howe (1864-1960)
Published: Birchard, 1918

W218. FIVE SONGS (1910)

1. When Stars Are in the Quiet Skies (E. Bulwer Lytton)
2. Love's Image (James Thomson)
3. Gifts (James Thomson)
4. When I Am Dead (Christina Rosetti [1830-1894])
5. O Love Stay by and Sing (Clarence B. Shirley)

Dedications: Ernestine Schumann-Heink (no. 2)/Ida May Chadwick (nos. 4 and 5)
Published: Schmidt, 1910

Selected Performances

W218a. 23 October 1910; Ernestine Schumann-Heink, contralto; Orchestra Hall, Chicago (no. 4 only).

W218b. 2 April 1913; Clarence Richter, vocalist; MacDowell Club concert; Jordan Hall, Boston (no. 5 only).

W218c. 21 April 1930; Rulon Y. Robison, tenor; "Concert of Compositions of George W. Chadwick"; New England Conservatory, Jordan Hall, (nos. 1 and 2 only).

W218d. 6 May 1930; Rulon Y. Robison, tenor; New England Conservatory, Jordan Hall, Boston (nos. 1 and 2 only).

W219. FIVE SONGS (1914)

1. The Voice of Philomel (See also: W271 and W103)
2. The Bobolink
3. Roses
4. When She Gave Me Her Hand
5. When Phillis Looks

Texts by: David Kilburn Stevens (1860-1946)
Dedications: Louise Homer (no. 1); Geraldine Farrar (nos. 2-4);
    Mrs. Richard Stevens (no. 5)
Holograph: NRU-Mus
Published: Schirmer, 1914

Selected Performance

W219a. 15 December 1919; Edith Woodman, soprano, Wallace Goodrich, piano; Recital Hall, New England Conservatory, Boston.

W220. A FLOWER CYCLE

1. The Crocus
2. The Trilliums
3. The Water Lily
4. The Cyclamen
5. The Wild Briar
6. The Columbine
7. The Foxglove
8. The Cardinal Flower
9. The Lupine
10. The Meadow Rue
11. The Jasmine
12. The Jacqueminot Rose

Texts by: Arlo Bates (1850-1918)
Dedication: Arlo Bates
Published: Ditson, 1892; reprinted, Earlier American Music, vol. 16.
        With an introduction by Steven Ledbetter. New York: Da
        Capo, 1980.

W221. FOUR CHRISTMAS SONGS FROM NOEL

1. A Voice from Yonder Manger (Paul Gerhardt [1656])
2. O Long and Darksome Was the Night (Ray Palmer)
3. O Holy Child, Thy Manger Streams (Danish traditional)
4. I Was a Foe to God (Gerhardt Tersteegen [1731])

For: S, A, T, B, respectively; piano or organ
Dedication: Carl Stoeckel (on orchestral score)
Published: Gray, 1912

(See also: W88)

W222. FOUR IRISH SONGS

1. Larry O'Toole (W. M. Thackeray)
2. The Lady of Leith (William Maginn)
3. Nora McNally (Anita Moor)
4. The Recruit (Robert William Chambers)

Dedications: F. Morse Wemple (no. 1); David Bispham (nos. 2 and 3);
        Herbert Witherspoon (no. 4)
Published: Schmidt, 1910 (publ. plate nos. 8932-8935)

W223. FULFILLMENT

Text by: David Kilburn Stevens (1860-1946)
Published: Schmidt, 1914

W224. THE GOOD SAMARITAN (Sacred)

With violin and organ accompaniment
Text by: James Montgomery
Published: Church, 1900

W225. GREEN GROWS THE WILLOW

Text by: Hamilton Aide

Dedication: Arthur Gordon Weld
Published: Schmidt, 1888

W226. HAIL, ALL HAIL THE GLORIOUS MORN (Sacred)

Text by: Ida S. Taylor
Published: Schmidt, 1892

W227. HARK! HARK, MY SOUL

Sacred song with organ accompaniment
Text by: Frederick William Faber (1814-1863)
Holograph: NRU-Mus
Published: Schirmer, 1903; reprint, Oakville, Ontario, Canada:
      Frederick Harris Music Co. [n.d.]

(See also: W129)

W228. HE MAKETH WARS TO CEASE (Sacred)

Text by: unknown
Published: Schmidt, 1892

W229. I HAVE NOT FORGOTTEN

Text by: W. M. Chauvenet
Published: Church, 1898

W230. IF I WERE YOU

Text: Hirsch [only name supplied]
Dedication: unknown
Holograph: not located

Neither a holograph nor a printed copy of this composition has been
located, but it has been recorded (See D72 and B146 [p. 113]).

W231. IN BARCELONA LIVED A MAID (Marco's Song from TABASCO)

Text by: Robert Ayres Barnet (1850?-1933)
Dedication: none
Published: Wood, 1894 (publ. plate no. 12)

(See also: W74)

W232. IN MY BELOVED'S EYES

Text by: W. M. Chauvenet
Dedication: Ida May Chadwick
Published: Scribner, 1897

(See also: W267)

Selected Performances

W232a. 21 November 1904; All-Chadwick concert; Herbert
Witherspoon, vocalist; Jordan Hall, Boston.

W232b. 10 March 1909; MacDowell Club concert; Jessica Swartz,
vocalist; Boston.

Bibliography

WB378. R. R. G. "Jordan Hall: Mr. Chadwick's Concert." *Boston
Evening Transcript* November 22, 1904: 15. Review of the
November 21, 1904 performance in Boston. This review does
not specifically consider this composition, but the writer says
of the event: "To turn to last night's concert, it must at once
be set down as a success." (See: W232a)

W233. IS MY LOVER ON THE SEA?

Text by: Barry Cornwall (1787-1874)
Published: New York: R. A. Saalfield, ca. 1876; Also published in
*Christmas Album. A Collection of Music for Young and Old
Adapted for Ye Xmas Time*; [same publisher], 1883. The
cover of the 1876 publication reads "By H. [*sic*] Chadwick";
but inside: "Music by George Chadwick. Olivet, Mich."

W234. JOSHUA (Humorous Song)

Text by: Richard Darwin Ware (1869-1931)
Published: Ditson, 1919 (publ. plate no. 73295)

A note on the printed version reads: "Pronounced Josh-u-ay"

(See also: W10, W82, W100, and W138)

W235. KING DEATH

Text by: unknown [probably Chadwick]
Dedication: Gardner S. Lamson
Published: Schmidt, 1885

W236. KISSING TIME

Text by: Eugene Field (1850-1895) (from *Lullaby Land: Songs of Childhood* [ca. 1895])
Published: Scribner, 1896

W237. LADY BIRD

Text: Southey [only name supplied]
Dedication: unknown
Holograph: not located

Neither a holograph nor a printed copy of this composition has been located, but it has been recorded (See B164 [p. 113] and D72).

W238. THE LAMENT (Egyptian Song from "Ben Hur")

Text by: Lew Wallace (1827-1905)
Dedication: James Means
Published: Schmidt, 1887

(See also: W216 [no. 12] and W252 [no. 7])

Selected Performance

W238a. 9 May 1888; Gardner S. Lamson, vocalist; at a performance of the Boston Orchestral Club; G. W. Chadwick, cond.; Music Hall, Boston.

W239. THE LAND OF COUNTERPANE

Text by: Robert Louis Stevenson (1850-1894)
Published in: *The Stevenson Songbook: Verses from A Child's Garden* by Robert Louis Stevenson with music by various composers. New York: Charles Scribner's Sons, 1898.

W240. THE LILY

Text by: Alessandro Salvini (trans. by T. R. Sullivan)
Dedication: James H. Ricketson
Published: Schmidt, 1887

(See also: W216 [no. 13])

Selected Performance

W240a. 14 October 1892; George Ellsworth Holmes, vocalist; Benefit performance at the home of Mrs. James B. Waller, Buena Park, Illinois.

Bibliography

WB379. "For the Children's Home at the Fair." *Chicago Tribune* October 15, 1892: 15. Notice that Chadwick's song was performed at the October 14, 1892 fundraising event. (See: W240a)

W241. LOCHINVAR (Ballad)

Text by: Sir Walter Scott (1771-1832)
Dedication: Max Heinrich
Published: Schmidt, 1896

(See also: W101)

W242. LYRICS FROM "TOLD IN THE GATE"

1. Sweetheart, Thy Lips are Touched with Flame
2. Sings the Nightingale to the Rose
3. The Rose Leans over the Pool
4. Love's Like a Summer Rose
5. As in the Waves without Number
6. Dear Love, When in Thine Arms I Lie
7. Was I Not Thine?
8. In Mead Where Roses Bloom
9. Sister Fairest, Why Art Thou Sighing?
10. Oh, Let Night Speak of Me (See also: WR5)
11. I Said to the Wind of the South
12. Were I A Prince Egyptian

Texts by: Arlo Bates (1850-1918)
Dedications: Max Heinrich (nos. 1, 7, and 10); Mrs. James C. Little
(no. 2); Harriet P. Sawyer (no. 3); Mrs. Halsey C. Ives (no.
4); G. Campanari (no. 5); I. M. C. [Ida May Chadwick]
(no. 6); "To Eoline" (no. 8); Perry Averill (no. 9.); Gertrude
Edmands (no. 11); William Lincoln Cosby (no. 12)
Published: Schmidt, 1897 (Edition Schmidt 71b); reprinted 1925

Selected Performances

W242a. 12 January 1898; Anna Miller Wood, vocalist; John C.
Manning, pianist; Steinert Hall, Boston (no. 6 only).

W242b. 9 February 1900; U. S. Kerr, baritone; G. W. Chadwick,
piano; Harvard Musical Association concert; Boston (no. 7
only).

W242c. 16 December 1906; Berrick van Norden, tenor; Chickering
concert; Boston (no. 12 only).

W242d. 23 January 1907; Celestine Cornelison, vocalist; Harris S.
Shaw, piano; MacDowell Club concert; Boston.

W242e. 30 September 1907; Jessie Swartz, vocalist; New England
Conservatory student recital; Jordan Hall, Boston (no. 11
only).

W242f. 27-30 December 1910 [precise date not listed]; Stephen
Townsend, baritone; Annual Meeting of the Music Teachers'
National Association; Boston University (no. 3 only).

W242g. August 1916 [precise date not found]; Reinald Werrenrath,
baritone; New York University, New York City (no. 10 only).

W242h. 21 April 1930; "Concert of Compositions of George W.
Chadwick"; Rulon Y. Robison, tenor; New England
Conservatory, Jordan Hall, Boston (no. 12 only).

W242i. 6 May 1930; Rulon Y. Robison, tenor; New England
Conservatory, Jordan Hall, Boston (no. 12 only).

Bibliography

WB380. "Music and Drama -- Steinert Hall: Mr. Noblos's Recital."

Boston Evening Transcript January 13, 1898: 5. Review of the January 12, 1898 performance. No specific mention of this composition. (See: W242a)

WB381. "Music Notes." *New York Times* July 30, 1916: 1/30. Announces a series of concerts to be given by Reinald Werrenrath in August, 1916 [precise dates not given]. (See: W242g)

WB382. *The Musician* 21/9 (September 1916): 56. Notice of Werrenrath's recital in July, 1916 [see WB381; the recital actually occurred later] which comprised 20 of the best (in the singer's estimation) American songs. (See: W242g)

W243. THE MILL

Text by: Miss [Mabel E.?] Mulock
Published: Schmidt, 1886 (publ. plate no. 876)

Bibliography

WB383. "Review of New Music." *The Musical Herald* 7/7 (July 1886): 224. This publication review notes that "The Mill" is included in *Wide Awake*, a volume of songs edited by Louis C. Elson [not located].

W244. THE MILLER'S DAUGHTER

Text by: Alfred Tennyson (1809-1892)
Dedication: Ida May Chadwick
Published: Schmidt, 1881 (publ. plate no. 229)

(See also: W12 and W252 [no. 8])

Selected Performance

W244a. 2 April 1886; Julian F. Witherell, piano; New England Conservatory student recital, Jordan Hall, Boston.

Bibliography

WB384. "New Music." *Boston Evening Transcript* November 12, 1881: 1. Publication announcement.

WB385. Elson, Louis C. "Review of New Music." *Musical Herald* 3/1 (January 1882): 25-26. Review of the publication. "A song of much lyric sentiment, in which the accompaniment is well developed, and the modulations (especially of the third verse) quite interesting. It will appeal to the best class of singers of English song."

WB386. "Concerts." *The Musical Herald* 7/5 (May 1886): 117. Post-concert announcement of the April 2, 1886 performance.

W245. MORNING GLORY

Text: Foresman [only name supplied]
Dedication: unknown
Holograph: not located

Neither a holograph nor a printed copy of this composition has been located, but it has been recorded (See B164 [p. 113] and D71).

W246. MY HEART AGAIN TO HOPE BEGINS (Fatima and Marco's Love Duet from TABASCO)

For: Soprano and tenor, piano
Text by: Robert Ayres Barnet (1850?-1933)
Dedication: none
Published: Wood, 1894 (publ. plate no. 12)

(See also: W74)

W247. O LOVELY HOME (Fatima's Song from TABASCO)

Text by: Robert Ayres Barnet (1850?-1933)
Dedication: none
Published: Wood, 1894 (publ. plate no. 14)

(See also: W74)

W248. PERIWINKLE BAY

Text by: David Kilburn Stevens (1860-1946)
Dedication: Alma Gluck
Published: Schmidt, 1914

W249. SACRED SONGS (1887)

1. When Our Heads Are Bowed with Woe (H. H. Milman)
2. O Mother Dear, Jerusalem (Francis Baker)
3. Let Not Your Heart Be Troubled (biblical)

Dedication: Adelaide Bothamly
Holograph: MBCM (nos. 1 and 3); DLC (no. 2)
Published: Schmidt, 1887 (publ. plate no. 1550 [no. 2 only])

W250. SAINT BOTOLPH

Text by: Arthur Macy (1842-1904)
Dedication: In honor of the 25th Anniversary of the Saint Botolph
      Club, Boston
Published: Wood, 1902; reprinted 1913 (chorus version)

(See also: W171)

W251. THE SEA KING

Text by: Barry Cornwall (1787-1874)
Dedication: Gardner S. Lamson
Published: Schmidt, 1885 (publ. plate no. 811)

W252. SEVENTEEN SONGS FOR ALTO OR BARITONE

1. Bedouin Love Song (Bayard Taylor) (See also: W206)
2. Allah Gives Light in Darkness (Henry Wadsworth Longfellow) (See
    also: W201 and W216 [no. 4])
3. He Loves Me (Newton MacIntosh) (See also: W216 [no. 3] and
    W255 [no. 2])
4. A Bonny Curl (Amelie Rives) (See also: W262 [no. 1])
5. The Maiden and the Butterfly (unknown) (See also: W261 [no. 2])
6. Nocturne (Thomas Bailey Aldrich) (See   also: W216 [no. 1] and
    W270 [no. 1])
7. The Lament (Lew Wallace) (See also: W216 [no. 12] and W238)
8. The Miller's Daughter (Alfred Lord Tennyson) (See also: W12 and
    W244)
9. O Love and Joy (Folk song) (See also: W269 [no. 1])
10. The Northern Days Are Short (Christina Rossetti) (See also: W269
    [no. 2])
11. Thou Art So Like a Flower (after Heine) (See also: W216 [no. 11]
    and W263 [no. 3])

12. I Know Two Eyes (Ballad) (unknown) (See also: W255 [no. 4])
13. In Bygone Days (John Leslie Breck) (See also: W216 [no. 6] and W255 [no. 3])
14. Sweet Wind that Blows (Oscar Leighton) (See also: W216 [no. 7] and W255 [no. 5])
15. Before the Dawn (Arlo Bates) (See also: W216 [no. 15] and W264 [no. 3])
16. The Danza (Arlo Bates) (See also: W216 [no. 5] and W255 [no. 1])
17. Song from the Persian (Thomas Bailey Aldrich) (See also: W216 [no. 2] and W270 [no. 2])

For: Alto or baritone
Dedication: none
Published: Schmidt, ca. 1918 (Edition Schmidt No. 38)

The popular song "The Danza" was arranged for chorus (SSA) by Jeanne Boyd (Schmidt, 1946).

Selected Performances

W252a. 2 February 1886; Miss Abbott, vocalist; G. W. Chadwick, accompanist; Boston Orchestral Club concert; Horticultural Hall, Boston (nos. 3, 12, and 16 only).

W252b. 4 February 1886; Mr. [James H.] Ricketson, tenor; Mr. [B. J.] Lang, piano; Cecilia Club concert; Music Hall, Boston (nos. 14 and 15 only).

W252c. 10 February 1886; Eugenia Sweet, vocalist; New England Conservatory student recital; Boston (no. 12 only).

W252d. 28 May 1886; Etta D. Trafton, vocalist; New England Conservatory student recital; Boston (no. 3 only).

W252e. 15 March 1887; George J. Parker, vocalist; Arthur Foote, piano; Chickering Hall, Boston (no. 17 only).

W252f. 19 November 1887; Frederick Jameson, tenor; Chickering Hall, New York City (nos. 3 and 14 only).

W252g. 12 July 1889; Maude Starvetta, vocalist; Exposition orchestra, Frank van der Stucken, cond.; Exposition Universelle, Trocadero Palace, Paris (no. 13 only [as an encore following the orchestra performance]).

W252h. 30 January 1909; Lila G. Byrne, vocalist; New England
Conservatory student recital; Jordan Hall, Boston (no. 3 only).

W252i. 13 April 1909; Clara Clemens, contralto; Mendelssohn Hall,
New York City (no. 16 only).

W252j. 28 February 1911; Edmont Clement, tenor; Carnegie Hall,
New York City (no. 14 only).

W252k. August 1916 [precise date not found]; Reinald Werrenrath,
baritone; New York University, New York City (no. 2 only).

W252l. 7 February 1926; Ernestine Schumann-Heink, contralto;
Handel & Haydn Society "Miscellaneous Programme";
Symphony Hall, Boston (nos. 2 and 16 only).

W252m. 8 March 1930; Mildred Kreuder, vocalist; Carol Hollister,
piano; under the auspices of the New York Madrigal Club;
Chalif Hall, New York City.

W252n. 21 April 1930; "Concert of Compositions of George W.
Chadwick"; Rulon Y. Robison, tenor; New England
Conservatory, Jordan Hall, Boston (no. 15 only).

W252o. 6 May 1930; Rulon Y. Robison, tenor; New England
Conservatory, Jordan Hall, Boston (no. 15 only).

Bibliography

WB387. "Theatres and Concerts -- Boston Orchestral Club." *Boston
Evening Transcript* February 3, 1886: 1. Review of the
February 2, 1886 program. (See: W252a)

WB388. "Theatres and Concerts -- The Cecilia." *Boston Evening
Transcript* February 5, 1886: 1. Review of the February 4,
1886 program. "Mr. Chadwick's songs . . . were heard with
manifest interest, if not delight . . . ." (See: W252b)

WB389. "Concerts." *The Musical Herald* 7/3 (March 1886): 85.
Announcement that the February 10, 1886 concert had occurred. (See: W252c)

WB390. "Concerts." *The Musical Herald* 7/7 (July 1886): 210.
Announcement that the May 28, 1886 concert had occurred.

(See: W252d)

WB391. "Theatres and Concerts." *Boston Evening Transcript* March
16, 1887: 1. Review of the March 15, 1887 performance.
Chadwick's "Song from the Persian" ". . . has much that is
lovely in it, albeit that it does not sound quite spontaneous,
nor as if the composer really had much to say." (See: W252e)

WB392. "The American Concerts." *New York Times* November 20,
1887: 2. Review of the November 19, 1887 concert. The
critic writes that "She Loves Me" is ". . . a really good song."
(See: W252f)

WB393. "Chat About Folks and Things." *Springfield* [Massachusetts]
Graphic April 1, 1893. Announcement that "Mr. Bailey" will
sing "Sweet Wind That Blows" and "Thou Art So Like a
Flower" at an upcoming recital, although exact dates are not
given.

WB394. "Concerts of the Week." *New York Times* April 11, 1909:
VI/7. Notice of Clara Clemens's recital, April 13, 1909.
(See: W252i)

WB395. "Music Notes." *New York Times* July 30, 1916: 1/30.
Announces a series of concerts to be given by Reinald
Werrenrath in August, 1916 [precise dates not given]. (See:
W252k)

WB396. *The Musician* 21/9 (September 1916): 56. Notice of Reinald
Werrenrath's recital in July, 1916 [although the date was
changed to August. See: WB395] which comprised 20 of the
best (in the singer's estimation) American songs. (See:
W252k)

WB397. "Mildred Kreuder Heard." *New York Times* March 9, 1930:
1/29. Review of Mildred Kreuder's recital of March 8, 1930.
" . . . the spirit of the text was interpreted with understanding."
(See: W252m)

W253. THE SHAMROCK BLOOMS WHITE (Francois's Lament from TABASCO)

Text by: Robert Ayres Barnet (1850?-1933)
Dedication: none

Published: Wood, 1894 (publ. plate no. 12)

(See: W74)

W254. SINCE MY LOVE'S EYES

Text by: W. M. Chauvenet
Dedication: Mrs. Gerrit Smith
Published: Church, 1898 (publ. plate no. 12806)

Selected Performance

W253a. 9 February 1900; U. S. Kerr, baritone; G. W. Chadwick,
piano; Harvard Musical Association concert; Boston.

W255. SIX SONGS (OP. 14) (1885)

1. The Danza (Arlo Bates) (See also: W216 [no. 5], W252 [no. 16] and
   WR1)
2. He Loves Me (Newton MacIntosh) (See also: W216 [no. 3] and
   W252 [no. 3])
3. In Bygone Days (John Leslie Breck) (See also: W216 [no. 6] and
   W252 [no. 13])
4. I Know Two Eyes (Ballad) (unknown) (See also: W252 [no. 12])
5. Sweet Wind That Blows (Oscar Leighton) (See also: W216 [no. 7]
   and W252 [no. 14])
6. Lullaby (unknown) (See also: W216 [no. 8])

Dedications: Jules Jordan (no. 1); Edward Bowditch (no. 2); Lizzie
    Barton Hall (no. 3); "To Adelaide" (no. 4); Olivia Bowditch
    (no. 5); Agnes Dana Dyer (no. 6)
Published: Schmidt, 1885; no. 1 reprinted in 1913; no. 4 revised and
    republished in 1914

Selected Performance

W255a. 2 February 1896; E. M. Abbott, vocalist; G. W. Chadwick,
    piano; Boston Orchestral Club concert; Chickering Hall,
    Boston (no. 4 only).

W256. SIX SONGS FOR MEZZO SOPRANO AND BARITONE (1902)

1. Euthanasia

    2. The Aureole
    3. Adversity
    4. The Wishing Stream
    5. The Honeysuckle
    6. The Stranger-Man

Texts by: Arthur Macy (except no. 3); W. M. Chauvenet (no. 3)
Holograph: NRU-Mus
Published: Schirmer, 1902 (publ. plate no. 16029)

New York Public Library holds Chadwick's autographed presentation copy to baritone David Bispham.

Selected Performances

W256a 10 March 1909; Jessica Swartz, vocalist; MacDowell Club concert, Boston (no. 6 only).

W256b. 6 March 1996; "The American Century" [New England Conservatory Music Festival]; Patrice Williamson, vocalist; Mei Sheun, piano; Williams Hall, New England Conservatory, Boston (no. 1 only).

W257. THE SOFT-SHELL CRAB

Text by: Elsie J. Cooley
Published: In *Children's Souvenir Song Book.* [Compiled by William L. Tomlins, Choral Director of the World's Columbian Exposition, Chicago, 1893.] London and New York: Novello, Ewer & Co., 1893 (pp. 52-53).

This song is incorrectly attributed to J. [*sic*] W. Chadwick. Some of the confusion may have been caused by the inclusion of a song by Mrs. H. H. A. Beach, "Singing Joyfully" (pp. 50-51), the text for which is by John White Chadwick.

W258. SONGS OF BRITTANY

    1. Loud Trumpets Blow
    2. Proudly Childe Haslin
    3. How Flowers Fade
    4. The Autumn Winds Are Chill (See also: W106)
    5. As Summer Wind
    6. Love is Fleeting (See also: W146)

7. My Sweetheart Gave a Crimson Blossom (See also: W155)
8. How Youth with Passion Plays
9. The Lark That Sang When Morning Broke (See also: W143)
10. Proudly at Morn the Hunter Rode
11. The Trumpet Sounds and Calls Away
12. The Distaff Whirled

Texts by: Arlo Bates (1850-1918)
Published: Schmidt, 1890 (publ. plate no. 2704; Edition Schmidt, no. 20); reprint, Huntsville, Texas: Recital Publications, 1986.

The printed composition notes that these songs are "arranged and harmonized from traditional Breton melodies."

W259. SORAIS' SONG

Text by: Rider Haggard (1856-1925)
Dedication: Clarence Hay
Published: Schmidt, 1888

Selected Performance

W259a. 9 February 1900; U. S. Kerr, baritone; G. W. Chadwick, piano; Harvard Musical Association concert; Boston.

W260. THAT GOLDEN HOUR

Text by: David Kilburn Stevens (1860-1946)
Dedication: Evan Williams
Published: Schirmer, 1914

W261. THERE IS A RIVER (Sacred)

Text by: unknown
Published: Schmidt, 1892

W262. THREE BALLADS

1. A Bonny Curl (Amelie Rives [1863-1945]) (See also: W252 [no. 4])
2. The Maiden and the Butterfly (unknown) (See also: W252 [no. 5] and WR2)
3. A Warning (Edward Breck)

Dedicatees: Eleanor Everest (no. 1); Annie P. Vinton (no. 2); "To Lutie" (no. 3).
Published: Schmidt, 1889 (publ. plate no. 1922-24)

W263. THREE LITTLE SONGS, OP. 11

1. Request (Barry Cornwall [1787-1874]) (See also: W216 [no. 10])
2. Gay Little Dandelion (unknown) (See also: W216 [no. 9])
3. Thou Art So Like A Flower (Du bist wie eine Blume) (after Heinrich Heine [1797-1856]) (See also: W216 [no. 11] and W252 [no. 11])

Dedication: Henry W. Dunham [no. 3]
Published: Schmidt, 1883 (publ. plate nos. 380-382); reprint, 1911 (publ. plate no. 9494 with English and German texts [no. 3 only])

W264. THREE LOVE SONGS, OP. 8

1. Rose Guerdon
2. Serenade (See also: W216 [no. 14])
3. Before the Dawn (See also: W216 [no. 15] and W252 [no. 15])

Texts by: Arlo Bates (1850-1918)
Published: Schmidt, 1882 (publ. plate nos. 503-505)

No. 3 has been arranged for voice and orchestra (2. 2. eh. 2. 2./4. 0. 0. 0./timp. harp. strings) by Val Coffey. Madison Heights, Michigan: Luck's Music Library, [n.d.].

Premiere

W264a. 4 February 1886; Mr. James H. Ricketson, tenor; Cecilia Society concert; Boston [precise location undetermined].

Other Selected Performance

W264b. 3 August 1915; Mrs. Arthur J. Hill, vocalist; San Francisco Musical Club concert; Held in the California Building of the Panama-Pacific Exposition grounds; San Francisco, Cal.

Bibliography

WB398. L. C. E. [Louis C. Elson]. "Review of New Music." *The*

Musical Herald 3/12 (December 1882): 336. Publication review. "The three songs are the best Lieder which the composer has yet given out . . . ."

WB399. Mason, Redfern. "As to Music and Musicians." *San Francisco Examiner* August 1, 1915: 26. Announcement of the August 3, 1915 performance, which is a concert devoted mainly to the music of Chadwick's student, Mabel Daniels. Mason notes that Daniels ". . . is thought highly of by George W. Chadwick." (See also: W264b)

WB400. Mason, Redfern. "Musical Club Gives Concert." *San Francisco Examiner* August 4, 1915: 9. Review of the August 3, 1915 performance ["Before the Dawn" only]. States that the Chadwick work was "sung and sung effectively. . . ." Also notes that Mrs. Chadwick was in the audience. (See also: W264b)

W265. THREE NAUTICAL SONGS FOR BARITONE

1. The Admirals (Richard Darwin Ware [1869-1931])
2. Drake's Drum (Henry Newbold) (Composed September 13, 1917) (See also: W99)
3. Pirate's Song (Arthur Conan Doyle [1859-1930]) (See also: W102)

Dedications: Reinald Werrenrath (no. 1); Charles Bennett (nos. 2 and 3)
Published: Ditson, 1920 (publ. plate nos. 73305, 73306 and 13474)

Selected Performance

W265a. 5 February 1926; Frederic Joslyn, baritone; Charles Touchette, piano; Jordan Hall, Boston.

Bibliography

WB401. "Boston Activities." *Musical America* 43/17 (February 13, 1926): 44. Notice of the performance of February 5, 1926. (See: W265a)

W266. THREE SONGS BY G. W. CHADWICK

1. So Far Away (unknown)
2. Good Night (unknown)

3. Across the Hills (P. W. Lyall)

Dedications: Mrs. G. M. Cummings (nos. 1 and 3); Jennie M. Noyes
      (no. 2)
Holograph: DLC
Published: Ditson, 1881 (publ. plate nos. 48267, 48278 and 48279);
      No. 2 was reprinted in 1909.

Printers' errors have led to confusion about Chadwick's authorship of
this set of songs. Nos. 1 and 2 were originally issued with attributions
to "J. [sic] W. Chadwick" on the cover sheet, although the inside cover
of no. 2 is correctly attributed to G. W. Chadwick. No. 3 is attributed
to G. W. Chadwick on both the cover and the inside page.

Selected Performance

W266a. 30 January 1883; New England Conservatory Graduates
      Concert; H. A. Moore, vocalist, W. P. Nickerson, pianist;
      [precise location undetermined]; (nos. 1 and 3 only).

Bibliography

WB402. "New Music." *Boston Evening Transcript* June 6, 1881: 6.
      Notice of publication of "Across the Hills."

WB403. "Musical Mention -- Boston and Vicinity." *Musical Herald*
      4/3 (March 1883): 84. Reports the performance of January 30,
      1883. (See: 266a)

W267. THREE SONGS FOR MEZZO-SOPRANO OR BARITONE

1. In My Beloved's Eyes (W. M. Chauvenet) (See also: W232)
2. The Brink of Night (W. M. Chauvenet)
3. Thou Art to Me (Arthur Macy [1842-1904])

Dedication: Ida May Chadwick (no. 2 only)
Holograph: NRU-Mus
Published: Schirmer, 1902 (publ. plate no. 16033-16035)

Selected Performances

W267a. 21 November 1904; Herbert Witherspoon, vocalist; All-
      Chadwick concert; Jordan Hall, Boston (no. 3 only).

W267b. 10 March 1909; Jessica Swartz, vocalist; MacDowell Club
concert; Boston (no. 3 only).

Bibliography

WB404. R. R. G. "Jordan Hall: Mr. Chadwick's Concert." *Boston
Evening Transcript* November 22, 1904: 15. Review of the
November 21, 1904 performance in Boston. This review does
not specifically consider this composition, but the writer says
of the event: "To turn to last night's concert, it must at once
be set down as a success." (See: W267a)

W268. TIME ENOUGH

Text: Braley [only name supplied]
Dedication: unknown
Holograph: not located
Neither a holograph nor a printed copy of this composition has been
located, but it has been recorded (See B164 [p. 113] and D70).

W269. TWO FOLK SONGS

1. O Love and Joy (anonymous) (See also: W252 [no. 9])
2. The Northern Days (Christina Rossetti [1830-1894]) (See also:
W252 [no. 10])

Dedication: Mrs. G. H. Stoddard
Published: Schmidt, 1892 (publ. plate no. 2394)

W270. TWO SONGS BY THOMAS BAILEY ALDRICH

1. Nocturne (See also: W216 [no. 1] and W252 [no. 6])
2. Song from the Persian (See also: W216 [no. 2] and W252 [no. 17])

Texts by: Thomas Bailey Aldrich (1836-1907)
Dedication: William J. Winch
Published: Schmidt, 1886 (publ. plate nos. 917-918)

W271. WHAT OTHER PEOPLE SAY (Pasha's Song and Chorus from TABASCO)

Text by: Robert Ayres Barnet (1850?-1893)
Published: Wood, 1894 (publ. plate no. 12)
(See also: W74)

W272. YESTERDAY

Text by: David Kilburn Stevens (1860-1946)
Dedication: Ernestine Schumann-Heink
Published: Schmidt, 1914 (publ. plate no. 10234-4)

II. Band Arrangements of Chadwick's Music by Chadwick and Others

WR1. THE DANZA

Arranged for: Band and vocalist
Arranged by: All parts bear the initials "E. G. C." [Edwin G. Clarke]
Manuscript parts (no score) at The Sousa Archive for Band Research,
        University of Illinois at Urbana-Champaign
Date: unknown

(See also: W255 [no. 1])

WR2. THE MAIDEN AND THE BUTTERFLY

Arranged for: Band and vocalist
Arranged by: Not indicated but all parts are in the hand of Herbert L.
        Clarke
Manuscript parts (no score) at The Sousa Archive for Band Research,
        University of Illinois at Urbana-Champaign
Date: unknown

(See also: W262 [no. 2])

WR3. MELPOMENE

Arranged for: Band
Arranged by: Frank J. Fiala
Manuscript score and parts held in the band library of The United States
        Marine Band ("The President's Own"), Washington, D. C.
Published: [n.p.]: Bovaco, 1992 [manuscript parts date from ca. 1910]

(See also: W11)

Selected Performance

WR3a. 16 March 1997; The United States Marine Band ("The President's Own"); Michael J. Colburn, cond.; Center for the Arts concert hall, George Mason University, Fairfax, Virginia.

WR4. THE NEW HAIL COLUMBIA MARCH (TABASCO)

Arranged for: Band
Arranged by: Hans Semper
Published: B. F. Wood, 1917

(See also: W74)

WR5. OH, LET NIGHT SPEAK OF ME

Arranged for: Band and vocalist
Arranged by: Not indicated but much of this arrangement is in John Philip Sousa's hand
Manuscript parts (no score) at The Sousa Archive for Band Research, University of Illinois at Urbana-Champaign
Date: unknown

(See also: W242 [no. 10])

WR6. RIP VAN WINKLE

Arranged for: Band
Arranged by: George Whitefield Chadwick (1854-1931)
Manuscript parts and full score (58 pp.) at The Sousa Archive for Band Research, University of Illinois at Urbana-Champaign
Date: unknown
(See also: W14)

WR7. SELECTION FROM BURLESQUE OPERA: TABASCO

Arranged for: Band
Arranged by: Joseph Bernard Claus (1833-1905)
Score and parts at The Sousa Archive for Band Research, University of Illinois at Urbana-Champaign
Date: 1894
Published: Boston: Jean White, 1894 (plate no. 756-25-2; by permission of B. F. Wood Publishing Company)
(See also: W74)

WR8. SINFONIETTA IN D MAJOR (Movement no. 2, "Canzonetta")

Arranged for: Band
Arranged by: E. Boccalari
Manuscript score (18 pp.) and parts at The Sousa Archive for Band
      Research, University of Illinois at Urbana-Champaign
Date: unknown

(See also: W17)

Selected Performances

WR8a. 4 January 1911; "Farewell Visit of Sousa and his Band," John
      Philip Sousa, cond.; Queen's Hall, London [Program held at
      The Sousa Archive for Band Research, University of Illinois
      at Urbana-Champaign].

WR8b. 17 April 1913 [possibly 1915]; John Philip Sousa and his
      Band, John Philip Sousa, cond.; Memorial Hall, [city
      undetermined]; [Program held at The Sousa Archive for Band
      Research, University of Illinois at Urbana-Champaign].

WR9. SYMPHONIC SKETCHES (Movement no. 1, "Jubilee")

Arranged for: Band
Arranged by: George Whitefield Chadwick (1854-1931)
Manuscript score (43 pp.) and parts at The Sousa Archive for Band
      Research, University of Illinois at Urbana-Champaign
Date: "12/14/07" appears at the end of the 2nd bass part

(See also: W19)

WR10. SYMPHONIC SKETCHES (Movement no. 1, "Jubilee")

Arranged for: Band
Arranged by: Joseph Bernard Claus (1833-1905)
Manuscript parts at DLC

(See also: W19)

WR11. SYMPHONIC SKETCHES (Movement no. 1, "Jubilee")

Arranged for: Band

Arranged by: Paul Hines
Manuscript score and parts held in the band library of The United States
      Marine Band ("The President's Own"), Washington, D. C.
Arrangement completed: May 13, 1946

The United States Marine Band ("The President's Own"), William F.
Santelmann, conductor, featured this work on its National Concert Tour
programs in 1953.

(See also: W19)

Other Selected Performances

WR11a. 1 April 1949; The United States Marine Band ("The
      President's Own"); Massachusetts Institute of Technology
      Mid-Century Convocation; William F. Santelmann, cond.;
      Boston Garden, Boston.

WR11b. 20 May 1980; The United States Marine Band ("The
      President's Own"); Colonel John R. Bourgeois, cond.; Tawes
      Theatre, University of Maryland, College Park, Maryland.

(See also: W19rr)

WR12. SYMPHONIC SKETCHES (Movement no. 1, "Jubilee")

Arranged for: Band
Arranged by: Howard Bowlin
Manuscript score and parts held in the band library of The United States
      Marine Band ("The President's Own"), Washington, D. C.
Date: August 17, 1988

The United States Marine Band ("The President's Own"), Colonel John
R. Bourgeois, conductor, featured this work on its National Concert
Tour programs in 1988 and 1995.

(See also: W19)

WR13. SYMPHONIC SKETCHES (Movement no. 4, "Vagrom Ballad")

Arranged for: Band
Arranged by: E. Boccalari

Manuscript score (36 pp.) and parts at The Sousa Archive for Band
Research, University of Illinois at Urbana-Champaign
Date: unknown

(See also: W19)

WR14. SYMPHONY NO. 2 (Movement No. 2, "Scherzo")

Arranged for: Band
Arranged by: George Whitefield Chadwick (1854-1931)
Manuscript score (29 pp.) and parts at The Sousa Archive for Band
Research, University of Illinois at Urbana-Champaign
Date: unknown

The score bears the the following inscription in J. P. Sousa's hand:
"Orchestra same key [F major]"

(See also: W21)

WR15. TABASCO MARCH

Arranged for: Band
Arranged by: E. N. Lafricain
Manuscript score: not located
Date: ca. 1893-1894

According to published reports, Chadwick provided advance sheets for
Lafricain to prepare a version of the march for military band. (See:
WB294)

(See also: W74)

WR16. TAM O'SHANTER

Arranged for: Band
Arranged by: John Philip Sousa (1854-1932)
Published score (96 pp.) with published parts is supplemented by
additional band parts (in Sousa's hand) that are intended to
replace the strings and fill out the rest of the band instrumen-
tation.
All materials are held at The Sousa Archive for Band Research,
University of Illinois at Urbana-Champaign
Date: unknown

(See also: W24)

Chadwick's presentation score to Sousa is inscribed: "[To] John Philip Sousa in token of a long and tried friendship from George W. Chadwick, Sept. 1925."

III. Chadwick's Arrangements of Music by Other Composers

WA1. Georg Frideric Handel, Sonata (No. 1) in A Major

Date arranged: unknown
Holograph score and parts: MBCM
Arranged for: 2 trumpets. organ. strings

Movements: Andante-Allegro; Adagio; Allegro

Selected Performance

WA1a. 17 December 1920; New England Conservatory Orchestra, Alfred Hamer, organ, G. W. Chadwick, cond.; Jordan Hall, Boston.

WA2. Georg Frideric Handel, Concerto in B-flat Major, No. 12

Date arranged: ca. 1903
Holograph score and parts: MBCM
Arranged for: Solo organ and orchestra

Movements: Pomposo; Larghetto; A tempo ordinario

Selected Performance

WA2a. 14 January 1927; New England Conservatory Orchestra, Albert W. Snow, organ, G. W. Chadwick, cond.; Jordan Hall, Boston.

WA3. Giuseppe Torrelli, Concerto for Two Violins

Date arranged: 1913
Ink holograph score and parts: MBCM
Arranged for: 2 solo violins. 2 trumpets. organ (ad lib.). strings

Movements: Allegro non troppo; Adagio; Andante; Adagio-Allegro

WA4. Antonio Vivaldi, Concerto for Three Violins in F

Date arranged: unknown
Holograph score and parts: MBCM
Arranged for: 3 solo violins. 3 trumpets. organ. strings

Discography

I. Orchestral Music

Aphrodite

D1. Reference Recordings RR-74CD (CD; 1996). Czech State Philharmonic Brno, Jose Serebrier, cond. Liner notes by Steven Ledbetter.

Elegy

D2. Reference Recordings RR-74CD (CD; 1996). Czech State Philharmonic Brno, Jose Serebrier, cond. Liner notes by Steven Ledbetter.

Euterpe

D3. Albany Records/Troy 030-2 (CD re-issue of LS-75-3; 1975).
Louisville Orchestra, Jorge Mester, cond.

D4. Louisville Orchestra First Edition Records LS-75-3 (33 1/3 rpm; 1975).
Louisville Orchestra, Jorge Mester, cond.

Melpomene

D5. Chandos 9439 (CD; 1996). Detroit Symphony Orchestra, Neeme Jarvi,
cond. Liner notes by Michael Fleming.

D6. Reference Recordings RR-64CD (CD; 1995). Czech State Philharmonic Brno, Jose Serebrier, cond. Liner notes by Steven Ledbetter.

D7.   Albany Records/Troy 103 (CD; 1993). Symphony Orchestra of
        America, Matthew H. Phillips, cond. Liner notes by Daniel
        Nightingale.

Rip van Winkle

D8.   Chandos 9439 (CD; 1996). Detroit Symphony Orchestra, Neeme Jarvi,
        cond. Liner notes by Michael Fleming.

Serenade for Strings

D9.   Albany Records/Troy 033 (CD; 1990). American Music Ensemble
        Vienna, Hobart Earle, cond.

Sinfonietta

D10.   The Library of Congress OMP-107, *Our Musical Past*, vol. 6 (CD;
        1990 [re-issue]). The Royal Philharmonic Orchestra, Karl Krueger,
        cond. Liner notes by Steven Ledbetter.

D11.   Society for the Preservation of the American Musical Heritage MIA-
        104 (33 1/3 rpm; 1959). American Arts Orchestra, Karl Krueger,
        cond. Liner notes by Karl Krueger.

Suite Symphonique

D12.   Refcrence Recordings RR-74CD (CD; 1996). Czech State Phil-
        harmonic Brno, Jose Serebrier, cond. Liner notes by Steven Ledbetter.

Symphonic Sketches

D13.   United States Marine Band USMB-CD-11, *Director's Choice* (CD;
        1996). United States Marine Band ("The President's Own"), Col. John
        R. Bourgeois, cond. "Jubilee" only [arranged for band].

D14.   Chandos 9334 (CD; 1995). Detroit Symphony Orchestra, Neeme Jarvi,
        cond. Liner notes by Bill F. Faucett.

D15.   Reference Recordings RR-64CD (CD; 1995). Czech State Philhar-
        monic Brno, Jose Serebrier, cond. Liner notes by Steven Ledbetter.

D16.   Mercury 434 337-2-CD (CD; 1994 re-issue of SR90018). Eastman-
        Rochester Orchestra, Howard Hanson, cond. Liner notes by David Hall.

D17. Telarc CD-80144 (CD; 1988). *American Jubilee*. Cincinnati Pops
Orchestra, Erich Kunzel, cond. "Jubilee" only. Liner notes by David
Loebel.

D18. Mercury SRI 75050 (33 1/3 rpm; 1975). Eastman-Rochester Orchestra,
Howard Hanson, cond. [Previously released as Mercury SR-90018.]

D19. Mercury MG 50337/SR-90337 (33 1/3 rpm; 1963). *Curtain Up!*
Eastman-Rochester Orchestra, Howard Hanson, cond. Movement no.
2, "Noel," only.

D20. Mercury SR 90049 (33 1/3 rpm; ca. 1960s). Eastman-Rochester
Orchestra, Howard Hanson, cond.

D21. Mercury SR-90018 (33 1/3 rpm; 1959). Eastman-Rochester Orchestra,
Howard Hanson, cond.

D22. Concord 3007 (33 1/3 rpm; 1957). Hamburg Philharmonia, Richard
Korn, cond. Movement no. 3, "Hobgoblin," only.

D23. Mercury MG-50104 (33 1/3 rpm; 1956). *American Music Festival*
series. Eastman-Rochester Orchestra, Howard Hanson, cond. Liner
notes by David Hall.

D24. Allegro ALG-3150 (33 1/3 rpm; 1955). Hamburg Philharmonia,
Richard Korn, cond. Movement no. 3, "Hobgoblin," only.

D25. Mercury MDS5-24 (One 7 1/2 ips stereo reel-to-reel tape; ca. 1950s).
Eastman-Rochester Orchestra, Howard Hanson, cond.

D26. Victor 12-0155-58 (78 rpm; before 1952). Eastman-Rochester
Symphony, Howard Hanson, cond. Movement No. 1, "Jubilee," only.

D27. Gramophone DB-3999 (78 rpm; before 1952). Eastman-Rochester
Symphony, Howard Hanson, cond. Movement No. 1, "Jubilee," only.

D28. Victor 18274 (78 rpm; before 1942). National Symphony Orchestra,
Hans Kindler, cond. Movement no. 2, "Noel," only.

D29. Gramophone ED-291 (78 rpm; before 1942). National Symphony
Orchestra, Hans Kindler, cond. Movement no. 2, "Noel," only.

D30. RCA Victor M608 (78 rpm; 1940s). Eastman-Rochester Orchestra,
Howard Hanson, cond. Movement no. 1, "Jubilee," only.

D31. Victor 15656 (in album M608) (78 rpm; 1939). Eastman-Rochester Symphony, Howard Hanson, cond. Movement No. 1, "Jubilee," only.

Symphony No. 2 in B-flat

D32. Chandos 9334 (CD; 1995). Detroit Symphony Orchestra, Neeme Jarvi, cond. Liner notes by Bill F. Faucett.

D33. New World Records NW-339-2 (CD; 1986). Albany Symphony Orchestra, Julius Hegyi, cond. Liner notes by Steven Ledbetter.

D34. Society for the Preservation of the American Musical Heritage MIA-134 (33 1/3 rpm; 1967). Royal Philharmonic Orchestra, Karl Krueger, cond. Liner notes by Karl Krueger.

Symphony in F (No. 3)

D35. Chandos 9253 (CD; 1994). Detroit Symphony Orchestra, Neeme Jarvi, cond. Liner notes by Bill F. Faucett.

D36. The Library of Congress OMP-107, *Our Musical Past*, vol. 6 (CD reissue of MIA-140; 1990). Royal Philharmonic Orchestra, Karl Krueger, cond. Liner notes by Steven Ledbetter.

D37. Society for the Preservation of the American Musical Heritage MIA-140 (33 1/3 rpm; 1968). Royal Philharmonic Orchestra, Karl Krueger, cond. Liner notes by Karl Krueger.

Tabasco March

D38. New World Records 80266-2 (CD reissue of NW-266; 1976). *The Pride of America -- The Golden Age of the American March*. The Goldman Band, Ainslee Cox, cond. Liner notes by Richard Franko Goldman.

Tam O'Shanter

D39. Chandos 9439 (CD; 1996). Detroit Symphony Orchestra, Neeme Jarvi, cond. Liner notes by Michael Fleming.

D40. Reference Recordings RR-64CD (CD; 1995). Czech State Philharmonic Brno, Jose Serebrier, cond. Liner notes by Steven Ledbetter.

D41. Desto D-421/DST-6421 (33 1/3 rpm; 1967). Vienna Symphony

Orchestra, Max Schoenherr, cond.

D42.   American Recording Society ARS-29 (33 1/3 rpm; 1953). Vienna
        Symphony Orchestra, Max Schoennherr, cond.

Theme, Variations, and Fugue

D43.   Nonesuch H-71200 (33 1/3 rpm; 1968). *Yankee Organ Music*.
        Richard Ellsasser, organ. Liner notes and organ specifications by Jason
        Farrow. (Arrangement for solo organ).

II. Chamber Music

String Quartet No. 1

D44.   Northeastern Records NR 236-CD (CD; 1988). The Portland String
        Quartet. Liner notes by Steven Ledbetter.

String Quartet No. 2

D45.   Northeastern Records NR 236-CD (CD; 1988). The Portland String
        Quartet. Liner notes by Steven Ledbetter.

String Quartet No. 3

D46.   Northeastern Records NR 235-CD (CD; 1988). The Portland String
        Quartet. Liner notes by Steven Ledbetter.

String Quartet No. 4

D47.   Northeastern Records NR 234-CD (CD; 1988). The Portland String
        Quartet. Liner notes by Steven Ledbetter.

D48.   Library of Congress nos. RWA 7343-7344 (reel tapes; recorded 1984).
        American String Quartet. [Recorded at the Music Division's "Festival
        of American Chamber Music," Coolidge Auditorium, Library of
        Congress, Washington, D. C.] (See also: W33d)

D49.   Library of Congress nos. RWA 5749-5750 (reel tapes; recorded May
        11, 1983). American String Quartet. [Recorded at a meeting of the
        International Association of Music Librarians, Coolidge Auditorium,

Library of Congress, Washington, D. C.] (See also: W33c)

D50. Vox SVBX-5301 (33 1/3 rpm; 1971) *The Early String Quartet in the U. S. A.* The Kohon Quartet.

D51. Vox Box CDX 5057 (CD; 1992 re-release of Vox SVBX-5301). *The Early String Quartet in the U. S. A.* The Kohon Quartet. Liner notes by R. D. Darrell.

D52. RCA Victor 15417B/Album M558 (78 rpm; before 1942). The Coolidge Quartet (Movement no. 2, "Andante semplice," only.)

D53. Library of Congress control no. 96703754/R (reel tape; recorded April 30, 1938). Coolidge Quartet. [Recorded at a concert under the auspices of the Elizabeth Sprague Coolidge Foundation, Coolidge Auditorium, Library of Congress, Washington, D. C.] (See also: W33b)

String Quartet No. 5

D54. Northeastern Records NR 234-CD (CD; 1988). The Portland String Quartet. Liner notes by Steven Ledbetter.

D55. Library of Congress nos. RWB 0372-0773 (reel tape; recorded May 10, 1985). Tremont String Quartet. [Recorded at the Music Division's *Festival of American Chamber Music*, Library of Congress, Coolidge Auditorium, Washington, D. C.]

Quintet for Piano and Strings

D56. Northeastern Records NR 235-CD (CD; 1988). The Portland String Quartet. Liner notes by Steven Ledbetter.

Piano

D57. Premiere Recordings [New York], American Piano Series No. 2. (CD; 1992). *Blue Voyage: Music in the Grand Tradition.* Ramon Salvatore, pianist. Liner notes by Steven Ledbetter. Contents: *Prelude Joyeaux, Le Crepescule, Le Ruisseau,* and *Dans Le Canot.*

Organ

D58. Orion ORS-78317 (33 1/3 rpm; 1978). William Osborne, organ. Contents: *Suite in Variation Form.*

D59.   Musical Heritage Society OR-A-263 (33 1/3 rpm; 1972). Janice Beck, organ. Contents: *Pastorale.*

D60.   Repertoire Recording Society RRS-12, *The American Collection* (33 1/3 rpm; 1973). Rollin Smith, organ. Contents: *Pastorale.*

D61.   Gloriae Dei Cantores GDCD 011, *Organ Music of America, vol. 2-- 1868-1908--The Boston Classicists* (CD; 1993). David Chalmers, organ. Contents: *Pastorale.*

III. Stage Works

Tabasco

D62.   *Music from the Source: New England Conservatory at 125.* (One commercially unavailable cassette recording; March 2, 1992). New England Conservatory Orchestra; John Moriarty, cond. Jordan Hall, Boston [Opening night concert celebrating the 125th anniversary of the conservatory.] Cassette held at New England Conservatory of Music, Boston. Contents: Overture only.

The Padrone

D63.   World premiere performance [Concert version] (One commercially unavailable cassette recording; September 29, 1995). Alexandra Gruber-Malkin, soprano; Jacqueline Pierce, mezzo-soprano; Jane Dutton, contralto; Barton Green and Chad Shelton, tenors; Thomas Woodman, baritone; Concora [chorus], Waterbury Chorale, Naugatuck Valley College Chorus, and the Waterbury Symphony Orchestra, Leif Bjaland, cond. Recorded at the Thomaston Opera House, Thomaston, Connecticut. Archival cassette held at New England Conservatory of Music, Boston.

IV. Choral Music

D64.   Northeastern Records 247-CD (CD; 1992). *Alleluia: Sacred Choral Music in New England.* The Harvard University Choir, Murray Forbes Somerville, cond. Contents: *Canzonetta* and *Sun of My Soul.*

V. Songs

D65.   Hyperion CDA66920 (CD; 1997). *Sure on This Shining Light:*
       20th-Century Romantic Songs of America. Robert White, tenor;
       Samuel Sanders, piano. Contents: *When Stars Are in The Quiet*
       Skies.

D66.   *The American Romantic, Featuring Songs of the Boston Composers*
       Group. A faculty recital by Rita V. Beatie, Jordan Hall, New England
       Conservatory, May 10, 1987. One commercially unavailable cassette
       recording held at New England Conservatory of Music, Boston.
       Contents: *Before the Dawn, Du bist wie eine Blume (Thou Art So*
       Like a Flower) and *Song from the Persian.*

D67.   Albany/Troy 034-2 (CD; 1991). *Songs of an Innocent Age: Music*
       from Turn of the Century America. American Song Series, vol. 3.
       Paul Sperry, tenor; Erma Vallecillo, piano. Contents: *Adversity,*
       Euthanasia, and *The Danza.*

D68.   Voyager VRLP-701S (33 1/3 rpm; 1976). Seattle Chamber Singers,
       George Shangrow, cond. Contents: *A Valentine.*

D69.   Duke University Press DWR-6418-18/DWRM-7501 (33 1/3 rpm;
       1966). John Kennedy Hanks, tenor; Ruth Friedberg, piano. Contents:
       Oh, Let Night Speak of Me.

D70.   Victor 36033 (78 rpm; before 1936). Ann Howard, soprano. Contents:
       Time Enough.

D71.   Victor 22621 (78 rpm; before 1936). Ann Howard, soprano. Contents:
       Morning Glory.

D72.   Victor 36032 (78 rpm; before 1936). Ann Howard, soprano. Contents:
       If I Were You and *Lady Bird.*

D73.   Victor 87172 (78 rpm; ca. 1912-1916). Ernestine Schumann-Heink,
       alto. Contents: *Allah.*

D74.   Victor 88409 (78 rpm; 1912). Geraldine Farrar, soprano; Victor
       Orchestra [conductor not listed]. Contents: *Love's Like a Summer*
       Rose [arranged for vocalist and orchestra by Lindermann].

D75.   Victor 87020 (78 rpm; ca. 1906-1910). Ernestine Schumann-Heink, alto; The Victor Orchestra [conductor not determined]. Contents: *The Danza.*

Discography
Bibliography

I. Orchestral Music

Aphrodite

DB1.   Faucett, Bill F. Review of Reference Recordings RR-74CD. *Palm Beach Post* July 20, 1997: 3J. "Chadwick's music is direct, lush, and usually clever and tuneful . . . . Aphrodite presents some of the best evocations of the sea in all of music . . . ." (See: D1)

DB2.   Dickinson, Peter. Review of Reference Recordings RR-74CD. *Gramophone* 75/889 (June 1997): 52-53. ". . . Aphrodite draws with equal conviction on [Wagner's] Tristan [und Isolde] or even Franck." (See: D1)

DB3.   Dyer, Richard. Announcement of release of Reference Recordings RR-74CD. "Classical Notes: Local Artists Put Their All on the Record." *Boston Globe* February 7, 1997: D17. (See: D1)

DB4.   Haller, Steven J. Review of Reference Recordings RR-74CD. *American Record Guide* 60/2 (March/April 1997): 113. "While [the] closing bars do betray the influence of Brahms, elsewhere the music is Chadwick at his best." (See: D1)

DB5.   Johnson, David. Review of Reference Recordings RR-74CD. *Fanfare* 20/4 (March/April 1997): 145-147. The central portion ". . . rises to an urgency bordering on the erotic--rather astonishing for a nineteenth-century, proper Bostonian." (See: D1)

DB6.   Snook, Paul A. Review of Reference Recordings RR-74CD. *Fanfare* 20/4 (March/April 1997): 144-145. "Without doubt, Aphrodite is a major addition to the late-Romantic recorded repertoire." (See: D1)

Elegy

DB7.   Faucett, Bill F. Review of Reference Recordings RR-74CD. *Palm Beach Post* July 20, 1997: 3J. "Chadwick's music is direct, lush, and usually clever and tuneful . . . . the unknown *Elegy* may well be one of Chadwick's best works." (See: D1)

DB8.   Dickinson, Peter. Review of Reference Recordings RR-74CD. *Gramophone* 75/889 (June 1997): 52-53. "The Elegy is dignified and restrained, a New Englander's expression of grief." (See: D1)

DB9.   Dyer, Richard. Announcement of release of Reference Recordings RR-74CD. "Classical Notes: Local Artists Put Their All on the Record." *Boston Globe* February 7, 1997: D17. (See: D1)

DB10.   Haller, Steven J. Review of Reference Recordings RR-74CD. *American Record Guide* 60/2 (March/April 1997): 113. " . . . the music flows more beguilingly than the usual funeral cortege and seems more evocative of the final resting place than the procession." (See: D1)

DB11.   Johnson, David. Review of Reference Recordings RR-74CD. *Fanfare* 20/4 (March/April 1997): 145-147. "It is a gorgeous piece, at once heartrending and uplifting." (See: D1)

DB12.   Snook, Paul A. Review of Reference Recordings RR-74CD. *Fanfare* 20/4 (March/April 1997): 144-145. ". . . sonorously moving . . . ." (See: D1)

Melpomene

DB13.   Achenbach, Andrew. Review of Reference Recordings RR-64CD. *Gramophone* 73/873 (February 1996): 46. ". . . Melpomene is a fine, often eloquent achievement whose slumbering, neo-Wagnerian character invites (and well withstands) comparison with, say, the tone poems of Franck or Dukas's early Polyeucte overture." (See: D6)

DB14.   Achenbach, Andrew. Review of Chandos 9439. *Gramophone* 74/877 (June 1996): 44. " . . . just a touch bland . . . ." (See: D5)

DB15. Bauman, Carl. Review of Albany Records/Troy 103. *American Record Guide* 57/3 (May-June 1994): 172. "From its Tristanesque opening (it even uses an English horn) to its end it maintains a properly somber atmosphere. . . . it is the real gem of the disc." (See: D7)

DB16. Haller, Steven J. Review of Reference Recordings RR-64CD. *American Record Guide* 58/6 (November-December 1995): 103-104. "This is not the Yankee rogue of Symphonic Sketches, but a heartfelt side of Chadwick's muse as moving as it is unexpected . . . ." (See: D6)

DB17. Haller, Steven J. Review of Chandos 9439. *American Record Guide* 59/5 (July-August 1996): 214-215. [This review mentions *Melpomene* only briefly.] (See: D5)

DB18. Johnson, David. Review of Reference Recordings RR-64CD. *Fanfare* 19/2 (November/December 1995): 233-234. " . . . Chadwick gives us one of the nineteenth century's more powerful musical depictions of tragic drama." (See: D6)

DB19. North, James H. Review of Chandos 9439. *Fanfare* 20/1 (September/October 1996): 343-344. " . . . almost Wagnerian . . . ." (See: D5)

DB20. Stryker, Mark. Review of Chandos 9439. "Slice of Americana -- DSO Handily Revives Work of 20th-Century Composers." *Detroit Free Press* (May 26, 1996): 4F. (See: D5)

DB21. Vroon, Donald. Review of Chandos 9439. *American Record Guide* 59/5 (July-August 1996): 214. " . . . thoroughly romantic and thoroughly enjoyable." (See: D5)

Rip Van Winkle

DB22. Achenbach, Andrew. Review of Chandos 9439. *Gramophone* 74/877 (June 1996): 44. " . . . the work as a whole contains little that lingers long in the memory, for all the solid craftsmanship on show." (See: D8)

DB23. Haller, Steven J. Review of Chandos 9439. *American Record Guide* 59/5 (July-August 1996): 214-215. ". . . conjures up amiable images of old Rip, including echoes of a barnyard dance . . . ." (See: D8)

DB24. North, James H. Review of Chandos 9439. *Fanfare* 20/1

(September/October 1996): 343-344. " . . . it suggests that its young composer was already competent and experienced in orchestral writing." (See: D8)

DB25. Stryker, Mark. Review of Chandos 9439. "Slice of Americana -- DSO Handily Revives Work of 20th-Century Composers." *Detroit Free Press* (May 26, 1996): 4F. This review only mentions that *Rip Van Winkle* is on the disc. (See: D8)

DB26. Vroon, Donald. Review of Chandos 9439. *American Record Guide* 59/5 (July-August 1996): 214. " . . . thoroughly romantic and thoroughly enjoyable." (See: D8)

Serenade for Strings

DB27. Johnson, David. Review of Albany Records/Troy 033-2. *Fanfare* 14/4 (March-April 1991): 180-181. "This Serenade delivers the goods. It's a superb piece of writing, making full use of divisi strings and thus achieving the same full-blooded sound as does Tchaikovsky in his String Serenade, op. 48." (See: D9)

DB28. Vroon, Donald R. Review of Albany Records/Troy 033-2. *American Record Guide* 54/2 (March-April 1991): 54. "It is not loaded with brilliant melodies, but it is brilliantly composed just the same." (See: D9)

Sinfonietta

DB29. Haller, Steven J. Review of OMP-107. *American Record Guide* 54/4 (July-August 1991): 44-45. ". . . energetic enough if without straying too far from the Old World mold . . . ." (See: D10)

DB30. Horowitz, Joseph. Review of OMP-107. "Beach, Chadwick: New World Symphonists." *New York Times* October 27, 1991: H/25. Discusses the musical style of the two composers and considers the new releases of their music. (See: D10)

DB31. McColley, Robert. Review of OMP 107. *Fanfare* 14/4 (March-April 1991): 181-182. ". . . it achieves coherence more by balance and contrast than by true symphonic development." (See: D10)

Suite Symphonique

DB32. Faucett, Bill F. Review of Reference Recordings RR-74CD. *Palm*

Beach Post July 20, 1997: 3J. "Chadwick's music is direct, lush, and usually clever and tuneful." His works ". . . can stand alongside the best compositions from the Romantic tradition without fear of comparison." (See: D12)

DB33.   Dickinson, Peter. Review of Reference Recordings RR-74CD. *Gramophone* 75/889 (June 1997): 52-53. ". . . sounds surprisingly like Elgar, especially in this key, since both composers drew on similar continental sources." (See: D12)

DB34.   Dyer, Richard. Announcement of the release of Reference Recordings RR-74CD. "Classical Notes: Local Artists Put Their All on the Record." *Boston Globe* February 7, 1997: D17. (See: D12)

DB35.   Haller, Steven J. Review of Reference Recordings RR-74CD. *American Record Guide* 60/2 (March/April, 1997): 113. "The Suite for the most part suggest a recycling of earlier material . . . ." (See: D12)

DB36.   Johnson, David. Review of Reference Recordings RR-74CD. *Fanfare* 20/4 (March April 1997): 145-147. "There is a certain amount of Richard Strauss in the cut of the first movement's themes. . . ." (See: D12)

DB37.   Snook, Paul A. Review of Reference Recordings RR-74CD. *Fanfare* 20/4 (March/April 1997): 144-145. ". . . the prevailing tone of this typically virile, forthright, yet soaring work is markedly Elgarian." (See: D12)

Symphonic Sketches

DB38.   Achenbach, Andrew. Review of Reference Recordings RR-64CD. *Gramophone* 73/873 (February 1996): 46. ". . . its warm-hearted, tuneful inspiration [emerges] as freshly as the day it was conceived." (See: D15)

DB39.   Guinn, John. Review of Chandos 9334. "CD Watch." *Detroit Free Press* (April 2, 1995): 8G. "Chadwick's Second Symphony and Symphonic Sketches are both competent, inoffensive pieces, but neither has very much to say." (See: D14)

DB40.   Haller, Steven J. Review of Reference Recordings RR-64CD. *American Record Guide* 58/6 (November-December 1995): 103-104.

". . . brash, bumptious and fairly bubbling over with high spirits. . . ."
(See: D15)

DB41.   Haller, Steven J.   Review of Chandos 9334. *American Record Guide*
58/4 (July-August 1995): 100-101. On movement no. 2, 'Noel':
"Chadwick allows the glorious melody to unfold with angelic purity
before building to an ecstatic climax." Also, conductor Jarvi's ". . .
manic romp is a marvel, in a sense celebrating the brash young turk
that was Chadwick . . . ." (See: D14)

DB42.   Johnson, David.   Review of Chandos 9334. *Fanfare* 18/6 (July/August
1995): 154-155. " . . . it is a symphony unlike any ever heard in the
nineteenth century." (See: D14)

DB43.   Johnson, David.   Review of Mercury Records 434337-2. *Fanfare* 19/1
(September/October 1995): 461. " . . . a unique, rousing, heart-
touching, echt-American evocation of Chadwick's masterpiece." (See:
D16)

DB44.   Johnson, David.   Review of Reference Recordings RR-64CD. *Fanfare*
19/2 (November/December 1995): 233-234. " . . . the playing is so
lively, humorous, and songful . . . ." (See: D15)

DB45.   Leland, Gerry.   Review of Telarc CD-80144. "Hear Music You Loved
in Movies." *Charlotte* [North Carolina] *Observer* (June 26, 1988): 2F.
"A fine album to get the patriotic juices flowing." (See: D17)

DB46.   March, Ivan.   Review of Mercury Golden Imports SRI 75050. "A
Mixed Bag of Mercury Golden Imports." *Gramophone* 60/718 (March
1983): 1060. "Chadwick was musically conservative and his suite,
while showing considerable skill and orchestral flair, reminds one of the
suites of Massenet with its comfortable tunefulness and easy-going
sentiment." (See: D18)

DB47.   Roos, James.   Review of Chandos 9334. "Neil Diamond Revives
Country-Pop Sound on Moon." *Miami Herald* (February 7, 1996): 2D.
" . . . among Chadwick's most arresting works, especially the
kaleidoscopic Jubilee." (See: D14)

DB48.   Trezise, Simon.   Article includes a review of Chandos 9334. "Music of
the American Dream." *Classic CD* 63 (July 1995): 24-28. "Chadwick's absorbing Symphonic Sketches . . . breathe fresh life into
Dvorak's symphonic forms, suggesting the wide open spaces and
dynamic vistas of the New World." (See: D14)

DB49. Trezise, Simon. Review of Chandos 9334. *Classic CD* 60 (April 1995): 59. Chadwick's works " . . . seem to breathe the pioneering spirit, the vast open spaces, and the vitality of the nascent New World of America." (See: D14)

DB50. Ulrich, Allan. Review of Chandos 9334. "A Bang-Up Selection for the Fourth." *San Francisco Examiner*, 30 June 1995, 17 (C). "[Conductor Neeme] Jarvi brings uncommon flair to these gems of our musical past." (See: D14)

DB51. Vroon, Donald R. Review of Mercury 434337-2. *American Record Guide* 58/1 (January-February 1995): 95-96. ". . . the whole is worth knowing and having, and no one should miss 'Jubilee'." (See: D16)

DB52. "Orchestra to Play 5 Hours Recording American Music." *Rochester Democrat and Chronicle* 11 May 1939. Notes the inclusion of Chadwick's "Jubilee" on a recording for RCA Victor [probably Victor 15656] intended for "world consumption." (See: D31)

Symphony No. 2 in B-flat

DB53. Guinn, John. Review of Chandos 9334. "CD Watch." *Detroit Free Press* (April 2, 1995): 8G. "Chadwick's Second Symphony and Symphonic Sketches [also on this disc] are both competent, inoffensive pieces, but neither has very much to say." (See: D32)

DB54. Haller, Steven J. Review of Chandos 9334. *American Record Guide* 58/4 (July-August 1995): 100-101. ". . . comfortably nestled in the European traditions of Brahms and Schumann." (See: D32)

DB55. Johnson, David. Review of Chandos 9334. *Fanfare* 18/6 (July/August 1995): 154-155. " . . . the supreme example of pre-Dvorak Americana." (See: D32)

DB56. Roos, James. Review of Chandos 9334. "Neil Diamond Revives Country-Pop Sound on Moon." *Miami Herald* (February 7, 1996): 2D. " . . . Brahmsian with distinctly American flavoring . . . ." (See: D32)

DB57. Trezise, Simon. Article includes a review of Chandos 9334. "Music of the American Dream." *Classic CD* 63 (July 1995): 24-28. This review does not consider the Second Symphony in detail. (See: D32)

DB58. Trezise, Simon. Review of Chandos 9334. *Classic CD* 60 (April 1995): 59. Chadwick's works " . . . seem to breathe the pioneering spirit, the vast open spaces, and the vitality of the nascent New World of America." (See: D32)

DB59. Ulrich, Allan. Review of Chandos 9334. "A Bang-Up Selection for the Fourth." *San Francisco Examiner* (30 June 1995): 17C. " . . . the Symphony still affords considerable pleasure in a retro way; he could hammer out those sweeping tunes with considerable extroversion." (See: D32)

DB60. Whittall, Arnold. Review of New World Records NW-339-2. *Gramophone* 65/772 (September 1987): 404. In an otherwise negative assessment of Chadwick, Whittall states, "There is some genuine vitality, resulting from an eager embrace of what was then an up-to-date and still evolving mode of expression." (See: D33)

Symphony in F (No. 3)

DB61. Achenbach, Andrew. Review of Chandos 9253. *Gramophone* (October 1994): 102. "Well made and richly orchestrated, here is a thoroughly engaging, warm-hearted symphony . . . ." (See: D35)

DB62. Guinn, John. Review of Chandos 9253. "CD Watch." *Detroit Free Press* (June 10, 1994): 11E. "Chadwick's well-crafted Third Symphony . . . is about as American as the Reichstag, but Jarvi and the DSO play it with dedication, respect and some flair." (See: D35)

DB63. Haller, Steven J. Review of OMP-107. *American Record Guide* 54/4 (July-August 1991): 44-45. " . . . there is still much Brahms in evidence--or perhaps more to the point, Chadwick's teachers Reinecke and Rheinberger [are in evidence]." (See: D36)

DB64. Haller, Steven J. Review of Chandos 9253. *American Record Guide* 57/6 (November-December 1994): 91-92. " . . . skillfully developed and orchestrated with considerable flair, rich in the shimmering glow of the horns." (See: D35)

DB65. Horowitz, Joseph. Review of OMP-107. "Beach, Chadwick: New World Symphonists." *New York Times* October 27, 1991: H/25. Discusses the musical style of the two composers and considers the new releases of their music. " . . . there is something discernibly American about Chadwick's relaxed mien; he is Brahms with his beard shaved off and grinning from ear to ear." (See: D36)

DB66. McColley, Robert. Review of OMP 107. *Fanfare* 14/4 (March-April

1991): 181-182. " . . . is highly original in thematic invention, development of ideas, and orchestration." (See: D36)

Tam O'Shanter

DB67.   Achenbach, Andrew. Review of Reference Recordings RR-64CD. *Gramophone* 73/873 (February 1996): 46. *Tam O'Shanter* is ". . . music of the utmost vividness and local colour. Chadwick's orchestral mastery is evident throughout . . . ." (See: D40)

DB68.   Achenbach, Andrew. Review of Chandos 9439. *Gramophone* 74/877 (June 1996): 44. " . . . an extremely persuasive account . . . ." (See: D39)

DB69.   Haller, Steven J. Review of Reference Recordings RR-64CD. *American Record Guide* 58/6 (November-December 1995): 103-104. "Chadwick at once sets the scene with a powerful depiction of the storm-swept winds . . . ." (See: D40)

DB70.   Haller, Steven J. Review of Chandos 9439. *American Record Guide* 59/5 (July-August 1996): 214-215. [This review does not consider *Tam O'Shanter* at length.] (See: D39)

DB71.   Johnson, David. Review of Reference Recordings RR-64CD. *Fanfare* 19/2 (November/December 1995): 233-234. " . . . a programmatic tone poem that can stand comparison with the best such works of Richard Strauss." (See: D40)

DB72.   North, James H. Review of Chandos 9439. *Fanfare* 20/1 (September/October 1996): 343-344. ". . . pretty hefty stuff . . . ." (See: D39)

DB73.   Stryker, Mark. Review of Chandos 9439. "Slice of Americana -- DSO Handily Revives Work of 20th-Century Composers." *Detroit Free Press* (May 26, 1996): 4F. [This review does not include mention of *Tam O'Shanter*.] (See: D39)

DB74.   Vroon, Donald. Review of Chandos 9439. *American Record Guide* 59/5 (July-August 1996): 214. " . . . thoroughly romantic and thoroughly enjoyable." (See: D39)

II. Chamber Music

DB75. Bauman, Carl. Review of Northeastern NR 236-CD, NR 235-CD, and NR 234-CD. *American Record Guide* 52/3 (May-June 1989): 37. "Each disc represents one creative period from his life so they offer fascinating insights into his growth as a composer." (See: D44, D45, D46, D47, D54 and D56)

DB76. Dickinson, Peter. Review of Northeastern Records NR 236-CD. *Gramophone* 68/809 (October 1990): 756. " . . . remarkable student works by a young American composer of considerable natural musicianship who was much admired by his teachers and German contemporaries." (See: D44)

DB77. Dyer, Richard. "Joiner to Keep Northeastern Records Operating." *Boston Globe* December 1, 1988: 89. This notice announces the continuation of operations at Northeastern recording company despite problems. Dyer notes that the Chadwick quartets are being distributed as part of the company's plan to address a neglected segment of the classical repertoire. (See: D44, D45, D46, D47, D54 and D56)

DB78. Kearns, William. Review of Northeastern NR 236-CD, NR 235-CD, and NR 234-CD. *American Music* 8/3 (Fall 1990): 378-380. Chadwick's quartets " . . . stretching from the composer's student years to those of his maturity, encompass a wealth of musical ideas, showing not only his own inventiveness but also suggesting the musical fecundity of the times themselves." (See: D44, D45, D46, D47, D54 and D56)

DB79. Turok, Paul. Review of Northeastern NR 236-CD, NR 235-CD, and NR 234-CD. *Ovation* 10/3 (April 1989): 59-60. "The performances are vital enough for the music to speak for itself, and the recordings are excellent." (See: D44, D45, D46, D47, D54 and D56)

DB80. Wiser, John. Review of Northeastern NR 236-CD, NR 235-CD, and NR 234-CD. *Fanfare* 12/5 (May-June 1989): 161-162. "This music is so firm of character and alive that a sense of discovery attends one's entire first hearing, and persists well beyond that." (See: D44, D45, D46, D47, D54 and D56)

III. Songs

DB81. McColley, Robert. Review of Albany-Troy 034-2. *Fanfare* 14/5
(May-June 1991): 338-339. This review contains no specific mention
of Chadwick's songs. (See: D67)

General Bibliography

B1.   Coffin, Charles Carleton. *The History of Boscawen and Webster from 1733 to 1878.* Concord, New Hampshire: Republican Press Association, 1878. Provides genealogical references to the Chadwick family, especially Edmund Chadwick, a participant at the Battle of Bunker Hill.

B2.   "Major and Minor." *The Musical Record* May 8, 1880: 199. Notice that Chadwick, newly returned from Europe, would reside in Boston.

B3.   "Musical." *Boston Evening Transcript* October 25, 1880: 1. Notes Chadwick's participation in an organ recital given by John A. Preston at Tremont Temple, Boston. In a four-hand fantasy by Hesse, "Mr. G. W. Chadwick gave able assistance . . . ."

B4.   "Here and There." *Church's Musical Visitor* 10/8 (May 1881): 218. "Mr. Geo. W. Chadwick, who recently returned from a course of musical study in Germany, has been appointed Musical Director of the Clarendon Street Baptist Church, of Boston . . . . We predict for our young countryman a brilliant career, if his present successes do not overcome him. From what we know of him, we have no fears in that direction, and shall watch his progress with much interest."

B5.   Clifford [only name supplied]. "Correspondence -- Boston" *Church's Musical Visitor* 10/10 (July 1881): 274-275. Clifford lists Chadwick as a newly-elected member of the board of directors of the Boston Philharmonic Society.

B6.   Clifford [only name supplied]. "Correspondence -- Boston" *Church's*

Musical Visitor (August 1881): 302. The author states that by year's end it is likely that Chadwick " . . . will be at the head of a department of practical composition" at New England Conservatory.

B7.   "Music and Drama." *Boston Evening Transcript* October 10, 1881: 6. This article provides information about the scheduled performances of John Knowles Paine's *Oedipus Tyrannus*, conducted by Chadwick. "Prof. Paine's music will be given by a large chorus of trained singers and an orchestra of thirty musicians." Performances were scheduled in Boston, New York and Philadelphia.

B8.   "Jottings." *Boston Evening Transcript* November 12, 1881: 4. Announcement regarding Paine's *Oedipus Tyrannus*. "The polyglot performances of *Oedipus* at the Globe Theatre [Boston], in January, will be under the musical direction of G. W. Chadwick."

B9.   "Music and Musicians." *Church's Musical Visitor* 11/3 (December 1881): 73. "Mr. Geo. W. Chadwick, the talented young composer, recently gave a fine concert in Lawrence, Mass., his old home, in which he was assisted by distinguished musical talent from Boston. Mr. Chadwick is about to assume the conductor's baton." [The program for the performance is not provided].

B10.   "Amusements -- Plays and Actors." *New York Times* January 22, 1882: 7. Announcement that *Oedipus Tyrannus*, with incidental music by John Knowles Paine, will be opening tomorrow [January 23] in Boston before showing in New York at Booth's Theatre. "Paine's music . . . will be rendered by a large orchestra lead [*sic*] by G. W. Chadwick."

B11.   "Theatres and Concerts -- Oedipus at the Globe." *Boston Evening Transcript* January 24, 1882: 1. Review of the performance of John Knowles Paine's *Oedipus Tyrannus* at the Globe Theatre, conducted by Chadwick. "Mr. Chadwick held his forces with a firm hand, and by his watchfulness prevented them from getting too far astray from each other."

B12.   "Amusements -- The Greek Play." *New York Times* January 31, 1882: 5. Review of the New York performance of Paine's *Oedipus Tyrannus*. No mention of Chadwick.

B13.   "Major and Minor." *The Musical Record* 178 (February 25, 1882): 339. On Chadwick's conducting of J. K. Paine's *Oedipus Tyrannus*: "Mr. G. W. Chadwick has few equals as an orchestral conductor."

B14. "Theatres and Concerts -- New England Conservatory." *Boston Evening Transcript* May 18, 1882: 1. Review of Chadwick's performance of Bach's St. Anne fugue in E-flat [BWV 552] at the 1000th concert performance presented by New England Conservatory. "Comment upon the performance would be entirely superfluous. The recognized merit of the musicians . . . is assurance that every number was executed in a style that reflected credit on the performer . . . ."

B15. "Major and Minor -- Chadwick." *The Musical Record* 191 (May 27, 1882): 575. Notice of Chadwick's appointment as organist of Park Street Church (Boston) for the coming year.

B16. "Musical Mention." *The Musical Herald* 3/11 (November 1882): 301. Report that "The Arlington Club will give three concerts during the season, probably in Horticultural Hall, under the direction of Mr. Chadwick."

B17. "Review of Recent Concerts -- The Club Concerts." *The Musical Herald* (February 1883): 53. On an Arlington Club concert directed by Chadwick: "His work was evident in the good singing of the club, and the concert was a very successful one." [This concert did not include works by Chadwick.]

B18. "Major and Minor." *The Musical Record* 243 (May 26, 1883): 64. Reviewing a concert by the Arlington Club, the writer states: "Mr. Chadwick may well be congratulated upon the proficiency of the club, whose singing is marked by precision and fulness [*sic*] of tone, and by a delightful clearness of enunciation."

B19. Perkins, Charles C. and John Sullivan Dwight. *History of the Handel and Haydn Society of Boston (1815-1890).* Boston: Mudge & Son, 1883-1893 (2 vols.); reprint, New York: Da Capo, 1977. Reports on the Handel & Haydn Society's performance of Chadwick's *Rip Van Winkle.* The work was ". . . heard with fresh interest, from the fact that the young composer, who had recently returned from his studies in Germany, conducted it in person. He was warmly received, and held the orchestra well in hand" (vol. 1, p. 412).

B20. Proteus [Louis Charles Elson]. "Music in Boston." *Church's Musical Visitor* 13/12 (December 1884): 324. On Boston's interest in music: "Boston is tending toward musical lectures. Mr. B. J. Lang is giving Symphonic Analysis at Chickering's, Mr. Chadwick is doing the same at his studio, Prof. J. K. Paine is giving historico-musical lectures once a week, [and] Mr. L. C. Elson is analyzing symphonies once a week at the New England Conservatory of Music."

B21. Jones, F. O. *A Handbook of American Music and Musicians*. Canaseraga, New York: Jones, 1886; reprint, New York: Da Capo, 1971. Includes an early biographical sketch and includes information on Symphony No. 1 and *Rip Van Winkle*. "Having given such early and substantial evidences of his talents, his future course will be watched with great interest" (p. 31).

B22. "Musical Matters -- Notes." *Boston Daily Advertiser* January 24, 1888: 4. This review of a Chickering Hall concert states that compositions by "S. [*sic*] W. Chadwick" were performed. "His new songs in a group of seven were sung by Mr. William J. Winch." The review does not offer the titles of the songs.

B23. Mathews, W. S. B. [William Smythe Babcock], ed. *A Hundred Years of Music in America: An Account of Musical Effort in America*. Chicago: G. L. Howe, 1889. Reprint, New York: AMS Press, 1970. Includes a biographical sketch and works list (p. 696-697). "[Chadwick] is a good organist and an excellent conductor, but it is as a composer that his work deserves especial mention."

B24. "George W. Chadwick of Boston Chosen." *Springfield Daily Republican* (Massachusetts) August 10, 1889: 6. Announcement of Chadwick's election as Music Director of the Hampden County Musical Association's Springfield Festival. ". . . Mr. Chadwick is a musician of unquestioned ability and a director of experience."

B25. "Music-Notes." *Boston Post* December 12, 1889: 4. General announcement. "The first concert [of the sixth season] of Mr. George Chadwick's admirable organization, the [Boston] Orchestral Club, this season, will be given tomorrow night in Association Hall."

B26. Goodrich, A. J. *Complete Musical Analysis*. Cincinnati: Church, 1889. Goodrich includes mention of several of Chadwick's works in a "compendium" chapter designed to lead to further study of various musical styles and concepts. Includes *Scherzino*, op. 7, no. 3 (p. 331), *Congratulations*, op. 7, no 1 (p. 332), *Melpomene* (p. 347), Quintet in E-Flat (p. 351), Symphony No. 2 (p. 350), and *Rip Van Winkle* (p. 350).

B27. Tiersot, Julien. *Musiques pittoresques: Promenades musicales a l'Exposition de 1889*. Paris: Library Fischbacher, 1889. Includes a brief (and not particularly positive) discussion of Chadwick's *Melpomene*, which the author heard at the July 12, 1889, concert in Paris conducted by Frank van der Stucken.

B28.   "General Music Notes." *The Musical Visitor* (May 1890): 122-123. This article notes that Chadwick's music is being included on a program in Washington, D. C. ". . . made up exclusively of American compositions." [The specific composition is not mentioned, and the details of this concert have not been located.]

B29.   Proteus [Louis Charles Elson]. "Music in Boston." *The Musical Visitor* (May 1890): 123-124. Comments on an early New England Conservatory Orchestra concert led by Chadwick at the Boston Music Hall. The music was " . . . performed in a manner that was absolutely professional, and which equalled the great concerts being given by the foreign conservatories in every particular." [No Chadwick compositions were on the program.]

B30.   "The Manuscript Society." *The Musical Record* 347 (December 1890): 3. This is an announcement that Chadwick is a member of New York's Manuscript Society. It also notes that he will conduct an overture at one of the Society's concerts. [Chadwick eventually conducted his own *The Miller's Daughter*.]

B31.   "Of Social Interest." *Springfield Graphic* (Massachusetts) November 26, 1892: 12. Report on Chadwick's relations with musicians involved with the Springfield Festival. "The musical association chorus is sadly in need of male voices, but it is safe to say that there are men who enjoy singing with the chorus who do not enjoy Mr. Chadwick's sarcasm, which at times verges on impoliteness."

B32.   "Music -- G. W. Chadwick." *The Whole Family* (October 1892): 23. This article includes a brief biography, commentary and photo. "Mr. Chadwick's compositions are distinguished by refinement, a love of melody, undoubted originality, and that wholesome conservative quality which may be called classicism."

B33.   "Chicago's Crowning Day -- The Dedicatory Exercises." *New York Tribune* October 22, 1892: 1. Although this article gives only brief mention of Chadwick, it is an excellent chronicle of the Dedication Ceremonies of Chicago's Columbian Exposition of 1892.

B34.   *Columbian Exposition, Dedication Ceremonies Memorial.* Chicago: The Metropolitan Art Engraving and Publishing Company, 1893.

This book details events surrounding the Dedication Ceremonies of Chicago's Columbian Exposition of 1892, including the performance of Chadwick's *Columbian Ode*.

B35. "Of Social Interest." *Springfield Graphic* (Massachusetts) March 18, 1893: 7. The writer briefly notes Chadwick's professional interest in a new talent, singer Mrs. Charles Rochat.

B36. "American Music -- Dr. Antonin Dvorak Expresses Some Radical Opinions." *Sunday Herald* (Boston) May 28, 1893: 23. Dvorak discusses his ideas regarding African and Indian melodies as the basis of an American music, followed by opinions solicited by various American composers, including Chadwick, who states: "I am not sufficiently familiar with the real negro melodies to be able to offer any opinion on the subject. Such negro melodies as I have heard, however, I should be sorry to see become the basis of an American school of composition."

B37. "Notes and Gossip." *The Musical Visitor* (March 1896): 89. "Mr. George W. Chadwick, the Boston composer, has been conducting concerts in St. Louis, Mo., at which compositions of his were performed, notably his Second Symphony."

B38. Elson, Louis C. *European Reminiscences, Musical and Otherwise.* Philadelphia: Presser, 1896; reprint, New York: Da Capo, 1972. Informative chapter on Leipzig, including discussion of Chadwick's teachers Reinecke and Jadassohn (chapter 3). Quotes Chadwick on studying with Jadassohn: " . . . after each lesson I wanted to run all the way home, to get at work on the points of the lesson at once!" (p. 264).

B39. Elson, Louis C. *The Realm of Music.* Boston: New England Conservatory, 1897. Elson notes that a problem in American composition is the proliferation of popular concert music which " . . . have impeded the acceptance of real music, composed by our Paines, Chadwicks . . . ."

B40. "Faelten is Out -- George W. Chadwick Will Now Succeed Him." *Boston Morning Journal* February 18, 1897: 1. ". . . there is a possibility that the newly-elected Director will not accept [the job]. He was first informed of his election by a [*Boston Morning*] *Journal* man, and he stated to the reporter that unless everything was made right [that is, unless his terms for employment were met] he should refuse to accept. This he made emphatic by repetition." In an interview with the reporter Chadwick stated: "The position of Director is filled with details calling for a vast amount of work and worry."

B41.   "Chadwick -- New Head of the Conservatory." *Boston Daily Advertiser* February 18, 1897: 1. Notice of Chadwick's election as the new Dean of the New England Conservatory. Chadwick " . . . is possessed of faculties which Mr. [Carl] Faelten [Chadwick's predecessor] lacked, and he brings to the position a reputation for ability which is not only national but established in musical centres abroad as well." The author also reports that Chadwick is presently organist and choirmaster at the Columbus Avenue Universalist Church.

B42.   "Change at the Conservatory -- George W. Chadwick Takes Place of Carl Faelten." *Boston Herald* February 18, 1897: 5. This article details the events leading up to Chadwick's election as the new Dean of New England Conservatory. Includes pencil sketch of Chadwick.

B43.   "Yale's Closing Exercises." *New York Daily Tribune* July 1, 1897: 7. The writer reports the details of the commencement ceremony at which Chadwick received an honorary M. A. degree. The exercises were held at Battell Chapel, Yale University, New Haven, Connecticut.

B44.   "Chadwick is Chosen! -- Zerrahn Will No Longer Conduct." *Worcester Telegraph* (Massachusetts) December 21 1897: 1. Notice of Chadwick's appointment as conductor of the Worcester Festival, succeeding the ousted Carl Zerrahn. Although Horatio Parker and Jules Jordan were among the candidates, Chadwick won the nomination unanimously. Chadwick ". . . comes to the Worcester festival with a well founded reputation; and his abilities in the conductor's chair were proved when members of the local chorus said that he brought out the beauties of H. W. Parker's 'Hora Novissima' better than did the composer himself."

B45.   "Expects to Accept Directorship -- Professor George Whitefield Chadwick of the New England Conservatory Will Conduct the Next Worcester Musical Festival and Its Preparation." [Unidentified newspaper clipping in the possession of the Chadwick family, ca. December 1897]. This announcement regards Chadwick's acceptance of the Worcester Festival conducting post. "While this offer is not exactly like lightning from a clear sky, because there has been a quiet intima-tion of it in musical circles, the official announcement of his appointment caused a little of a surprise."

B46.   Cutter, Benjamin. *Exercises in Harmony: Simple and Advanced Supplementary to the Treatise on Harmony by G. W. Chadwick.* Boston: New England Conservatory of Music, 1899. Continues and expands upon Chadwick's harmony text.

B47.   Krehbiel, Henry E. "Music in America -- The Present State of the Art of Music." In *Music and Musicians,* edited by Albert Lavignac. New York: Holt, 1899. Biographical sketch and appreciation. "In Mr. Chadwick . . . there is a noticeable tendency which promises to disclose something idiomatic which, if pursued, will eventually give characteristic colour to the American school. At present the fruits of this tendency are not obvious enough to excite special comment . . . ." (p. 494).

B48.   Finck, Henry T. *Anton Seidl: A Memorial by His Friends.* New York: Scribners, 1899; reprint, New York: Da Capo, 1983. In an essay by Seidl titled "The Development of Music in America," he notes that the achievements of Paine, MacDowell, Chadwick, and Templeton Strong "augur well for the future productions of American composers" (p. 207).

B49.   Hughes, Rupert. *Contemporary American Composers.* Boston: L. C. Page, 1900. Includes a biography, works list, and photo. Also includes a reprint of no. 1 of his *Two Folk Songs* (1892) and program notes for *Melpomene.* Chadwick holds a place " . . . among the foremost of the foremost American composers" (p. 210).

B50.   Finck, Henry T. *Songs and Song Writers.* New York: Scribner's Sons, 1900. Includes a discussion of several songs with remarks about them from Chadwick. Finck believes Chadwick's songs to be " . . . some of the most original produced in America."

B51.   "Music and Musicians." *The Sunday Times* (London) March 10, 1901: 6. At a Popular Concert in Royal Albert Hall, singer Madame Amy Sherwin " . . . was thrice recalled after songs by Chadwick and Liza Lehmann." The titles of the songs performed are not provided. The accompanist was Henry Bird.

B52.   "Max Heinrich and Richard Strauss' Enoch Arden." *Music* 20 (November 1901): 396-402. Interview with baritone Max Heinrich (1853-1916), a proponent of Chadwick's music. "Do I do anything of Chadwick's? Certainly. Everything that Mr. Chadwick has ever written I think I know. I think I was perhaps the man who first sang Mr. Chadwick's songs."

B53.   Williams, Rev. Wolcott B. *A History of Olivet College, 1844-1900.*
        Olivet, Michigan: Olivet College, 1901. This book provides infor-
        mation about Olivet College and the Michigan Conservatory, with only
        brief mention of Chadwick.

B54.   Mathews, W. S. B. [William Smythe Babcock]. "A Few Boston
        Notes." *Music* 21/2 (January 1902): 102-106. A general report on
        Boston's musical scene. "I hear that Mr. Chadwick, having
        accomplished something as director of the New England Conservatory
        to re-establish that very large school in the estimation of Bostonians, is
        now able to find a little time for himself, and his ambition is again
        awakening to put forth original works surpassing even the best of those
        which have already distinguished him."

B55.   "In New Jordan Hall." *Boston Globe* June 23, 1903: 8. Announce-
        ment regarding New England Conservatory's first commencement
        ceremony in the new Jordan Hall. "The occasion marks the formal
        opening of the hall, which is considered one of the best of its kind in
        New England." Also notes that the key address will be given by
        Chadwick.

B56.   Mathews, W. S. B. [William Smythe Babcock]. "The American
        Composer and American Concert Programs." *The Musician* 8/6 (June
        1903): 204. In an insightful essay on the state of music in America,
        critic Mathews states: "[Renowned singer] David Bispham once told
        me that he considered Chadwick one of the greatest songwriters in the
        world . . . ."

B57.   "No Other Like It -- Jordan Hall, Conservatory of Music, Dedicated."
        Boston Daily Globe October 21, 1903: 1. This article details the
        dedication ceremonies surrounding the opening of Jordan Hall and
        Chadwick's role in the activities. Chadwick conducted his *Melpomene*
        overture at the dedication concert.

B58.   Brown, T. Allston. *A History of the New York Stage* (3 vols.) New
        York: Dodd & Mead, 1903; reprint, New York: Benjamin Blom, 1964.
        Includes a cast listing of Chadwick's *Tabasco*, which opened at The
        Broadway Theatre on May 14, 1894. [See vol. 3, page 413.]

B59.   Elson, Louis C. *The History of American Music.* London:
        Macmillan, 1904. This is the most thorough of the early biographical
        essays and the basis for many of the later ones. Relies on direct quotes
        from Chadwick and Jadassohn. A rarely seen photo faces page 229
        (Plate VIII). Elson quotes Chadwick as follows: "I believe in a sound

contrapuntal education, then as much harmonic breadth as possible. I believe in form, but not formality" [emphasis Chadwick's] (p. 172).

B60.   Daniels, Mabel. *An American Girl in Munich.* Boston: Little, Brown, 1905. This memoir by one of Chadwick's composition students discusses Chadwick as a teacher and compares his methods to her mentor in Munich, Ludwig Thuille, who had been one of Chadwick's classmates at the Leipzig Conservatory.

B61.   Elson, Louis C., editor. *Famous Composers and Their Works.* Boston: J. B. Millet Company, 1906. Chadwick is discussed in a chapter titled "Some Orchestral Masterpieces," wherein Elson declares Chadwick's Third to be the best among his symphonies (p. 194). Elson also states: " . . . his symphonic work has an especial interest from the fact that he has managed to impart a distinctly American character to some of his movements, which gives them more of a national flavor than many of the symphonies by native composers" (p. 194). In the chapter titled "Standard Oratorios," *Phoenix expirans* is considered " . . . one of the gems of modern composition" (p. 215).

B62.   Noelte, A. Albert. "The Conservatory Orchestra." *The Neume* 3 (Published by the New England Conservatory, Class of 1907): 39-42. Recounts the genesis and development of the New England Conservatory's student orchestra with emphasis on Chadwick's contributions.

B63.   Gilman, Lawrence. *Stories of Symphonic Music.* New York: Harper and Brothers, 1907. Provides brief program notes for the orchestral works *Melpomene*, *Euterpe*, *Adonais*, and *Cleopatra*.

B64.   Reinecke, Carl. "My Pupils and Myself." *The Etude* 26/1 (January 1908): 7-8. A remembrance by Reinecke of his pupils who " . . . have achieved success and now bear noted names." Reinecke states that Chadwick is " . . . now rightfully considered one of the most important of American composers." Includes photo (p. 8).

B65.   "The World of Music." *The Etude* 26/2 (February 1908): 138. General announcement. "Mr. Chadwick, director, and Mr. Ralph L. Flanders, manager of the New England Conservatory of Music, have been reelected for a term of five years."

B66.   Green, Janet, ed. *The American History and Encyclopedia of Music*, Musical Biographies, vol. 1. New York: Irving Squire, 1908. S.v. "Chadwick, George Whitefield." Includes a brief biographical sketch.

B67. Upton, George P. *Musical Memories*. Chicago: McClurg, 1908. A discussion of music at the World's Columbian Exposition with references to performances of the *Columbian Ode* and the Second Symphony.

B68. *Heart Songs*. With a Foreword by Joe Mitchell Chapple. Boston: Chapple Publishing Company, 1909; reprint, New York: Da Capo, 1983, with a new Introduction by Charles Hamm. This book indicates that Chadwick served on the committee which conferred awards on individuals who helped the publisher identify America's best 400 songs. Victor Herbert also served on the committee.

B69. "Music and Drama." *Boston Evening Transcrpt* May 19, 1909: 21. This article reviews an American Music Society concert at which Chadwick conducted Edward Burlingame Hill's *The Nuns of Perpetual Adoration* (18 May 1909, Jordan Hall, Boston). The program ". . . was well chosen and admirably carried out."

B70. Hudson, Wylna Blanche. "Boston." *Musical Courier* 58 (May 26, 1909): 38. This article reviews an American Music Society concert at which Chadwick conducted Edward Burlingame Hill's *The Nuns of Perpetual Adoration* (18 May, 1909, Jordan Hall, Boston). No mention of Chadwick.

B71. A. E. "Youthful Musicians' Score." *Musical America* 15/17 (March 2, 1910): 31. Notice of a performance by the New England Conservatory Orchestra, led by Chadwick. [Repertoire not listed.]

B72. "Pen Pictures of Clubs and Federation Folk." *Public Ledger* (Philadelphia) March 30, 1911: 2. Reports on activities held during the 1911 meeting of the National Federation of Musical Clubs at which Chadwick's *Suite Symphonique* was awarded a prize. The article notes Chadwick's attendance at a reception and that the composer Mabel Daniels was a student of his at New England Conservatory.

B73. "Horatio W. Parker Wins Metropolitan Prize Competition." *Musical America* 13/26 (May 6, 1911): 1. This article chronicles the Metropolitan Opera composition competition of 1911 for which Chadwick was a judge along with Alfred Hertz, Charles Martin Loeffler, and Walter Damrosch.

B74. Farwell, Arthur. "Noted Composers Honored at Great Norfolk Festival." *Musical America* 14/6 (June 17, 1911): 1, 3-4. Although this article includes only brief mention of Chadwick, it is a thorough chronicle of the Norfolk Festival, which presented a number of premieres of Chadwick's music. Includes photos.

B75.   Llewelyn, Louise. "The Development of the Music Conservatory in America." *Musical America* 14/7 (June 24, 1911): 13-14. Llewelyn considers conservatories in America with special emphasis on Chadwick and New England Conservatory. Topics discussed include the state of music in America and music competitions. In an interview with Chadwick, the composer states: "I believe that women and women's clubs . . . are doing more for the country in the dissemination of good music than any other element." Includes photo.

B76.   Thomas, Rose Fay. *Memoirs of Theodore Thomas.* New York: Moffat, Yard, 1911. Includes a letter (dated January 5, 1905) from Chadwick to Mrs. Theodore Thomas, written upon Thomas's death: " . . . I can truly say that I have never had any other teacher or friend in my whole career, from whom I absorbed so much knowledge, in stimulation or in courage to fight for a high standard and for an ideal" (pp. 567-568). Also notes that Chadwick was awarded a "Master Artist" medal from the World's Columbian Exposition (pp. 378-379).

B77.   Elson, Louis C., ed. *Modern Music and Musicians* (6 vols.) New York: University Society, Inc.: 1912. In a section titled "MacDowell's Contemporaries," Elson notes that Chadwick ". . . has given expression to a conservative but increasingly modernistic tendency in a series of programmatic symphonic works, chiefly distinguished by musicianly workmanship, a rather severe formalism, and at times a remarkable dramatic power and pleasing orchestral color" (p. 493). Includes photo (p. 492).

B78.   O. D. [Olin Downes]. "Boston's Clever Student Orchestra." *Musical America* 15/23 (April 13, 1912): 40. Discusses the growth and success of the New England Conservatory orchestra on its 10th anniversary. The orchestra was founded by Chadwick.

B79.   *The Harvard Musical Association (1837-1912).* Prepared by the Association. Boston: Ellis, 1912. Lists Chadwick as a "resident member" from 1881 through 1897 (p. 36).

B80.   "Music in America, Special Articles." In *University Musical Encyclopedia: A History of Music* (vol. 2). New York: The University Society, 1912. Brief biography and appreciation with consideration of Chadwick's relationship to the Boston composers (pp. 54-80, esp. 72-73). Includes photo in frontispiece.

B81.   "General News Items." *The Musician* 19/6 (June 1914): 423-424.
Announces that Chadwick " . . . has written a chorus for male voices
[*The Vikings Last Voyage*] which is to be sung at the 50th anniversary
of the Concordia Singing Society of Leipzig, next fall. Mr. Chadwick
was a member of the society during his student days, and has kept an
honorary connection since then."

B82.   "General News Items." *The Musician* 19/8 (August 1914): 559-560.
Reports on the meeting of the Oliver Ditson Society for the Relief of
Needy Musicians of which Chadwick was a trustee. "This fund is to
help in case of destitution . . . ."

B83.   Elson Louis C. "Old Times in American Music." *The Musician* 19/12
(December 1914): 805 [continued p. 866]. "Even today the good
influence [of a conservative European musical education] is still at work
in the compositions of . . . [Chadwick] . . . ; for I hold such works as
the *Melpomene* overture . . . to be much more important to our
musical advance than the wild strivings after intense modernism which
have been recently displayed by some of the younger and less balanced
American composers."

B84.   Hughes, Rupert. *American Composers*. Boston: The Page Company,
1914; reprint, New York: AMS Press, 1973. Chadwick is discussed in
in Part Three/Chapter 3, "The Academics" (pp. 210-221), and in Part
Two/Chapter 1, "The Orchestral Masters" (pp. 477-479). Includes a
photo and a facsimile of Chadwick's autograph.

B85.   "Society Notes." *San Francisco Examiner* (July 25, 1915): 22.
Describes a sight-seeing and social event attended by the Chadwicks
during their trip to California's Panama-Pacific Exposition.
Apparently, Mrs. Chadwick named a lake ("Imp's Bathtub") on Mount
Diablo, which " . . . has assumed new significance . . . with the Boston
woman's adaptable appellation."

B86.   "Society Notes -- Music Notes." *San Francisco Examiner* (July 25,
1915): 24. Notes that while in California, Chadwick attended the
convention of the California Music Teachers' Association.

B87.   Farwell, Arthur, and W. Dermot Darby, eds. *Music in America*. Vol.
4, The Art of Music. New York: National Society of Music, 1915.
Farwell briefly discusses Chadwick's music and his role in the erection
of New England Conservatory's Jordan Hall. " . . . Chadwick always
preserves a certain severe formalism which precludes the possibilities of
his capitulation either to the impressionist vagaries of modern French

music or the polyphonic complexities of the Germans of today" (p. 337).

B88. Gilbert, Henry F. "The American Composer." *Musical Quarterly* 1/1 (1915): 169-180. No specific mention of Chadwick, but important information about the Norfolk [Connecticut] Festival, at which Chadwick premiered several of his compositions.

B89. Farwell, Arthur. "American Music After Fifteen Years." *Musical America* 22 (July 31, 1915): 10. Farwell documents his discussion with Chadwick regarding the lot of the American composer in modern times.

B90. "General News Items." *The Musician* 21/3 (March 1916): 188-190. Notes Chadwick's impressions of the West based on his recent tour: "He praises, in the highest terms, the qaulity [*sic*] of the California voice."

B91. "General News Items." *The Musician* 21/11 (November 1916): 707. Notice that music by Chadwick will appear on a New York Symphony tour (Walter Damrosch, conductor) of the Pacific coast from March 19 through May 22, 1917. [Specific compositions are not mentioned.]

B92. Baker, Benjamin. "Artfully Applying Architectural Acoustics to Music." *Boston Evening Transcript* January 22, 1916: II/8. Baker chronicles the efforts to perfect the acoustics in Boston's Symphony Hall. Chadwick took part in an experiment to determine the acoustical acceptibility of various room designs.

B93. Huneker, James Gibbons. *The Philharmonic Society of New York and its Seventy-Fifth Anniversary: A Retrospect.* New York: Printed for the Philharmonic Society, 1917. This brief history of performances by the Philharmonic lists works performed through the 1917 season, including Chadwick's *Melpomene* (p. 53), *Euterpe* (p. 99) and *Stabat Mater Speciosa* (p. 99).

B94. Goepp, Philip H. "The Rise of the American Symphony." *The Etude* 35/5 (May 1917): 305-306. Goepp writes that Chadwick's symphonies ". . . are distinguished for virile buoyancy of temper and a prodigal flow of sustained melody. So clear is the Celtic strain . . . . that one is tempted to say that the true Scotch symphonies were written in America."

B95. " 'Americans Must Utilize Music, Like Germans' Say Sinfonians."

Musical Accent February 28, 1918 (unsigned article found in Sousa Press Book [box 26], United States Marine Band Library ["The President's Own"]). This article includes a discussion of the music fraternity Phi Mu Alpha Sinfonia's attempt to make music a more important aspect of the war effort. During a meeting of the fraternity's Alpha chapter, Chadwick ". . . who was one of the founders of the fraternity in 1898, and who suggested the name of 'Sinfonia,' gave some interesting reminiscences of the appearance of the European national bands at the great Peace Jubilee in Boston . . . ."

B96.   Downes, Olin. "American Composers Are Heard." *Boston Evening Post* October 12, 1919: 10. Downes comments on the Worcester Festival's "Festival of American Music," which brought out many musicians. "Probably in the whole history of American music there were never so many American musicians herded together and roped in in [*sic*] the same space." Chadwick's *Judith* was a featured presentation of the festival.

B97.   Gunn, Glenn Dillard. "The Present Status of American Music." In *Studies in Musical Education, History and Aesthetics*, Series 13: Proceedings of the 40th Annual Meeting of the Music Teachers National Association. Hartford, Connecticut: Published by the Association, 1919. " . . . the prestige of the New England Conservatory has been a factor in the success of George Whitefield Chadwick, and . . . his brilliant talents have not suffered by reason of that connection."

B98.   Bispham, David. *A Quaker Singer's Recollections.* New York: Macmillan, 1920. The well-known singer recounts his career and discusses his devotion to presenting music by American composers, including Chadwick.

B99.   *Massachusetts Society of the Sons of the American Revolution: Roll of Membership with Ancestral Records.* Boston: Published by the Society, 1920. Records Chadwick as member no. 13,980 (p. 103).

B100.   Perry, Bliss. *The Life and Letters of Henry Lee Higginson.* Boston: Atlantic Monthly Press, 1921. Notes Chadwick's speech at Boston Symphony Orchestra founder Henry Lee Higginson's 80th birthday dinner, 18 November 1914 (p. 461).

B101.   Jordan, Jules. *The Happenings of a Musical Life.* Providence, Rhode Island: Palmer Press, 1922. A musician relates anecdotes about Chadwick (p. 42) and discusses a performance of *Phoenix expirans* by the Arion Club (p. 36). Jordan was Chadwick's only serious competition in the bid for directorship of New England Conservatory.

B102. Lahee, Henry Charles. *Annals of Music in America.* Boston: Marshall Jones, 1922; reprint, Freeport, New York: Books for Libraries Press, 1970. This chronological listing of significant events in American music history (mostly premieres and important performances) refers to numerous compositions by Chadwick. Lahee includes a complete list of Chadwick's referenced compositions (pp. 205-206).

B103. Johnstone, Arthur Edward. Preface to *The Aspen* by George W. Chadwick. St. Louis: Art Publications Society ("Progressive Series Compositions, Cat. #816"), 1924. Includes a brief biographical sketch and a discussion of Chadwick's pedagogical piece, *The Aspen* for solo piano. Discussion of the composition includes "Poetic Idea," "Form and Structure," "Interpretation," and a glossary of musical terms used in the composition.

B104. Engel, Carl. "George W. Chadwick." *Musical Quarterly* 10 (1924): 438-457. Includes important (if not always correct) biographical material by a colleague who knew Chadwick well, a discussion of his music, and a works list. "Mr. Chadwick is first and foremost a symphonic composer. The orchestra is the medium he prefers to all others. In it he expresses himself most fully, most happily. He thinks and hears orchestrally. His instrumental methods are not mere borrowed devices. They are the outcome of a distinctive instrumental imagination" (p. 451-452).

B105. Otis, Philo Adams. *The Chicago Symphony Orchestra: Its Organization, Growth and Development, 1891-1924.* Chicago: C. F. Summy, 1924. Includes remarks about Chadwick's various visits to Chicago, and the Symphony's performances of his music.

B106. Elson, Louis C. *The History of American Music.* New York: Franklin, 1925; reprint, Lenox Hill, 1971. Includes a thorough and appreciative biographical sketch and appraisal of his work. "In chamber music, Chadwick has achieved the best that America can show to-day" (p. 175).

B107. Goepp, Philip H. *Great Works of Music.* Garden City, New York: Garden City Publishing Company, 1925. Includes a florid analysis of *Suite Symphonique* with three musical examples (pp. 342-350).

B108.   Parker, W. J. "Mollenhauer Resigns Baton of Boston People's Symphony; Mason is Successor." *Musical America* 42/23 (September 26, 1925): 4. Parker notes that Chadwick has been engaged to conduct one concert by the People's Symphony Orchestra during the 1925-1926 season. [Neither further information nor a review has been located.]

B109.   "Boston." *Musical America* 43/1 (October 24, 1925): 171. The article discusses registration week at New England Conservatory for the coming year and Chadwick's mandate to his faculty. The writer states: "Upon the teachers of harmony Mr. Chadwick impressed the desirability of teaching [harmony] through the fingers [i.e., on the piano], even if with some necessary sacrifice of the quantity of paperwork. 'If they can do it on the pianoforte, they can do it on paper' was his succinct generalization."

B110.   Colles, H. C., ed. *Grove's Dictionary of Music and Musicians*, 3rd ed. New York: Macmillan, 1927. S.v. "Chadwick, George Whitefield" by W. J. Henderson. Contains a brief biography and an abridged works list. "Above all things else he draws clear and engaging melodic outlines in all his music."

B111.   Hipsher, Edward Ellsworth. *American Opera and Its Composers.* Philadelphia: Presser, 1927; reprint, New York: Da Capo, 1978. Includes biographical information and a discussion of *Love's Sacrifice*, *Judith*, and *Tabasco* (pp. 118-122). Hipsher has good insight into Chadwick's dramatic and choral style. "Mr. Chadwick has a facile sense of the theatrical in its better qualities. The dramatic instinct is native to his manner of thought" (p. 120).

B112.   Railey, Julia Houston. *Mater Musica: The New England Conservatory, 1867-1927.* Boston: New England Conservatory, 1927. An appreciation of Chadwick and a list of his accomplishments. Includes an engraving of the famous Joseph Rodefer DeCamp portrait. "No other man in America has so distinguished a roster of pupils . . . ."

B113.   Pratt, Waldo Selden, ed. *Grove's Dictionary of Music and Musicians, American Supplement* (revised). New York: Macmillan, 1928. S.v. "Chadwick, George Whitefield." Contains a brief biography with an annotated works list. Also quotes important recollections by Edward Burlingame Hill, a former Chadwick student: "He invariably lays a firm constructive foundation in his compositions in larger forms, in order that he may be free to elaborate detail as he pleases."

B114.   Upton, William Treat. "Changing Types of Song, 1876 to 1926, and the Most Significant American Compositions of Fifty Years." In *Proceedings of the Music Teachers National Association*, edited by Karl W. Gehrkens, 47-55. Hartford, Connecticut: Published by the Association, 1929. Notes Chadwick's success in songwriting: " . . . adequate technique, worthy ideas worthily expressed . . . ."

B115. Upton, William Treat. "The Modern Tendency in Song Writing." *The Musician* 34/3 (March 1929): 14 [continued p. 34]. Treat states that with Chadwick and Arthur Foote " . . . at last we find sincerity of feeling, coupled with adequate technique, worthy musical ideas worthily expressed . . . ." Refers to "The Danza," "Allah," "Sweetheart, Thy Lips are Touched with Flame," and "Oh, Let Night Speak of Me."

B116. "George W. Chadwick is Feted by the 'Bohemians'." *Musical America* 49/23 (December 10, 1929): 7. This article reports on a celebration of Chadwick's 75th birthday presented by the Bohemian Club [probably held at Harvard Hall]: "Rubin Goldmark, president [of the club], introduced the guest in his usual humorous vein and referred to him as The Grand Old Man of American composers and the active head of one of our most notable institutions. Mr. Chadwick responded with a witty allusion to the string quartet [No. 5] of his about to be played as being a relic of the Ice Age."

B117. Rosenfeld, Paul. *An Hour with American Music*. Philadelphia: J. B. Lippincott Co., 1929. Chadwick and his music are usually unfavorably compared to Edward MacDowell in Rosenfeld's essay. "The passion of [Chadwick's] Aphrodite . . . resides chiefly in its title, which must be held in mind [when] listening to the tone poem. Failing, one might easily mistake the intention of the music, and suppose it an affectionate meditation on the fine old virtues of the composer's aunt. The spirits and recklessness of his Tam O'Shanter are equally a matter of convention . . . ."

B118. Slonimsky, Nicolas. "Composers of New England." *Modern Music* 6 (February/March 1930): 24-27. Slonimsky writes that Chadwick and his colleague Arthur Foote " . . . have upheld New England's fame as a musical center without furthering the advance of a national idiom."

B119. "Chadwick's Fiftieth Anniversary as Conservatory Director." *The Musician* 35/6 (June 1930): 17. Remarks on a program that included *Rip Van Winkle*, a scene from *Judith*, and two movements from the Third Symphony [The headline erroneously states it is a celebration of his directorship, which began in 1897. The occasion was actually a celebration of his arrival on the Boston musical scene in 1880 following his European sojourn.]

B120. "George W. Chadwick, Noted Musician, Dies." *New York Times* April 5, 1931: II/26. This brief obituary includes an abbreviated listing of Chadwick's most important compositions.

B121. "Rites Tomorrow in Boston for G. W. Chadwick." *New York Herald Tribune* April 6, 1931: 19. The writer of this obituary includes important biographical details and seems to have had personal knowledge of Chadwick's early life. "In his early youth he pumped the organ in a church and when the regular organist became ill one day young Chadwick exchanged the [pump] handle for the bench." Also, "In his days at high school Mr. Chadwick composed waltzes and light overtures for small bands."

B122. "Editorials -- George Whitefield Chadwick." *Christian Science Monitor* April 8, 1931: 16. "Under his leadership a development of the school [New England Conservatory] took place which was comparable to that of Harvard under Eliot . . . . The influence of his artistic integrity and personal character on the musical culture of the United States will be permanent."

B123. "Funeral -- George W. Chadwick." *Boston Herald* April 8, 1931: 17. This obituary notes that the services were to be held at Trinity Church, followed by burial at Mount Auburn Cemetery. Also lists pallbearers and ushers.

B124. J. A. H. "Chadwick Dies at his Boston Home." *Musical America* 51/7 (April 10, 1931): 4. Obituary includes a biographical sketch and an appreciation of his life. Also includes a reproduction of the portrait by Joseph Rodefer De Camp.

B125. "Obituary -- George W. Chadwick." *Musical Courier* 102/15 (April 11, 1931): 21. Brief obituary recounts his career, noting that he once held a position as organist at St. John's Church, Boston.

B126. Downes, Olin. "George Whitefield Chadwick -- Passing of Dean of American Composers Marks End of Epoch in Native Tonal Art -- Varied and Productive Career." *New York Times* April 12, 1931: IX/7. This lengthy essay is one of the most important obituaries and appreciations that Chadwick received following his death. "With him a whole epoch in American music culminated. . . . When all is said and done, he more than any other one man gives his creative period its stamp and character and represents most completely the body of serious American music . . . . It is impossible to think of a more honest and accomplished musician, or one who, without pretense or megalomania, accomplished as much for the development of his native art." This article includes a portrait.

B127. "Memorial to Chadwick." *New York Times* May 20, 1931: V/28. Recounts the May 19 Chadwick memorial concert at Jordan Hall which featured *Adonais* and *Phoenix expirans*, performed by the New England Conservatory chorus and orchestra, directed by Wallace Goodrich. "The hall was crowded by those anxious to pay tribute to the memory of the distinguished musician."

B128. MacDougall, Dr. Hamilton C. "George W. Chadwick: An Appreciation of a Distinguished Life." *The Diapason* 22 (May 1, 1931): 8. An informative appreciation by one of Chadwick's former counterpoint students at New England Conservatory. "I have left to the last what seems to me Chadwick's most remarkable quality of mind and music, his youth. He was 76 years old as time goes, but a most active and original mind, a most vivid personality, [and] an intense vitality gave youth to his music."

B129. M. A. [Margaret Anderton]. "The Passing of George W. Chadwick." *The Musician* 36/5 (May 1931): 10. Obituary with portrait. "Mr. Chadwick was all that was best in the music output of the United States, and as a creative composer with a long list to his credit, had ever unmistakably shown his mastery of his art . . . ."

B130. "Chadwick Memorial Held in Boston." *The Musician* 36/6 (June 1931): 4. Recounts the May 19 Chadwick memorial program [see B127]. Also notes that the program was broadcast on radio.

B131. Dunham, Henry Morton. *The Life of a Musician.* New York: Richmond Borough Publishing Company, 1931. This memoir by a former organ teacher at New England Conservatory includes an account of the ouster of conservatory director Carl Faelten and the assumption of the directorship of the conservatory by Chadwick.

B132. Mason, Daniel Gregory. *Tune In, America.* New York: Knopf, 1931; reprint, Freeport, New York: Books for Libraries Press, 1969. Includes information regarding performances of Chadwick's music on various orchestra programs around the United States.

B133. Howe, M. A. DeWolfe. *The Boston Symphony Orchestra, 1881-1931.*

Boston: Houghton Mifflin, 1931. Includes a roster of Chadwick's works which were performed by the Boston Symphony Orchestra (pp. 191-192), and notes that Chadwick delivered lectures on music being performed by the group during its 4th season (p. 68). Also provides a great deal of information about the Boston music scene as Chadwick would have known it.

B134.   Birchard, Clarence C. "America -- A Treasure House of Folk Music." *The Musician* 36/9 (September 1931): 7. Remarks by one of Chadwick's publishers about the opportunities available to American composers who would use vernacular musics as a basis for their own work. "The jazz music is the type that Chadwick spoke about as 'alley music' or 'hand-organ' music of his day, which put the breath of musical life into the young Chadwick."

B135.   Hadley, Henry K. *Commemorative Tribute to Chadwick.* New York: American Academy of Arts and Letters [publication no. 77], 1932 (pp. 99-106). "His integrity as a man and musician, his gift of humor, his wit--sometimes caustic, but underneath always intensely human--are well known, while the depth of his emotions, [and] the spontaneity of their expression, are abundantly reflected in his works."

B136.   Howe, Mark A. DeWolfe. *A Venture in Remembrance.* Boston: Little, Brown, 1932. Although this volume does not mention Chadwick specifically, it contains a good deal of information about Boston culture, especially the club life that became important to Chadwick's middle and later years. Includes descriptions of those clubs which boasted Chadwick as a member, the Tavern Club and the Saint Botolph Club (pp. 296-301).

B137.   Stanford, Charles Villiers, and Cecil Forsythe. *A History of Music.* New York: Macmillan, 1932; reprint, New York: Macmillan, 1950. Includes a brief appreciation of Chadwick and his music. "He has a directness of thought, a humour, and a power of seeing himself as others see him that smack more of London or Paris than of Boston."

B138.   Salter, Sumner. "Early Encouragements to American Composers." *Musical Quarterly* 18/1 (January 1932): 76-105. Includes a listing of concerts of American music. The author mentions performances of Chadwick's *Scherzino* (p. 79), *Melpomene* (p. 81), Quintet in E-Flat (p. 84), *The Miller's Daughter* (p. 88), and *Lovely Rosabelle* (p. 89).

B139.   Miller, Eleanor. *The History and Development of the New England Conservatory of Music* (2 vols.) B. M. Thesis, New England

Conservatory, 1933. Includes a chapter on Chadwick with special emphasis on his role as director of New England Conservatory (pp. 259-262). Notes that Chadwick studied organ with Dudley Buck.

B140.   Fisher, William Arms. *Music Festivals in the United States: An Historical Sketch.* Boston: The American Choral and Festival Alliance, Inc., 1934. Contains information about several festivals with which Chadwick was involved, including the Worcester County Musical Association [Worcester Festival] (pp. 26-28) and the Litchfield County Choral Union [Norfolk Festival] (pp. 47-49). Notes several performances of his works from those festivals, as well as mention of a performance of Chadwick's *Land of Our Hearts* at the Lawrence (Kansas) Music Festival (p. 54).

B141.   Grant, Robert. *Fourscore: An Autobiography.* Boston: Houghton Mifflin Company, 1934. Although this book, written by one of Chadwick's librettists, does not refer to him directly, it provides an important and insightful glimpse into Boston's literary and social circles. Grant, an exact Chadwick contemporary, also chronicles political currents in Boston.

B142.   Langley, Allen Lincoln. "Chadwick and the New England Conservatory of Music." *Musical Quarterly* 21 (1935): 39-52. Written by a former New England Conservatory student. Provides a great deal of information about Chadwick as teacher and conductor, and recounts the inner workings of the conservatory during Langley's association with it (1914-1920). On Chadwick's leadership of the conservatory orchestra: "Never an expert with the baton, and often depending on the orchestra's instinct for the incisive attack which his stick was far from unequivocally evoking, he nevertheless was a man who, despite imperfections of conducting technique, knew all there was to know in other respects about the repertoire he chose. Erudition of the thorough German sort was evident; so, too, a determination that discipline should be always maintained" (p. 41).

B143.   Hanson, Howard. "American Procession at Rochester." *Modern Music* 13 (March-April, 1936): 22-28. Report on the history of Rochester's American Composers' Concerts. On *Tam O'Shanter*: " . . . though it may not be typically American, it is certainly neither Gallic nor Latin!"

B144.   Ewen, David. *Composers of Yesterday.* New York: Wilson, 1937. Ewen provides a brief biography with an abbreviated works lists and photo (pp. 92-94). "At one time, Chadwick was esteemed the foremost American composer of his day. Towards the end of his life, however, his reputation drooped, and while the charm of some of his music still held a particular appeal, it had ceased to exert an important influence in our musical development."

B145. Foote, Arthur. "A Bostonian Remembers." *Musical Quarterly* 23 (1937): 37-44. An interesting memoir of musical life in Boston in the latter half of the nineteenth century by one of Chadwick's closest friends. Important passages regarding camaraderie among the school of Boston composers. "One of my cherished remembrances is of the meetings several times a year of Chadwick, Parker, Whiting, and myself, at which we offered manuscript compositions for criticism, sometimes caustic, always helpful" (p.41).

B146. McCusker, Honor. *Fifty Years of Music in Boston.* Boston: Trustees of the Public Library, 1938. McCusker's brief biographical sketch includes previously published critical comments by John Sullivan Dwight, John Tasker Howard, and Philip Hale regarding Chadwick's compositional style.

B147. Monroe, Harriet. *A Poet's Life.* New York: Macmillan, 1938. This memoir by the poet of the *Columbian Ode* for the Chicago Columbian Exposition of 1892, which Chadwick set to music, does not mention the composer. However, it does detail circumstances surrounding the Exposition, including the Dedication Ceremony rehearsals and performance, led by Theodore Thomas.

B148. Mason, Daniel Gregory. *Music in My Time and Other Reminiscences.* New York: Macmillan, 1938 ; reprint, Westport, Connecticut: Greenwood Press, 1970. Includes an excerpt of a note from Chadwick to Mason regarding the latter's piano quintet. Reveals interesting thoughts about Chadwick's attitude toward critics, criticism, and his own music (p. 176).

B149. Homer, Sidney. *My Wife and I: The Story of Louise and Sidney Homer.* New York: Macmillan, 1939. This memoir by one of Chadwick's former students gives insight into the older composer and his importance in American music. "Could New England have anything to say [in the art of music]? George Chadwick had quietly shown that it could, that there was a poetry in prosaic, repressed New England which could find expression in that strange medium called music. The performance of his Rip van Winkle overture by the Boston Symphony Orchestra can be called a landmark in American musical life" (p. 33).

B150.   Upton, George, and Felix Borowski. *The Standard Concert Guide*.
         Garden City, New York: Blue Ribbon Books, 1940. Includes analytical
         program notes on Symphony No. 3, *Thalia, Euterpe, Melpomene,
         Adonais, Tam O'Shanter*, and *Symphonic Sketches* (pp. 125-134).
         Also includes information on premiere performances.

B151.   Howard, John Tasker. *Our Contemporary Composers: American Music
         in the Twentieth Century*. New York: Thomas Y. Crowell, 1941;
         reprint, Freeport, New York: Books for Libraries Press, 1975.
         Biographical sketch with photo (pp. 11-12). "Chadwick had the
         craftsmanship of [John Knowles] Paine, and beyond that a genuine
         spark of inspiration; in his music one hears now a sly chuckle, now the
         voice of real emotional warmth."

B152.   Semler, Isabel Parker. *Horatio Parker*. New York: Putnam's Sons,
         1942; reprint, New York: Da Capo, 1973. Includes correspondence
         between the Parkers and the Chadwicks which indicates the depth of
         their personal and professional relationship. Recalling his trip to
         Britain (December 12, 1901), Parker wrote to Ida May Chadwick that
         her husband " . . . seems to have left a luminous trail of good-will
         behind him," noting regards were sent from a number of esteemed
         British musicians (p. 139).

B153.   Atherton, Percy Lee. "Boston Days (1909-1922): Some Engeliana." In
         A Birthday Offering to Carl Engel, ed. Gustave Reese, 27-34. New
         York: Schirmer, 1943. This excellent essay on the Boston musical
         scene notes that Chadwick was a charter member of the city's
         Composer's Club (p. 31).

B154.   Hanson, Howard. "Twenty Years' Growth in America." *Modern Music*
         20 (January-February, 1943): 95-101. Conductor/composer Hanson
         essays musical tradition in American music and disputes the idea that
         American art is primarily German-influenced. "It is first of all an
         Anglo-Saxon tradition which appears in the works of Chadwick. It
         is furthermore a scholarly tradition evidenced by high technical
         standards . . . ."

B155.   Starr, Harris E., ed. *Dictionary of American Biography*, vol. 21
         (Supplement I -- to December 31, 1935). New York: Charles
         Scribner's Sons, 1944. S.v. "Chadwick, George Whitefield," by John
         Tasker Howard. Biographical sketch and works list. "Chadwick . . .
         more than any other of his Boston colleagues, put his own native
         Yankee humor into his works" (vol. 21, p. 161).

B156. Morin, Raymond. *The Worcester Music Festival: Its Background and History, 1858-1946*. Worcester, Massachusetts: Worcester County Musical Association, 1946. Includes a chronicle of Chadwick's tenure as conductor of the festival in chapter 8, "George W. Chadwick Takes the Baton (1898-1901)." Also includes information about festival guest artists, repertoire, critical reception, and newspaper reviews. Chadwick's " . . . third season as Festival conductor achieved for him total acceptance by a chorus that had been firm in its devotion to [his predecessor on the podium] Carl Zerrahn."

B157. Foote, Arthur. *An Autobiography*. Norwood, Massachusetts: Plimpton, 1946; reprint, New York: Da Capo, 1979 [with an introduction and notes by Wilma Reid Cipolla.] Provides commentary on the popularity of *Melpomene*, the St. Botolph Club (of which Chadwick was a member) and New England Conservatory. Although Chadwick is not discussed at length, this memoir by Chadwick's close associate provides much insight into a composer's life during that era.

B158. Goodrich, Wallace. "Personal Recollections of the New England Conservatory of Music." Typed manuscript, 1947. Spaulding Library, New England Conservatory of Music, Boston. Goodrich, director of the conservatory from 1931 to 1942, details conservatory activities from 1867 to 1947. Includes information about Chadwick, especially with reference to his role as conservatory director.

B159. Amory, Cleveland. *The Proper Bostonians*. New York: Dutton, 1947; reprint, Orleans, Massachusetts: Parnassus Imprints, 1984. While this book does not mention Chadwick, it does contain valuable information about Major Henry Lee Higginson, as well as several of Chadwick's librettists, and Chadwick's most important critic, Henry T. Parker of the *Boston Evening Transcript*. Especially noteworthy is the description of events surrounding Higginson's 80th birthday celebration, at which Chadwick delivered a speech.

B160. Finney, Theodore M. *A History of Music* (revised edition). New York: Harcourt, Brace & Co., 1948. Brief [and not entirely correct] biography and short listing of works. "Most of Chadwick's music has been performed, and much of it published."

B161. Eaton, Quaintance. *Musical U. S. A.* New York: Allen, Towne and Heath, 1949. Brief mention of Chadwick, but a great deal of valuable information on musical Boston. Eaton discusses most of the city's major musical personalities. "Perhaps the grandest of the grand old

men of his generation was George Whitefield Chadwick . . .; he was
certainly one of the most original composers of his time . . . ."

B162.   Johnson, Earle H. *Symphony Hall, Boston.* Boston: Little, Brown,
1950. Includes a complete roster of Chadwick's works performed by
the Boston Symphony Orchestra through 1949.

B163.   Hanson, Howard. *Music in Contemporary American Civilization.*
Lincoln: University of Nebraska Press, 1951. Hanson discusses
Chadwick briefly within the framework of a discussion of American
symphonists from the 1880s to 1920.

B164.   Clough, Francis F. and G. J. Cuming. *The World's Encyclopedia of
Recorded Music.* London: Sidgwick & Jackson, 1952. Includes a
listing of Chadwick's recorded music (p. 113).

B165.   Copland, Aaron. *Music and Imagination.* New York: Mentor Books,
1952. Includes Copland's thoughts on his predecessors. On Chadwick
and the New England composers: "They loved the masterworks of
Europe's mature culture not like creative personalities but like the
schoolmasters that many of them became." (See also: B231)

B166.   Hamm, Charles. Program notes for *Symphonic Sketches*, no. 1
"Jubilee." Cincinnati Symphony Orchestra program book, January
11/12, 1952. Includes a brief essay on Chadwick and an insightful
essay on "Jubilee." Especially important is his explanation of the
". . . 'Juba', a Southern Negro contraction of 'Jubilee,' [which] was
used to designate a certain type of dance-song . . . . Chadwick
unquestionably knew of the "Juba," and possibly incorporated
suggestions of it into this piece."

B167.   Darack, Arthur. Program notes for *Symphonic Sketches*, no. 2 "Noel."
Cincinnati Symphony Orchestra program book, December 19/20,
1952. Program notes for "Noel" quote Edward Burlingame Hill, a
former Chadwick student and friend, at length: "His [Chadwick's] chief
attributes are fluency and beauty of melodic inventiveness, mastery of
part-writing, [and] a logical and coherent grasp of form. His harmonic
structure is solid, yet he always manages to obtain effects that are
romantic, poetic or dramatic in color without resorting to the devices of
ultra-modern eccentricity."

B168.   Woerner, Karl H. "Chadwick, George Whitefield." In *Die Musik in
Geschichte und Gegenwart*, ed. by Friedrich Blume. Kassel and Basel:

Barenreiter, 1952: vol. 2, col. 1011-1013. This German-language essay includes a brief biography and an abbreviated works list.

B169.   Howard, John Tasker. *Our American Music: Three Hundred Years of It.* 3rd ed. New York: Thomas Y. Crowell, 1954. Howard includes an entertaining sketch of Chadwick's life and works. ". . . there is a steadiness in Chadwick's music that is always dependable, a freshness that is a matter of spirit rather than of style or idiom" (p. 330). Includes a photo.

B170.   *Bio-Bibliographical Index of Musicians in the United States of America Since Colonial Times.* Washington, D. C.: The Library of Congress, 1956; reprint, New York: American Musicological Society Press, 1972. This bibliography documents mention and/or discussion of Chadwick in a number of books on diverse aspects of American music history. The inclusion of a portrait and/or musical examples is also noted.

B171.   Downes, Irene, ed. *Olin Downes on Music.* New York: Simon and Schuster, 1957. This volume includes references to Chadwick and a reprint of Downes's article "Two Novelties by Symphony" (here re-titled "Two New Americans' Compositions Are Heard,"), Boston Post, April 14, 1911. The article features a review of *Suite Symphonique.*

B172.   Campbell, D. G. *George W. Chadwick: His Life and Works.* Ph.D. Dissertation, Eastman School of Music, Rochester, New York, 1957. Includes a brief biography, analyses of the music according to genre, and additional chapters on Chadwick's compositional style, harmonic technique, orchestration, and his influential harmony textbook.

B173.   Yellin, Victor Fell. *The Life and Operatic Works of George Whitefield Chadwick.* Ph.D. Dissertation, Harvard University, 1957. The most extensive biography available with valuable genealogical information and information gleaned from the author's personal interviews with Chadwick's family and friends. Yellin includes important essays on the stage works and details their genesis, analyzes musical elements, and chronicles performances.

B174.   Howard, John Tasker and George Kent Bellows. *A Short History of Music in America.* New York: Thomas Y. Crowell, 1957; reprint, New York: Apollo Editions, 1969. Includes a biographical sketch with commentary. Chadwick's " . . . own work, while somewhat academic, had a spark of genuine inspiration . . . . He added life to the forms he

used, and gave us something vital. There is a freshness in his music
that is a matter of spirit rather than of style or idiom" (pp. 157-160).

B175.   Murphy, Howard A. *Teaching Musicianship: A Manual of Methods
and Materials.* New York: Coleman-Ross Company, 1962. Includes
results from a survey which indicate that Chadwick's *Harmony* (1902)
was still being used in at least six colleges as late as 1947 (p. 246).

B176.   Downes, Olin. "American Chamber Music." In *Cobbett's Cyclopedic
Survey of Chamber Music* (2nd ed.), vol. 1, edited by Walter Willson
Cobbett, pp. 11-18. London: Oxford, 1963. Downes discusses
Chadwick's chamber works, including the Quintet in E-Flat, and the
Fourth and Fifth String Quartets. "Chadwick, in certain compositions,
comes much nearer to what may be considered American . . . than many
who have more loudly professed artistic allegiance to a national ideal."

B177.   Engel, Carl. "Chadwick, George Whitefield." In *Cobbett's Cyclopedic
Survey of Chamber Music* (2nd ed.), vol. 1, edited by Walter Willson
Cobbett, pp. 237-238. London: Oxford, 1963. Engel includes a biographical sketch and discussion of the music. " . . . Chadwick deserves
to rank as a pioneer in the musical development of America." On the
Fifth Quartet: "Chadwick's humour is marked, but never heavy or
grotesque; the music is sparkling and fluid in spite of its designedly
jerky rhythm . . . ."

B178.   Fitzpatrick, Edward John. *The Music Conservatory in America.* Ph.D.
Dissertation, Boston University, 1963. Fitzpatrick refers to Chadwick
and New England Conservatory in his chapter titled "George W.
Chadwick, The Third Director" (p. 361). Most citations refer to
Chadwick in his role as conservatory director.

B179.   Mattfeld, Julius. *A Handbook of American Operatic Premieres, 1731-
1962.* Detroit: Information Service, 1963. Includes references to *Judith*
(p. 51) and *Love's Sacrifice* (p. 57).

B180.   Thompson, Oscar, editor-in-chief. *The International Cyclopedia of
Music and Musicians.* New York: Dodd, Mead, and Co., 1964. S.v.
"Chadwick, George Whitefield." Includes a brief biography and an
abridged works list.

B181.   Eaton, Quaintance. *The Boston Opera Company.* New York:
Appleton-Century, 1965; reprint, New York: Da Capo, 1980. Notes
Chadwick's presence at the cornerstone-laying ceremony of the Boston
Opera House, 30 November 1908 (p. 13). Also notes that one of his

compositions [*Judith*, in its piano-vocal version] was encased in a bronze casket inside the cornerstone, along with works by other noted Boston composers (p. 14).

B182. Aborn, Merton Robert. *The Influence on American Musical Culture of Dvorak's Sojourn in America*. Ph.D. Dissertation, Indiana University, 1965. Aborn notes that Chadwick was a judge for the National Conservatory composition contest in the Fall of 1892 in the "Grand Opera" category. Other judges at the competition were Dvorak, Arthur Nikisch, Anton Seidl, J. K. Paine, Dudley Buck, and B. J. Lang.

B183. Blom, Eric. *Grove's Dictionary of Music and Musicians* (5th ed.) New York: St. Martin's Press, 1966. S.v. "Chadwick, George Whitefield," by W. J. Henderson. Includes a biography and an abridged works list. "[Chadwick] exerted a potent educational influence" (vol. 2, pp. 150-151).

B184. Forner, J.[ohannes], H. Schiller and M. Wehnert. *Hochschule fur Musik Leipzig (1843-1968) Gegrundet als Conservatorium der Musik*. Leipzig: n.p. [1968]. Contains a reproduction of part of Chadwick's Lehrerzeugniss, or transcript/reference letter, which was issued to him by the Leipzig Conservatory following the completion of his course of studies.

B185. Sablosky, Irving. *American Music*. Chicago: University of Chicago Press, 1969. Sablosky's brief consideration of Chadwick largely interprets him as "traditional."

B186. Stopp, Jacklin B. "The Secular Cantata in the United States: 1850-1919." *Journal of Research in Music Education* 17/4 (Winter 1969): 388-98. Stopp briefly discusses several of Chadwick's cantata-like works and provides a listing which includes publication information, performance requirements, librettist, and timings for *The Lily Nymph*, *Lovely Rosabelle*, *Columbian Ode*, *Phoenix Expirans*, and *The Viking's Last Voyage* (p. 396).

B187. "A Century of Music in New England." In printed program for *Festival of New England Composers, Past and Present*, held 5-9 May 1971, at New England Conservatory, Boston. Includes a brief outline of American music in New England with discussion about Chadwick and his music, as well as others in the Boston school of composition.

B188. Lowens, Margery Morgan. *The New York Years of Edward MacDowell*. Ann Arbor, Michigan: University Microforms, 1971.

Numerous references to Chadwick, including a letter from Chadwick to MacDowell declining the latter's invitation to teach his class at Columbia University (p. 41). Also provides information on Chadwick's conducting of works by MacDowell (p. 218).

B189. Ives, Charles. *Memos.* Edited by John Kirkpatrick. New York: Norton, 1972. Ives records his experience with Chadwick, who was guest speaking at one of Horatio Parker's music classes at Yale University. Ives notes that ". . . at the time (1897-8) Chadwick was the big celebrated man of American music." (pp. 183-184).

B190. Dart, Harold. "An Introduction to Selected New England Composers of the Late Nineteenth Century." *Music Educators' Journal* 60/3 (November 1973): 47-53, 89-92. This fine introduction to the Second New England School of composers includes a brief biography of Chadwick, an excerpt from the Third Symphony (p. 51), a photo (p. 50), an assessment of his music, and a discography (p. 53).

B191. Krueger, Karl. *The Musical Heritage of the United States: The Unknown Portion.* New York: Society for the Preservation of the American Musical Heritage, Inc., 1973. Includes a brief biography, an appreciation of selected works, and a photo (p. 193).

B192. Homer, Anne. *Louise Homer and the Golden Age of Opera.* New York: William Morrow, 1974. This biography of a leading American contralto includes references to Chadwick regarding Homer's attempts to enter New England Conservatory. On Homer's impending audition: " . . . Chadwick wouldn't be an easy man to sing for, but there wasn't another musician in Boston who was as influential (pp. 84-84).

B193. Yellin, Victor Fell. "Chadwick, American Musical Realist." *Musical Quarterly* 61 (1975): 77-97. An extended analysis of Chadwick's life and several compositions, including *Tam O'Shanter*, *Symphonic Sketches* and *The Padrone*. The article provides an important analysis of Chadwick's students years in Europe and considers the role of realism in his music.

B194. Haas, Robert Bartlett, ed. *William Grant Still and the Fusion of Cultures in American Music.* Los Angeles: Black Sparrow, 1975. Haas briefly notes that Still studied with Chadwick for four months (p. 6).

B195. Clarke, Garry E. *Essays on American Music.* Contributions in American Music, no. 62. Westport, Connecticut: Greenwood Press,

1977. Clarke provides general remarks about the New England school of composers. "Chadwick and many of his contemporaries were thoroughly trained composers who produced works that could at least be compared to their European models" (p. 77).

B196.   Gillespie, John. *Nineteenth Century American Piano Music.* New York: Dover Publications, 1978. Includes brief biographical commentary and an introduction to a reprint of no. 2 of his *Two Caprices* for piano.

B197.   Ledbetter, Steven. "Chadwickiana at the New England Conservatory." Paper presented at the annual mid-Winter meeting of the Music Library Association, Paine Hall, Harvard University, 2 March 1978. [Copy deposited at New England Conservatory.] Includes a survey of Chadwick's music with an important discussion of the stage works, especially *Judith, Tabasco* and *The Padrone.* Chadwick ". . . was as eclectic as any American composer of his time, drawing models of procedure from the best examples he knew, examples that were almost invariably European."

B198.   Dennison, Sam, curator. *The Edwin A. Fleisher Collection of Orchestral Music in the Free Library of Philadelphia: A Cumulative Catalog, 1929-1977.* Boston: G. K. Hall, 1979. A listing of Chadwick's printed music held by the Free Library of Philadelphia. Includes: number of movements, publishers' information, number of pages in score, performance information, and timings (pp. 156-158).

B199.   Hoopes, Donelson F. *Childe Hassam.* New York: Watson-Gupthill, 1979. Hoopes notes that Chadwick had met Hassam and purchased the first painting the artist ever sold (p. 58).

B200.   Lawrence, Vera Brodsky, ed. *The Wa-Wan Press* (5 vols.) New York: Arno Press, 1979. Lawrence notes that Chadwick served on the executive board of Arthur Farwell's Wa-Wan Press (p. 29).

B201.   Kingman, Daniel. *American Music: A Panorama.* New York: Schirmer, 1979. Includes a brief biography, a listing of Chadwick's important students, and a short discussion of his music with emphasis on *Symphonic Sketches* (pp. 436-437). Chadwick produced " . . . perhaps the most 'American'-sounding work to come out of the New England group of composers" (p. 437).

B202.   Ledbetter, Steven. *Introduction to Songs to Poems by Arlo Bates by George W. Chadwick.* New York: Da Capo, 1980. Ledbetter discusses

Chadwick's song style with emphasis on *A Flower Cycle* and *Lyrics from "Told in the Gate."* Ledbetter also provides information about the sources of Bates's poems and about Bates himself.

B203.   Loucks, Richard. *Arthur Shepherd, American Composer.* Provo, Utah: Brigham Young University Press, 1980. This book includes references to Chadwick by Shepherd, who had studied with him at New England Conservatory. Shepherd described " . . . a fresh, American spirit and outlook . . . ." that was occurring at the conservatory under Chadwick's leadership (p. 6).

B204.   Sadie, Stanley, ed. *The New Grove Dictionary of Music and Musicians.* New York and London: Macmillan, 1980. S.v. "Chadwick, George Whitefield," [vol. 4, pp. 105-106] by Victor Fell Yellin. Includes a biography, an abbreviated works list, and a bibliography.

B205.   St. Amand, Sylvia A. "George Chadwick and Springfield's Golden Era." In *Springfield City Library Bulletin* (March 1980): 19-21. Provides biographical details and information on Chadwick's role as conductor of the Springfield Festival. Also includes a photo (p. 20).

B206.   Davis, Ronald L. *A History of Music in American Life* (3 vols.). Malabar, FL: Krieger, 1980. Volume 2 (pp. 85-88) contains a brief biography and mention of his most important works.

B207.   Cohn, Arthur. *Recorded Classical Music.* New York: Schirmer, 1981. This discography includes entries/reviews of: *Euterpe*; *Symphonic Sketches*; *Tam O'Shanter*; *Tabasco*; *Pastorale in E-flat Major*; *Theme, Variations and Fugue*; the Fourth String Quartet; and "Oh, Let Night Speak of Me."

B208.   Zuck, Barbara. *A History of Musical Americanism.* Ann Arbor: UMI Research Press, 1981. This book contains several passing references to Chadwick with regard to his role in creating an American style of music. Also documents several performances of his music, notably the Paris performance of *Melpomene* conducted by Frank van der Stucken (p. 50). Chadwick and his contemporaries ". . . perpetuated the European traditions and schools of musical thought" (p. 39).

B209.   Krummel, Donald W., et al. *Resources of American Music History: A Directory of Source Materials from Colonial Times to World War II.* Urbana: University of Illinois Press, 1981. Cites the locations of various Chadwick source materials, including holographs, printed music, and personal effects. See Krummel catalogue nos. 195B, 227B, 227C, 317, 636, 646, 705, 863, 951, 1061A, 1080, 1111, 1159, 1359, 1534, and 1580.

B210.   Martin, George. *The Damrosch Dynasty: America's First Family of Music*. Boston: Houghton Mifflin, 1983. Notes Chadwick's relationship with Walter Damrosch (p. 285), and chronicles events surrounding the Metropolitan Opera's 1909 competition, at which both men served as judge. Other judges included Charles Martin Loeffler and Alfred Hertz.

B211.   Yellin, Victor Fell. "George Chadwick and Populist Music." Paper delivered as part of the "Musicology Lecture Series," State University of New York--Buffalo, April 11, 1983. An enlightening discussion of Chadwick's populist philosophies and its realization in his music. Also includes a discussion of "The Boston Myth," biographical details, excerpts from Chadwick's infamous speech before the Music Teachers National Association (1877), and references to *Rip Van Winkle*, *Symphonic Sketches*, *The Peer and the Pauper*, the Second Symphony, and *A Quiet Lodging*.

B212.   Yellin, Victor Fell. Review of *A History of Musical Americanism* by Barbara Zuck. In *American Music* 1/1 (Spring 1983): 70-76. Within the framework of this book review, Yellin provides insightful comments on Chadwick's "Germanism," and the basis of his American style. ". . . Chadwick's mature style combines the craft he perfected in the remarkably short time of his two years in Germany as a student with his Yankee tunesmith heritage and an appreciation of the Slavic, Italian, and especially, the French schools."

B213.   Levy, Alan Howard. *Musical Nationalism: American Composers' Search for Identity*. Westport, Connecticut: Greenwood Press, 1983. Numerous references to Chadwick, particularly in the chapter titled "The German Orthodoxy." Mentions *The Padrone*, *Symphonic Sketches*, *Tam O'Shanter*, and *Tobasco* [*sic*]. " . . . Chadwick, Parker, and Paine were simply damn good composers, irrespective of style. Their absence from the twentieth-century concert stage reflects extramusical prejudices over which a late-nineteenth-century composer could not possibly have exerted any control" (p. 6).

B214.   Hamm, Charles. *Music in the New World*. New York: Norton, 1983. Hamm includes a biographical sketch and a discussion of Chadwick's music. On Chadwick's songs " . . . there was nothing distinctive about these pieces . . . ." (p. 54). And, "Not even his most successful compositions, solid and serious though they may have been, broke new ground . . . ." (p. 332).

B215. Ledbetter, Steven. *George W. Chadwick: A Sourcebook.* Revised preliminary version. Unpublished typescript deposited at New England Conservatory, 1983. This invaluable tool for Chadwick research includes a chronology of Chadwick's life, bibliographical entries for most of Chadwick's compositions (including composition dates, premiere dates, instrumentation, manuscript locations, excerpts from selected reviews), and several references to Chadwick's journals and letters.

B216. Arvey, Verna [Mrs. William Grant Still]. *In One Lifetime.* Fayetteville, Arkansas: University of Arkansas Press, 1984. This personal memoir by the wife of the African-American composer William Grant Still provides several enlightening comments about Chadwick as teacher: "Chadwick's method of teaching was wise and unusual. The student merely worked out his own ideas, which the teacher afterward criticized and discussed in detail" (p. 63).

B217. Dox, Thurston. *American Oratorios and Cantatas: A Catalog of Works Written in the United States from Colonial Times to 1985.* Metuchen, New Jersey and London: Scarecrow, 1986 (2 vols.) Includes a detailed citation for *Judith* and selected reviews (catalog no. OR84, vol. 1, pp. 41-42).

B218. McKinley, Ann. "Music for the Dedication of the World's Columbian Exposition in Chicago, 1892." *American Music* 3 (Spring 1985): 42-51. McKinley discusses the musiç programs for the Exposition and details events surrounding the production of Chadwick's *Columbian Ode.* Also includes excerpts from letters that Chadwick wrote to Theodore Thomas, the Expostion music director.

B219. Moore, MacDonald Smith. *Yankee Blues: Musical Culture and American Identity.* Bloomington, Indiana: Indiana University Press, 1985. Moore briefly notes that Arthur Farwell had studied composition with Chadwick "unsatisfactorily," and that later on Chadwick would not "lend his name" to Farwell's Wa-Wan Press enterprise (p. 78-79). [Although it seems that later on Chadwick did, in fact, lend his name as a director. See: B227].

B220. Pappin, Gay Gladdin. *The Organ Works of George Whitefield*

Chadwick. D.M.A. Thesis, Louisiana State University, 1985. [Not consulted.]

B221. Hitchcock, H. Wiley, and Stanley Sadie, eds. *The New Grove Dictionary of American Music*. New York: Macmillan, 1986. S.v. "Chadwick, George Whitefield," [vol. 1, pp. 384-396] by Victor Fell Yellin [text] and Steven Ledbetter [works list]. This article comprises the most comprehensive encyclopedic treatment of Chadwick, with sections entitled "Early Years Up to 1880," "1880-97," "1897-1931," and "Style." Included is a succinct biography with a full acount of his most important works and the major events of his life. Also included is an extensive works list and photo. "His best works show him to have been a pioneer in freeing American musical expression from German conservatory style" (p. 387).

B222. Tischler, Barbara. "One Hundred Percent Americanism and Music in Boston During World War I." *American Music* 4/2 (Summer 1986): 164-176. Tischler presents a discussion of anti-German sentiment during the years surrounding World War I and its impact on orchestra programming. This is an excellent essay on Boston's musical life at the time, but only briefly mentions Chadwick (p. 173).

B223. Mazzola, Sandy. "Bands and Orchestras at the Columbian Exposition." *American Music* 4/4 (Winter 1986): 411-415. Mazzola provides information regarding performance preparations for the World's Columbian Exposition. Includes information about performing organizations, programs, attendance records, and Exposition financial details with regard to music.

B224. Tischler, Barbara L. *An American Music: The Search for an American Musical Identity*. New York: Oxford University Press, 1986. Tischler mentions Chadwick with regard to his work at the World's Columbian Exposition and Hanson's production of Chadwick's music at the Eastman Festival of American Music (Rochester, New York).

B225. Francombe, Leona. "The Boston Sound Revisited." *Symphony Magazine* 38/3 (June/July 1987): 42-45, 124-125. A fine introduction to the culture of Boston and the music of the Second New England School. "With George Whitefield Chadwick a purely American sound began to emerge . . . ."

B226. Chase, Gilbert. *America's Music* (revised 3rd edition). Urbana: University of Illinois Press, 1987. Includes a brief biographical sketch and remarks about the music, with emphasis on the "American" works (pp. 386-390; photo faces p. 386). "The wide range of his cultural, aesthetic, and social concerns is reflected in his copious and varied compositional output" (p. 388).

B227. Culbertson, Evelyn Davis. "Arthur Farwell's Early Efforts on Behalf of American Music, 1889-1921." *American Music* 5/2 (Summer 1987): 156-175. Notes Chadwick's membership as a founding board member of Farwell's Wa-Wan Press, along with Frank Damrosch, Lawrence Gilman, and Charles Martin Loeffler.

B228. Grout, Donald Jay. *A Short History of Opera* (3rd ed.) New York: Columbia University Press, 1988. Grout mentions Chadwick only briefly. "The operas of George Whitefield Chadwick (1854-1931) attracted little attention outside his native Boston . . . ."

B229. Hitchcock, H. Wiley. *Music in the United States: A Historical Introduction* (Third Edition). Englewood Cliffs, New Jersey: Prentice Hall, 1988. This book comprises the best textbook treatment of Chadwick and his music (pp.145-148). "Chadwick is notable among the [Second New England School] group for his sympathy--reflected, however, unevenly in his works--for the American vernacular tradition's music . . . ."

B230. Williams, David Russell. *Conversations with Howard Hanson*. Arkadelphia, Arkansas: Delta, 1988. Williams records Hanson's views on a number of composers of the Boston school. "Chadwick . . . wasn't very much influenced by anybody; he was a very independent fellow" (p. 16).

B231. Copland, Aaron and Vivian Perlis. *Copland Since 1943*. New York: St. Martin's Press, 1989. Includes Copland's reflections on discoveries made while exploring Harvard's Widener Library: "There I examined scores of George Chadwick and was rather surprised to find how varied in style his orchestral works were. I made a note at the time: 'I am convinced that there are many amusing discoveries awaiting the more adventurous musicologist' " (p. 178).

B232. Rockwell, John. "Paine and Chadwick Return to Favor." *New York Times* January 15, 1989: H/23. Rockwell discusses the position in music history of both J. K. Paine and Chadwick, and their recent "discovery" on orchestra programs and on recordings. " . . . this pleasing, well-crafted, warmly accessible music should appeal to modern symphony audiences."

B233.   Schabas, Ezra. *Theodore Thomas*. Urbana: University of Illinois Press, 1989. Refers to Chadwick with emphasis on his role in the events of the World's Columbian Exposition.

B234.   Tyler, Linda. *Edward Burlingame Hill: A Bio-Bibliography*. Westport, Connecticut: Greenwood Press, 1989. Tyler briefly mentions Hill's study with Chadwick at New England Conservatory. Also includes references to performances of Hill's compositions conducted by Chadwick (pp. 43-44).

B235.   Block, Adrienne Fried. "Dvorak, Beach and American Music." In *A Celebration of American Music: Words and Music in Honor of H. Wiley Hitchcock*, ed. by Richard Crawford, R. Allen Lott, and Carol Oja. Ann Arbor: University of Michigan Press, 1990. Includes a discussion of Chadwick's thoughts about Dvorak and the creation of an American musical style (see p. 259).

B236.   Ledbetter, Steven. "Two Seductresses: Saint-Saens's Delilah and Chadwick's Judith." In *A Celebration of American Music: Words and Music in Honor of H. Wiley Hitchcock*, ed. by Richard Crawford, R. Allen Lott, and Carol Oja, pp. 449-459. Ann Arbor: University of Michigan Press, 1990. A comparative analysis of *Judith* and *Samson et Delilah*; includes a good discussion of *Judith*'s compositional history and critical reception.

B237.   Yellin, Victor Fell. "Prosodic Syncopation." In *A Celebration of American Music: Words and Music in Honor of H. Wiley Hitchcock*, ed. by Richard Crawford, R. Allen Lott, and Carol Oja, pp. 449-459. Ann Arbor: University of Michigan Press, 1990. Yellin discusses the rhythmic properties of English and Anglo-Celtic speech patterns while citing instances of Chadwick's use of them in *Judith* (p. 455). While Chadwick is not the topic of this article, it is important for an understanding of his rhythmic style.

B238.   Kearns, William K. *Horatio Parker, 1863-1919: His Life, Music, and Ideas*. Metuchen, New Jersey: Scarecrow Press, 1990. Kearns provides numerous references to Chadwick as both teacher and friend to Parker. Among his several teachers, Parker " . . . named Chadwick, only nine years older, as most influential" (p. 6).

B239.   Abraham, Gerald, ed. *The New Oxford History of Music*, "Romanticism (1830-1890)," vol. 9. New York: Oxford University Press, 1990. S.v. "Britain and the U. S.," by Nicholas Temperley. The author provides a brief discussion of Chadwick and his music.

"Chadwick . . . perhaps awaits upward re-evaluation." Chadwick writes " . . . effective melodies . . . his harmonies and accompaniment textures are quite varied, though in all cases German-derived" (p. 778). Includes a musical example, "The Cardinal Flower" from Chadwick's *A Flower Cycle*: " . . . this is a resourceful song."

B240.   Yellin, Victor Fell. *Chadwick: Yankee Composer*. Washington and London: Smithsonian Institution Press, 1990. The first book-length study available on Chadwick is divided into two parts, "Chadwick: The Man," and "Chadwick: The Music." The first section deals with Chadwick's biography. While Yellin employs much of the information from his 1957 dissertation, there is still a good deal of new information presented here. The discussion of the music includes a survey of Chadwick's works in all genres; of course, Yellin is particularly at home with Chadwick's stage works. Numerous photos, plates, and 86 musical examples. The "Notes" section serves as the bibliography.

B241.   Negri, Gloria. "Brook Farm Being Spruced Up for 150th Birthday." *Boston Globe* June 9, 1991: 32. Negri writes that recorded works by American composers, including Chadwick, are being played at the Brook Farm celebration in an attempt to set a proper nineteenth-century mood.

B242.   Faucett, Bill F. "Musical Skylarking: Influences on the Symphonic Style of George Whitefield Chadwick." Paper read at the Southern Chapter Meeting of the American Musicological Society, Hattiesburg, Mississippi, February 22, 1991. Discusses sources of Chadwick's orchestral style with references to composers including Dvorak, Wagner, Mendelssohn, and others.

B243.   Faucett, Bill F. Review of *Chadwick: Yankee Composer*, by Victor Fell Yellin. In *Notes* 48/2 (December 1991): 493-495. Review of Yellin's important monograph, the first book-length study of Chadwick. "Yellin does not discuss Chadwick's entire output but readers will find a sampling large enough--generously peppered with musical examples--to satisfy an initial curiosity about this composer's imaginative style" (p. 495). [See also: B240]

B244.   Tawa, Nicholas. *The Coming of Age of American Art Music: New England's Classical Romanticists*. Westport, Connecticut: Greenwood Press, 1991. The first book-length study of the New England compo-sers, this work includes 28 pages devoted to Chadwick's life and music (pp. 103-130). This is a good survey of the better known composi-tions, and one of the few recent discussions of his songs. "Chadwick

remains an artist of sturdy integrity and splendid individuality"
(p. 128).

B245.   Bomberger, E. Douglas. *The German Musical Training of American Students, 1850-1900.* Ph.D. Dissertation, University of Maryland, 1991. Bomberger provides an excellent sketch of Chadwick's musical education at the Leipzig Conservatory (pp. 70-79), and notes that, in the case of Chadwick, the conservatory's tradition of public composition exams ". . . produced noteworthy results, and could even be argued to have launched his career as a professional composer" (pp. 78-79).

B246.   Borroff, Edith. *American Operas: A Checklist.* Warren, Michigan: Harmonie Park Press, 1992. Includes a listing of Chadwick's stage works with dates of performances, number of acts, librettists, and publication information (p. 53).

B247.   Faucett, Bill F. *The Symphonic Works of George Whitefield Chadwick.* Ph.D. Dissertation, Florida State University, 1992. Includes a biographical sketch, analytical discussion of Symphony Nos. 1-3, *Symphonic Sketches*, *Sinfonietta*, and *Suite Symphonique*, and a discography. [See also: B265]

B248.   Guinn, John. "DSO's New Schedule Resonates with Change." *Detroit Free Press* March 10, 1992: 4D. Guinn notes that Detroit Symphony Orchestra music director Neeme Jarvi's new three-year recording contract with the Chandos label will likely result in recordings of Chadwick's music.

B249.   Sadie, Stanley, ed. *The New Grove Dictionary of Opera.* London: Macmillan, 1992. S.v. "Chadwick, George W(hitefield)," [vol. 1, pp. 813-814] by Steven Ledbetter. Includes a brief biography, an essay on Chadwick's stage works, a stage works list, and a bibliography.

B250.   Tawa, Nicholas. *Mainstream Music of Early Twentieth Century America.* Westport, Connecticut: Greenwood Press, 1992. Includes passing references to Chadwick, especially with regard to his influence upon the generation of composers that followed him.

B251.   Epstein, Dena J. "Frederick Stock and American Music." *American Music* 10/1 (Spring 1992): 20-52. Includes references to performances of works by Chadwick, and a complete roster of his music performed by the Chicago Symphony Orchestra from 1905 to 1942.

B252.   Faucett, Bill F. Program notes for Symphony in F Major (No. 3).
         American Symphony Orchestra, *Bard Music Festival Rediscoveries*
         program, "Dvorak," Annandale-on-Hudson, New York, August 13-15
         and 20-22, 1993: 44-45. Faucett provides notes on the sources,
         history, and structure of the Third Symphony.

B253.   Fox, Pamela. Review of *Chadwick: Yankee Composer*, by Victor Fell
         Yellin. In *American Music* 12/1 (Spring 1994): 89-93. Concise
         summation of Yellin's text with emphasis on general traits of
         Chadwick's compositional style. [See also: B240]

B254.   Garofalo, Robert J. *Frederick Shepherd Converse (1871-1940): His
         Life and Music*. Metuchen, New Jersey: Scarecrow Press, 1994.
         Garofalo provides several important references to Chadwick, who had
         been a long-time teacher, friend and colleague of Converse's. Particu-
         larly important was Chadwick's role in convincing Converse to study
         with Rheinberger (p. 7). The author also notes that Chadwick was a
         member of the Board of Directors of the Boston Opera Company (p.
         34).

B255.   "National Symphony to Try Winter in Maine." *San Jose Mercury
         News* (November 24, 1994): 3D. Notes that the National Symphony
         Orchestra, led by associate conductor Barry Jekowsky, will perform
         music by New England composers, including Chadwick, on its upcom-
         ing "American Residency" program in Maine [specific works are not
         listed].

B256.   Ledbetter, Steven. "What Might Have Been . . ." Program notes for
         the world premiere [concert version] of *The Padrone*. Waterbury
         Symphony Orchestra, Leif Bjaland, cond.; Concora [chorus], Richard
         Coffey, cond. Thomaston Opera House, Thomaston, Connecticut,
         September 29, 1995. An excellent synopsis of the *The Padrone* with
         an appreciation of the composer and his career as an opera composer.
         "Chadwick's *Padrone* was utterly different [from earlier American
         operas]: it was realistic, down-to-earth, based on an actual social
         problem and humanizing it with a dramatic story and fast-moving
         music."

B257.   Slonimsky, Nicolas. *Music Since 1900* (5th ed.) New York:
         Schirmer, 1995. Slonimsky provides references, usually humorous, to
         the following Chadwick compositions: *Adonais* (p. 4), *Judith* (p. 15),
         Cleopatra (p. 52), *Symphonic Sketches* (p. 78), *Aphrodite* (p. 129),
         The Pilgrims (p. 217), *The Padrone* (p. 710). Also an obituary (p.
         333). On *Aphrodite*: " . . . in nine well-defined sections, with foamy

harps, humid strings, and zephyr-wafted woodwinds assaulted by Wagnerophallic trombones and mating trumpets . . . ."

B258. Farwell, Arthur. *"Wanderjahre of a Revolutionist" and Other Essays on American Music.* Edited by Thomas Stoner. Rochester, New York: University of Rochester Press, 1995. Farwell includes several references to Chadwick, his former teacher of composition, and also considers Chadwick's role in Farwell's American Music Society.

B259. Ledbetter, Steven. "George W. Chadwick and the American Orchestral Tradition." Liner notes to Reference Recordings RR-64CD, Czech State Philharmonic, Jose Serebrier, cond. [Includes *Tam O'Shanter*, *Melpomene*, and *Symphonic Sketches*], 1995. An excellent essay on Chadwick as an orchestral composer, with emphasis on the works featured on the recording. Chadwick was ". . . one of the most important pioneers of a tradition of orchestral music that had begun in the generation before him, one that he and his contemporaries brought to full flower in a rich stage of late romanticism."

B260. McPherson, Bruce, and James Klein. *Measure by Measure: A History of New England Conservatory from 1867.* Boston: The Trustees of New England Conservatory of Music, 1995. An excellent general history of the conservatory's growth featuring two chapters concerning Chadwick's relationship with the institution. "George Whitefield Chadwick: The Unanimous Choice" (Chapter 4) details the events leading up to Chadwick's election as the conservatory's director; "George Whitefield Chadwick: An American School" (Chapter 6) chronicles Chadwick's visions for the development of the conservatory and their realization. Contains numerous photographs.

B261. Struble, John Warthen. *The History of American Classical Music: MacDowell through Minimalism.* New York: Facts on File, 1995. Includes a biographical sketch and a photo. " . . . his primary genre was orchestral portraiture, in which he excelled all his contemporaries, including MacDowell."

B262. Bjaland, Leif. "Pushing American Buttons." *Symphony* 47/1 (January-February 1996): 7-9. Written by the conductor of the world premiere performance of Chadwick's *The Padrone*, this article chronicles Bjaland's interest in music by the New England composers and discusses the events leading up to *The Padrone*'s 1995 concert production in Thomaston, Connecticut, with the Waterbury Symphony Orchestra.

B263.   Faucett, Bill F. "Re-Evaluating Chadwick's Orchestral Works: A Taxonomy and Reception History." Paper read at the Southern Chapter Meeting of the American Musicological Society, Tampa, Florida, February 2, 1996. Discusses aspects of Chadwick's orchestral style and its evolution with emphasis on the development of nationalistic, modernistic, and dramatic elements. This paper also considers Chadwick's music as viewed by contemporary critics.

B264.   Crawford, Richard. "Edward MacDowell: Musical Nationalism and an American Tone Poet." *Journal of the American Musicological Society* 44/3 (Fall 1996): 528-560. Crawford places MacDowell within the circle of Boston composers by using statements made by Chadwick regarding the collegiality among musicians of the era. Crawford's insightful comments rely mostly on information gleaned from Chadwick's introduction to W. L. Hubbard's *History of American Music*.

B265.   Faucett, Bill F. *George Whitefield Chadwick: His Symphonic Works.* Lanham, Maryland and London: Scarecrow Press, 1996. The most comprehensive study available of Chadwick's symphonies and symphony-like compositions, including Symphonies Nos. 1-3, *Symphonic Sketches, Sinfonietta*, and *Suite Symphonique*. After a biographical sketch, the book discusses each work's history, analyzes the music in detail, and provides commentary on their critical reception. Includes plates and numerous music examples. "Chadwick's symphonic works constitute the most important body of orchestral compositions before World War I. They are, in terms of craftsmanship, ingenuity, and sheer quantity, unparalleled" (p. 160).

B266.   Tawa, Nicholas. "Ives and the New England School." In *Charles Ives and the Classical Tradition*, edited by Geoffrey Block and J. Peter Burkholder. New Haven: Yale University Press, 1996. Tawa discusses Chadwick at length, arguing that his influence directly and indirectly on Ives was great. "[Ives] undoubtedly took into account Chadwick's high reputation as a composer and [Horatio] Parker's admiration for his compositions, which would have led Ives to become familiar with his music" (p. 58).

B267.   Freeman, Charles S. "Elements of Realism in Chadwick's *The Padrone*." Paper read at the Southern Chapter meeting of the American Musicological Society, Tuscaloosa, Alabama, February 21, 1997. Freeman considers Chadwick's opera with emphasis on the composer's text setting and use of vernacular musical materials, and considers its place in the realistic artistic movement of Chadwick's day. Freeman also includes a good summary of the plot.

Bibliography of Writings by Chadwick

C1.   "The Popular Music -- Wherein Reform is Necessary." In *The Proceedings of the Music Teachers' National Association, 1877*. Delaware, Ohio: G. H. Thompson, Job Printer, 1877: 34-39. Reprinted in *The Vox Humana* 6/3 (June 1877). Chadwick's famous youthful tirade against composers of popular music: "Those who furnish the popular music have not paid, either in money or in mental discipline, the price of true and first-class musicians."

C2.   "Americans in Music." *The Musical Visitor* (December, 1892): 335. In statements derived from an interview with Chadwick, he discusses composition competitions and the position of the American composer in society. "As yet we can be said to have no school of American music, and the concert programs made up entirely of American music show a distinct lowering of the proper standard."

C3.   "How Do Composers Think Music [?]" *The Musical Visitor* 22/7 (July 1893): 181. This essay quotes Chadwick at length and gives insight into his compositional aesthetic. ". . . the musical idea is a fact, and its function, like any other artistic or poetic idea, is the expression of truth and beauty. . . . Every musical composition (if it be worthy of the name) is an art problem in which, with certain conditions given, and certain materials at hand, a certain result is to be obtained."

C4.   *Harmony: A Course of Study*. Boston: B. F. Wood Music Co., 1897

[88th edition printed by B. F. Wood in 1925]; reprint, New York: Da Capo, 1975. Chadwick's highly influential textbook on harmony intended for use by college-level students. ". . . if the effect justifies the means, any rule may be disregarded. This usually involves considerations other than purely harmonic ones; orchestral color, rhythm, and the dramatic effect often give striking significance to harmonic combinations and progressions which would otherwise be offensive, or at least unsatisfactory . . . ."

C5.   *Key to Chadwick's Harmony.* Boston: B. F. Wood, 1902. Provides solutions and insights to his *Harmony: A Course of Study.*

C6.   "Musical Atmosphere and Student Life." *New England Conservatory Magazine* 9/4 (May 1903): 138-141. Provides interesting comments on contemporary musical conditions compared to German and European conditions. Chadwick also discusses opportunities for education which are available to enterprising students. ". . . I believe that this atmosphere [of art and of the serious study of music] now exists in this country, and in this city of Boston, if the student is really earnest and serious enough to take advantage of it" (p. 139).

C7.   "Faculty Reminiscences." *The Neume* 1 (Class of 1905, The Neume Board): 101-113. Chadwick comments on the legendary conductor, Hans von Bulow (p. 106).

C8.   "A Touch of Beethoven." *The Neume* 3 (Class of 1907, The Neume Board): 35-37. A tongue-in-cheek account of Chadwick's conversation with the statue of Beethoven which stands at New England Conservatory. Contains important biographical information. Chadwick writes that Beethoven had ". . . brought back to my recollection the happy, careless days in the old Music Hall and the old Conservatory--when everything was before us, when the hearing of a masterpiece, his [Beethoven's] masterpieces--for the first time, was an event to be marked with a white stone" (p. 36).

C9.   "Edward MacDowell." *The Neume* 4 (Class of 1908, The Neume Board): 126-127. Chadwick's appreciation of MacDowell and his music. On the Suite in A Minor, op. 42: ". . . the writer still remembers the delight of the musicians and the audience which was created by its striking rhythmic vitality and unique instrumentation" (p. 126).

C10.   "American Composers." In *The American History and Encyclopedia of Music.* Vol. 8, *History of American Music,* edited by William Lines

Hubbard, pp. 1-15. An insightful essay regarding the tradition of serious music in the U. S. Chadwick's omission of his own contribution to the field is rectified by the editor at the end of the article.

C11. "The Curriculum of a School of Music." In *Studies in Musical Education, History, and Aesthetics, Proceedings of the Music Teachers National Association* (3rd Series). Hartford, Connecticut: Published by the Association, 1909: 65-77. Reprinted, *The Neume* 5 (Class of 1909, The Neume Board): 121-130. A discussion of Chadwick's ideal curriculum includes courses available in ear training, "rudiments," harmony, composition, history, piano, organ, and singing.

C12. "The Evolution of the Musical Idea." Address delivered to The MacDowell Club (Boston), March 10, 1909. Not located; this topic is announced on the program of a MacDowell Club concert.

C13. Untitled address delivered to the Litchfield County Choral Union [Norfolk, Connecticut], June 11, 1909. Reprinted in J. H. Vaill, ed. *Litchfield County Choral Union.* Norfolk, Connecticut: Litchfield County University Club, 1912. Chadwick recounts music's role in his upbringing and describes the state of music in the United States. He then praises the efforts of the Litchfield County Choral Union and its efforts on behalf of the highly-regarded Norfolk Festival.

C14. "The Conservatory Orchestra." *The Neume* 8 (Class of 1912, The Neume Board): 113. Chadwick provides an historical overview of the New England Conservatory Orchestra, which he founded, and provides information about its personnel and repertoire.

C15. "Notes on the Norfolk Meeting." Undated, unidentified article inserted into Chadwick's 1914 *Journal.* Chadwick comments on the appearance of Finnish composer Jean Sibelius at the 26th annual meeting of the Litchfield County Choral Union, Norfolk, Connecticut.

C16. "Mr. Chadwick on the Symphonic Orchestra." Dated November 18, 1914, this unidentified article was inserted into Chadwick's 1914 *Journal.* This address was delivered on the occasion of Boston Symphony Orchestra founder Henry Lee Higginson's 80th birthday.

C17. *Horatio Parker.* New Haven: Yale University Press, 1921; reprinted, New York: AMS Press, 1972. [Much of this book was first delivered as a paper before the American Academy of Arts and Letters (July 25, 1920), and printed in: *Commemorative Tribute to Horatio Parker.* New York: American Academy of Arts and Letters, 1922, publication no.

23.] Chadwick's brief biography of his longtime friend chronicles Parker's education and career, and provides insights into his most important compositions.

C18. "Et Arcadia Ego." *Boston Herald* May 29, 1923: 14. In Chadwick's sentimental response to a chronicle of the arts and its role on Boston's Park Street in the *Herald* column, "As the World Wags," he recalls the good old days when he was just starting to gain a reputation as a professional composer. Regarding his Park Street Church studio, he recalls, "To that room came, among others, Horatio Parker and Arthur Whiting, with their fugues and canons. Perhaps they brought with them more than they carried away from their teacher."

C19. *Solfeggio Studies with Piano Accompaniment.* Boston: New England Conservatory, 1926. This volume includes exercises for classroom use.

C20. "Tributes to [*sic*] Eminent Men and Women to Theodore Presser." *The Etude* 44/1 (January 1926): 10. Chadwick's appreciation of his friend and one-time benefactor includes some important biographical information about his early years in Germany. Chadwick's eldest son, Theodore, was named after Presser.

C21. "Music." In *Fifty Years of Boston: A Memorial Volume Issued in Commemoration of the Tercentenary of 1930.* Compiled by the Subcommittee on Memorial History and edited by Elisabeth M. Herlihy. Boston: 1932 (pp. 319-334). A detailed history of music in Boston with sections titled: "Conditions Before 1880," "The Symphony Orchestra," "Other Orchestras," "Opera," "Chamber Music in Boston," and "Educational Opportunities." On the Boston Orchestral Club, which Chadwick led from 1888: "Somewhat more rigid discipline was enforced and more pretentious programs were performed [than at the Boston Symphony Orchestra concerts]. But after 1893 ". . . subscriptions fell off, interest languished and the club was discontinued."

Song Title Index

Song titles are listed alphabetically and indexed by their Work ("W") number. The placement of individual songs located in a collection are referenced following the Work number.

Choral Music Index

Titles are listed alphabetically and indexed by their Work ("W") number. The placement of individual compositions located in a collection are referenced following the Work number.

Abide with Me W104
Angel of Peace W131/10
Art Thou Weary W105
As the Hart Pants W189/1
At the Bride's Gate W186/2
Autumn Winds Are Chill, The W106
Awake Up My Glory W107

Ballad of Trees and the Master, A W108
Beatitudes, The W109
Behold the Works of the Lord W110
Behind the Lattice W192/2
Blessed Be the Lord W188/2
Bluebells of New England, The W111
Book of Choruses for High Schools and Choral Societies, A W112
Boy and the Owl, The W126/1
Brightest and Best W113
Buie Annajohn W112/5
Busy Lark W114

Caravan Song W112/2
Child is Born in Bethlehem, A (Carol from Noel) W115, W131/11
Chorus of Hebrews (Chorus from Judith) W116, W131/14
Chorus of Pilgrim Women W112/6
Christmas Greeting, A W117, W131/12

General Index

Hines, Paul, WR11
Hipsher, Edward Ellsworth, B111
Hitchcock, H. Wiley, B221, B229,
    B235, B236, B237
Hobson, Mary, W70a
Hochschule fur Musik (Munich), 4
Hollis Street Church, W76a
Hollister, Carol, W252m
Holmes, George Ellsworth, W240a
Holmes, Mabel Metcalf, W43b-c
Holmes, Malcolm, W1g
Holmes, Oliver Wendell, W131/10
Holt, Charlotte, W70b
Homer, Louise, W69g, W88a, W103,
    W219, B192
Homer, Sidney, B149
Hoopes, Donelson F., B199
Hopekirk, Helen, W43
Horowitz, Joseph, DB30, DB65
Hosmer, Lucien, W74, WB296
Howard, Ann, D70-72
Howard, John Tasker, B146, B151,
    B169, B174
Howe, Julia W., W210
Howe, Mark A. DeWolfe, W80, W94,
    W125, W184, W217, B133,
    B136
Howe, Stewart, W71b
Hubbard, Eliot, W73a-b, W206a
Hubbard, William Lines, WB39,
    WB202, C10, B264
Hudson-Alexander, Caroline, W90d
Hughes, Rupert, B49, B84
Human, T., W32
Humphrey, Homer, W65
Huneker, James Gibbon, B93
Hyatt, Alfred H., W112/2, W112/7

Indianapolis, Symphony Orchestra,
    W8j, W19w, W19ii
Ingham, John Hall, 9, 16, W83,
    W112/1, W142
Irving, Washington, 12, W14
Isaacs, Kevin Jay, WB370

Ives, Charles, B189, B266
Ives, Mrs. Halsey C., W242

Jadassohn, Salomon, 3, 4, W31, B38,
    B59
Jameson, Frederick, W252f
Janpowlski, A., W69b
Jarvi, Neeme, W14n, W19kk-mm,
    W21j, W22m, D5, D8, D14,
    B248
Jefferson, Joseph, W14
Jeffords, Geneva, W91c
Jekowsky, Barry, B255
Jenks, Francis H., WB333, WB361
Jepson, Harry B., W81, W137
Johnson, David, DB5, DB11, DB18,
    DB27, DB42-44, DB36,
    DB55, DB71
Johnson, Earle H., B162
Johnson, Katherine, W69j
Johnson, Thor, W14n, W19bb-cc,
    W19ee
Johnstone, Arthur Edward, B103
Johnstone, Lela B., W88d
Jones, F. O., B21
Jones, Floyd, W70b
Jordan, Jules, W255, B101
Joslyn, Frederic, W265a
Juch, Emma, W84b-c
Judson, George W., WB29, WB190,
    WB191, WB321

Karidoyanes, Steven, W19ss
Kearns, William, DB78, B238
Keble, John, W181
Kelley, Edgar Stillman, WB67
Kerr, U. S., W101e, W205a, W206b,
    W214a-b, W242b, W253a,
    W259a
Kimmelmann, Michael, WB215
Kindler, Hans, D28-29
Kingman, Daniel, B201
Kirkpatrick, John, B189
Klein, James, B260

Orchestra of America, W71c
Orcutt, William Dana, W199
Ormond, Lilla, W96, W200
Orpheus Club (Philadelphia), W187
Orpheus Club (Springfield, Mass.),
    W170
Osborne, William, D58
Otis, Philo Adams, B105
Owen, Hugh, W90f

Page, Joshua, W12
Page, Tim, WB150
Paine, John Knowles, 3, 5, WB52,
    WB102, WB158, B7-8, B10-
    13, B20, B48, B151, B182,
    B213, B232
Palmer, Maurine, W88h
Palmer, Ray, W221/2
Panama-Pacific International Expo-
    sition, W8f, W11x, W15c,
    W19e, W264b, B85
Pappin, Gay Gladdin, B220
Park Street Church (Boston), 5, B15,
    C18
Parker, George J., W91a, W252e
Parker, Henry T., WB8, WB17, WB21
    WB23, WB31, W7, WB45,
    WB112, WB115, WB121,
    WB128, WB129, WB132,
    WB135, WB172, WB242,
    WB257, WB308, WB359,
    B159, B213
Parker, Horatio, 7, 9, WB67, W13,
    WB102, W24, W58, W90b,
    W187, B44, B73, B145,
    B189, C17, C18, B238, B266
Parker, Isabella G., W77, W92, W122,
    W175
Parker, Louise, W71c
Parker, Stanley, W73
Parker, W. J., WB188, WB309, B108
Parker, William Stanley, W73b
Parmenter, Ross, WB280
Patee, Elaine, W88j

Peabody, Josephine, W112/6
Peck, Samuel Minturn, W192/2
Pelletier, Wilfrid, W19gg
People's Symphony Orchestra, W2b,
    W8g, W14h, W17g, W18h,
    W19j, W21d, W21e, W97b,
    W98a, W99a, W101g,
    W101l, W103a, B108
Perkins, Charles C., B19
Perlis, Vivian, B231
Perner, Antoinette, W70a, W88e
Perry, Bliss, B100
Perry, Lilla Cabot, W186
Petersilea, Carlyle, 2
Phares, Keith, W71b
Philadelphia Orchestra, W18a, W69f
Philharmonic Society of Montreal,
    W84, W84b
Phillips, Matthew H., D7
Phi Mu Alpha Sinfonia, 7, B95
Phippen, Joshua, W91a
Piatt, Aurora, W68c-d
Pierce, Jacqueline, W71a, D63
Pittsburgh Symphony Orchestra,
    W19z
Plutarch, W6
Plymouth (Mass.) Philharmonic,
    W19ss
Polly, Hildred, W88d
Poole, Clara, W90c
Portland String Quartet, W35h, D44-
    47, D54, D56
Potter, Mildred, W90e
Powers, Francis Fisher, W90b
Pratt, Charles Stuart, W131/7, W203
Pratt, Waldo Selden, B113
Prescott, Rev. George J., W127
Presser, Theodore, C20
Preston, A., W52
Preston, John A., W188a, B3
Proctor, George, W43a
Pugsley, Richard, J. W7b, W10a

Rabaud, Henri, W83b

Stuart, Mason, W21e
Stucken, Frank van der, W11b, W11f,
    W11i, WB52, W12b, W252g,
    B27, B208
Sturgis, Richard Clipston, W73b
Stutco, T. E., W74a
Sullivan, T. R., W216/13, W240
Sundelius, Marie, W90e
Swartz, Jessica, W69d, W232b,
    W242e, W256a, W267b
Sweet, Eugenia, W252c
Symphony Capelle (Copenhagen),
    W11c
Symphony Orchestra of America, D7

Tampa Bay Chamber Orchestra, W16c
Tavern Club, B136
Tawa, Nicholas, B244, B250, B266
Taylor, Bayard, W161, W168,
    W189/3, W206, WB377,
    W252/1
Taylor, Ida S., W226
Taylor, W. L., W203
Temperley, Nicholas, B239
Tennyson, Alfred, W12, W244,
    W252/8
Tersteegen, Gerhardt, W221/4
Thackeray, W. M., W187/2, W222/1
Thayer, Eugene, W59
Thayer, Rodney, W74a
Theodore Thomas Orchestra, 2, W18,
    W101d, W101h-i
Thiele, Ernest, W32b
Thomas, George W., W74b-c
Thomas, Rose Fay, B76
Thomas, Theodore, W11g-h, W11n,
    W13b, W21c, W22, W22b,
    W22h, W88a, B76, B147,
    B218, B233
Thomson, James, W218/2-3
Thompson, Kara Shay, W71b
Thompson, Oscar, WB20, B180
Thuille, Ludwig, B60
Thursday Morning Musical Club

(Boston), W191, W192
Ticknor, Howard Malcolm, WB46
Tiersot, Julien, B27
Tily, Herbert J., W69f
Timberlake, Craig, W153
Tischler, Barbara, B222, B224
Todhunter, John, W69j, W96, W200
Todi, Giacopone da, W191/1
Toedt, Mrs. Theodore, W90b
Tomlins, William L., W89a, W209,
    W210, W257
Torelli, Giuseppe, WA3
Touchette, Charles, W265a
Townsend, Stephen, W101b, W101f,
    W242f
Trafton, Etta D., W252d
Treble Clef Club (Philadelphia), W78,
    W123, W134a, W135
Tremont String Quartet, W34i, D55
Trench, Richard Chevenix, W90
Tresahar, John, W68e
Trezise, Simon, DB48-49, DB57-58
Troutbeck, G. E., W131/1
Tucker, C. B., W74a
Tuesday Morning Singing Club (New
    York), W186, W186a
Turner, Ross Sterling, W25, W179
Turok, Paul, DB79
Tyler, Linda, B234

Ulrich, Allan, DB50, DB59
United States Marine Band, W19rr,
    WR3a, WR11, WR11a-b,
    WR12, D13
Upton, George P., B67, B150
Upton, William Treat, B114, B115

Vaill, J. H., WB184, WB319
Vallecillo, Erma, D67
Van Yorx, Theodore, W84e
Vaughn, Grace, W74b-c
Victor Orchestra, D74-75
Vie Joyeuse, La, W18
Vienna Symphony Orchestra, D41-42

About the Author

BILL F. FAUCETT, whose specialty is American music, teaches in West Palm Beach, Florida, where he is also a music critic for *The Palm Beach Post*. He is the author of *George Whitefield Chadwick: His Symphonic Works* (1996).

ISBN 0-313-30067-4

90000>

EAN

9 780313 300677

HARDCOVER BAR CODE